BRAINTEASING
IQ PUZZLES

BRAINTEASING IQ PUZZLES

CHARTWELL
BOOKS, INC.

This edition printed in 2009 by
CHARTWELL BOOKS, INC.
A Division of **BOOK SALES, INC.**
276 Fifth Avenue Suite 206
New York, New York 10001 USA

Copyright © 2008 Arcturus Publishing Limited
26/27 Bickels Yard, 151–153 Bermondsey Street,
London SE1 3HA

ISBN-13: 978-0-7858-2454-1
ISBN-0-7858-2454-5

Printed in Singapore

INTRODUCTION

Thinking can be fun, as this book proves. Within these pages you will find more than 580 puzzles offering a mixture of challenges at different levels of difficulty to test your mental agility.

The puzzles range from those concerning location – where to place dominoes, for example – through mathematics to logical and perceptual puzzles. None of the puzzles requires specific knowledge of a subject, beyond a basic grasp of maths. What you will need to solve them is logical thinking allied to concentration.

The six sections of the book are not graded by difficulty, although if taken in isolation some puzzles in Section 6 might seem more difficult than those in Section 1. If you start with Section 1 and work your way progressively through the book, you should find that you are able to solve puzzles in the later sections in the same time, or less, than puzzles in the earlier sections as your mind becomes attuned to thinking logically.

With some puzzles taking minutes to solve and others providing tougher competition, you will never know what to expect and so never be bored.

The solutions to all the puzzles can be found at the back of the book.

1

A standard set of 28 dominoes has been laid out as shown. Can you draw in the edges of them all? The check-box is provided as an aid and the domino already placed will help.

0-0	0-1	0-2	0-3	0-4	0-5	0-6
✓	✓	✓	✓	✓	✓	✓

1-1	1-2	1-3	1-4	1-5	1-6	2-2
✓	✓	✓	✓	✓	✓	✓

2-3	2-4	2-5	2-6	3-3	3-4	3-5
✓	✓	✓	✓	✓	✓	✓

3-6	4-4	4-5	4-6	5-5	5-6	6-6
✓	✓	✓	✓	✓	✓	✓

2

Draw walls to partition the grid into areas (some walls are already drawn in for you). Each area must contain two circles, area sizes must match those numbers shown next to the grid and each '+' must be linked to at least two walls.

3,   3,   6,   6,   7

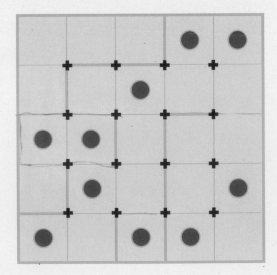

Every row and column in this grid originally contained one heart, one club, one diamond, one spade and two blank squares, although not necessarily in that order.

Every symbol with a black arrow refers to the first of the four symbols encountered when travelling in the direction of the arrow. Every symbol with a white arrow refers to the second of the four symbols encountered in the direction of the arrow.

Can you complete the original grid?

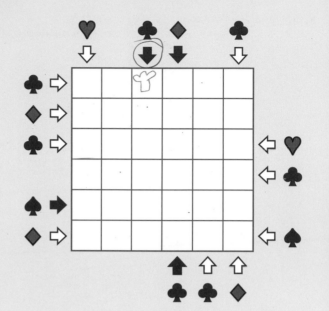

4

The blank squares below should be filled with whole numbers between 1 and 30 inclusive, any of which may occur more than once, or not at all.

The numbers in every horizontal row add up to the totals on the right, as do the two long diagonal lines; whilst those in every vertical column add up to the totals along the bottom.

							115
3			30	4	17		99
18	21			29		15	125
28	27		8		18	7	101
	20	16	9	22		15	117
1		28	14	2	3	22	87
	21	18		13	7	17	110
24		30	10	16	11		101
103	143	121	110	95	80	88	48

5

Draw in the missing hands on the final clock.

2:58am

12:09pm

10h 49mn

9:20

6:31

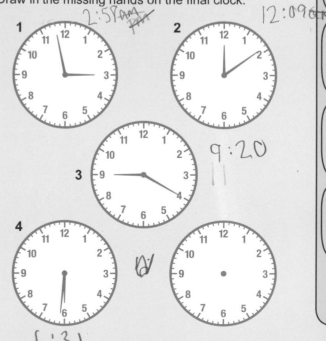

Can you place the hexagons into the grid, so that where any hexagon touches another along a straight line, the number in both triangles is the same? No rotation of any hexagon is allowed!

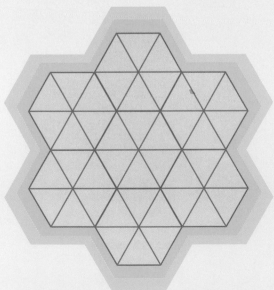

Twelve L-shapes like the ones here need to be inserted in the grid and each L has one hole in it.

There are three pieces of each of the four kinds shown here and any piece may be turned or flipped over before being put in the grid. No pieces of the same kind touch, even at a corner.

The pieces fit together so well that you cannot see any spaces between them; only the holes show.

Can you tell where the Ls are?

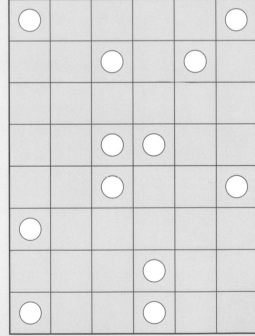

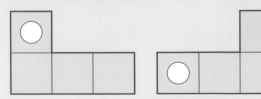

S E C T I O N

1

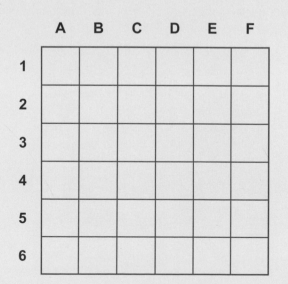

8

In this puzzle, an amateur coin collector has been out with his metal detector, searching for booty. He didn't have time to dig up all the coins he found, so has made a grid map, showing their locations, in the hope that if he loses the map, at least no-one else will understand it…

Those squares containing numbers are empty, but where a number appears in a square, it indicates how many coins are located in the squares (up to a maximum of eight) surrounding the numbered one, touching it at any corner or side. There is only one coin in any individual square.

Place a circle into every square containing a coin.

						0			
	0	2	2	2			3	4	
				2					
				3			2	4	
	1				1				3
		2		3			1		
	3			2					
0				3		3			1
				2					0
	3				0	2			

9

The grid should be filled with numbers from 1 to 6, so that each number appears just once in every row and column. The clues refer to the digit totals in the squares, eg A 1 2 3 = 6 means that the numbers in squares A1, A2 and A3 add up to 6.

1 C 1 2 = 3

2 D 4 5 = 3

3 E 3 4 5 = 8

4 F 3 4 = 10

5 D E F 1 = 12

6 D E 2 = 9

7 A B 3 = 7

8 A B 4 = 4

9 A B 5 = 9

10 D E 6 = 5

11 A 1 2 = 10

	A	B	C	D	E	F
1						
2						
3						
4						
5						
6						

Each of the small squares in the grid below contains either A, B or C. Each row, column, and diagonal line of six squares has exactly two of each letter. Can you tell the letter in each square?

Across

1   The Bs are next to each other
2   The Cs are between the As
3   No two letters the same are directly next to each other
4   No two letters the same are directly next to each other
5   The As are between the Cs
6   The As are between the Cs

Down

1   The Cs are next to each other
2   Each A is directly next to and below a C
3   The As are lower than the Cs
4   The Bs are next to each other
5   The As are lower than the Cs
6   The As are between the Bs

The object of this puzzle is to trace a single path from the top left corner to the bottom right corner of the grid, travelling through all of the cells in either a horizontal, vertical or diagonal direction.

Every cell must be entered once only and your path should take you through the numbers in the sequence 1-2-3-4-5-6-1-2-3-4-5-6, etc.

Can you find the way?

1	2	5	6	2	3
3	4	4	2	1	4
1	5	3	1	5	1
2	6	6	4	6	2
3	4	5	3	4	3
5	6	1	2	5	6

Can you place the vessels into the diagram? Some parts of vessels or sea squares have already been filled in. A number to the right or below a row or column refers to the number of occupied squares in that row or column.

Any vessel may be positioned horizontally or vertically, but no part of a vessel touches part of any other vessel, either horizontally, vertically or diagonally.

Empty Area of Sea: ≈

Aircraft Carrier: ◀■■▶

Battleships: ◀■▶ ◀■▶

Cruisers: ◀▶ ◀▶ ◀▶

Submarines: ● ● ● ●

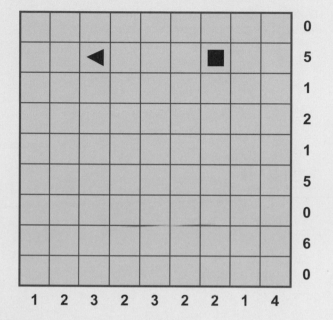

Column totals: 1 2 3 2 3 2 2 1 4

Row totals: 0 5 1 2 1 5 0 6 0

13

Can you fill each square in the bottom line with the correct digit?

Every square in the solution contains only one digit from each of the lines above, although two or more squares in the solution may contain the same digit.

At the end of every row is a score, which shows:

a the number of digits placed in the correct finishing position on the bottom line, as indicated by a tick; and

b the number of digits which appear on the bottom line, but in a different position, as indicated by a cross.

SCORE

2	1	2	8	✓✓
2	1	2	3	✓
1	4	5	8	✓
7	3	5	2	✗
6	6	8	5	✓
				✓✓✓✓

14

Draw a single continuous loop, by connecting the dots. No line may cross the path of another.

The figure inside each set of any four surrounding dots indicates the total number of surrounding lines.

```
.   .   .   .   .   .   .   .   .   .
  1                       3
.   .   .   .   .   .   .   .   .   .
      3   0   3       1       3
.   .   .   .   .   .   .   .   .   .
  1                   0       3
.   .   .   .   .   .   .   .   .   .
  1   0   2               0   1       2
.   .   .   .   .   .   .   .   .   .
    1           1                   1
.   .   .   .   .   .   .   .   .   .
          2   1
.   .   .   .   .   .   .   .   .   .
  2           3           0   1
.   .   .   .   .   .   .   .   .   .
  3       2   1   0   1       2       0
.   .   .   .   .   .   .   .   .   .
      2   1                   0
.   .   .   .   .   .   .   .   .   .
  1   2   2       0                   0
.   .   .   .   .   .   .   .   .   .
  2           1   0   2       3   1
.   .   .   .   .   .   .   .   .   .
  2           3   2
.   .   .   .   .   .   .   .   .   .
```

A B C D E F G H I J K L M N O P Q R S T U V W X Y Z
1 2 3 4 5 6 7 8 9 10 11 12 13 14 15 16 17 18 19 20 21 22 23 24 25 26

15

Each horizontal row and vertical column should contain different shapes and different numbers.

Every square will contain one number and one shape and no combination may be repeated anywhere else in the puzzle.

1   2   3   4   5

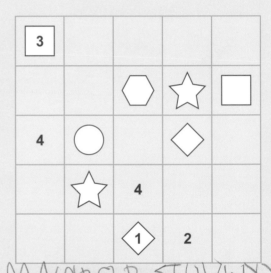

16

Given that the letters are valued 1-26 according to their places in the alphabet, can you crack the mystery code to reveal the missing letter?

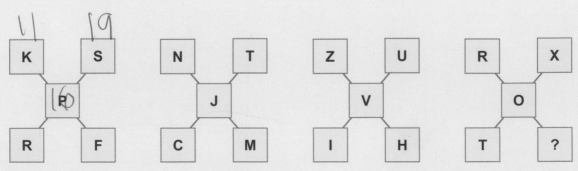

A set of dominoes is to be placed in four rows as shown below. The numbers indicate which values are shown on all the dominoes in each column and the relevant half of the domino in every row. Find out where each domino is placed by carefully comparing rows and columns to determine the possible positions of certain dominoes: for instance, if any column contains only one 6, then the domino 6/6 isn't in that column.

A set of dominoes consists of:

0/0, 0/1, 0/2, 0/3, 0/4, 0/5, 0/6, 1/1, 1/2, 1/3, 1/4, 1/5, 1/6, 2/2,

2/3, 2/4, 2/5, 2/6, 3/3, 3/4, 3/5, 3/6, 4/4, 4/5, 4/6, 5/5, 5/6, 6/6.

	0, 1, 2, 4, 5, 5, 6, 6.	0, 0, 2, 4, 4, 5, 5, 5.	0, 0, 1, 1, 1, 2, 2, 4.	0, 2, 2, 2, 3, 3, 4, 4.	0, 2, 3, 3, 5, 6, 6, 6.	1, 1, 3, 4, 4, 5, 6, 6.	0, 1, 1, 3, 3, 3, 5, 6.
1, 1, 1, 3, 4, 5, 6.							
2, 3, 3, 4, 4, 6, 6.							
0, 0, 2, 3, 3, 4, 6.							
0, 0, 1, 1, 4, 5, 5.							
0, 0, 1, 5, 5, 5, 6.							
0, 1, 2, 3, 5, 6, 6.							
1, 2, 2, 3, 3, 4, 4.							
0, 2, 2, 2, 4, 5, 6.							

Place the eight tiles into the puzzle grid so that all adjacent numbers on each tile match up. Tiles may be rotated through 360 degrees, but none may be flipped over.

2	2
1	3

2	3
4	3

2	2
2	4

4	2
4	1

1	3
2	1

3	1
4	4

1	1
3	3

3	2
1	4

(grid with handwritten 2, 2 / 1 in top-left cells, and 1 1 / 4 3 in lower-right cells)

Place all twelve of the pieces into the grid. Any may be rotated or flipped over, but none may touch another, not even diagonally. The numbers outside the grid refer to the number of consecutive black squares; and each block is separated from the others by at least one white square. For instance, '3 2' could refer to a row with none, one or more white squares, then three black squares, then at least one white square, then two more black squares, followed by any number of white squares.

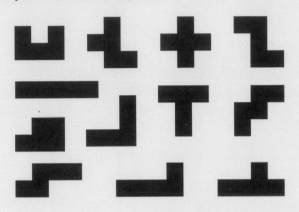

S
E
C
T
I
O
N

1

20

In the diagram below, which letter should replace the question mark?

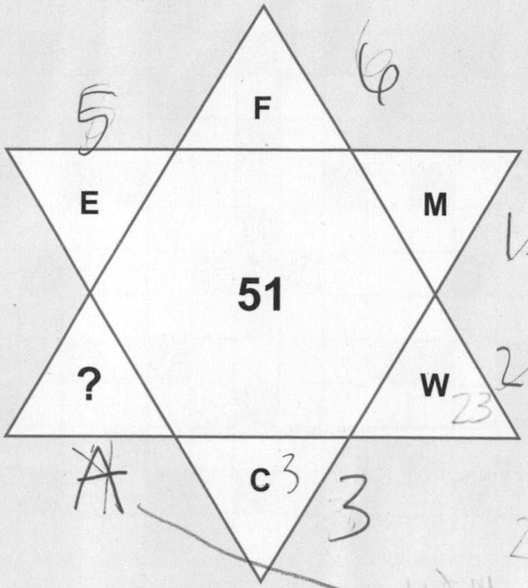

F

E

M

51

?

W

C

21

In the square below, change the positions of six numbers, one per horizontal row, vertical column and long diagonal line of six smaller squares, in such a way that the numbers in each row, column and long diagonal line total exactly 96. Any number may appear more than once in a row, column or line.

14	9	10	23	14	14
25	26	18	21	30	4
22	9	12	28	21	10
21	9	30	4	17	24
9	8	6	11	32	6
14	23	26	2	10	14

22

Every brick in this pyramid contains a number which is the sum of the two numbers below it, so that F=A+B, etc. Just work out the missing numbers!

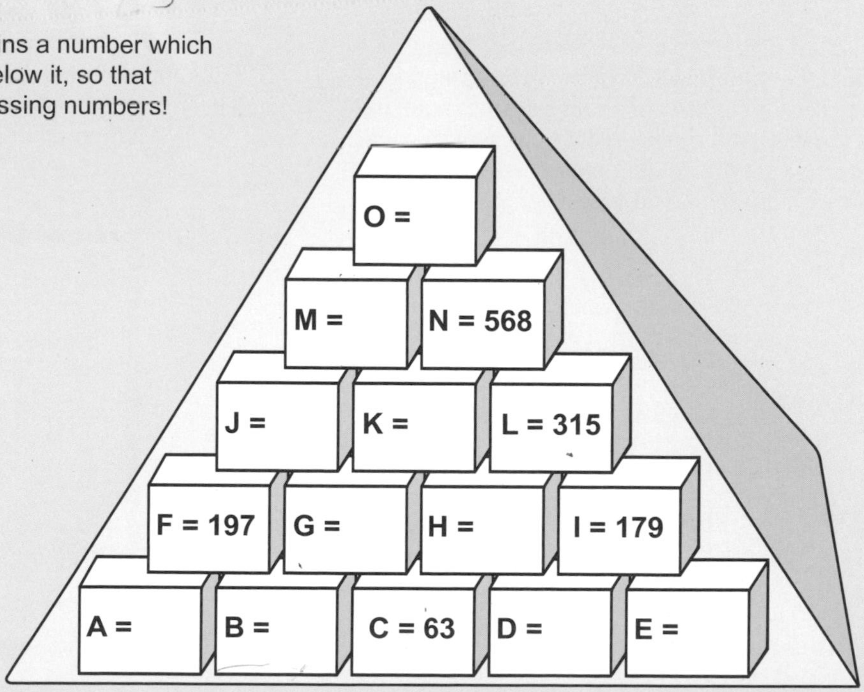

O =

M =   N = 568

J =   K =   L = 315

F = 197   G =   H =   I = 179

A =   B =   C = 63   D =   E =

With the starters already given, can you fit all of the remaining listed numbers into this grid? Take care, this puzzle may not be as easy as it looks!

18	398	2837	7765	64722
23	583	3346	7783	96369
25	785	3456	8367	115235
46	837	3737	8635	204891
60	897	4636	8735	252307
68	919	4894	8850	267843
90	1003	4988	9491 ✓	278710
92	1079	5174	9523	376361
226	1130	5743	26438	433790
246	1496	6505	54667	551168
248	1830 ✓	6963	56796	614793
325	2756	7688	61704	753340

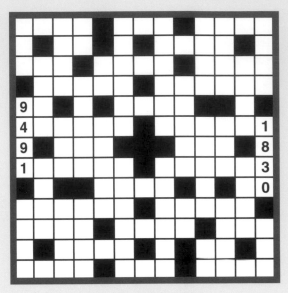

The chart gives directions to a hidden treasure behind the centre black square in the grid. Move the indicated number of spaces north, south, east and west (eg 4N means move four squares north) stopping at every square once only to arrive there. At which square should you start?

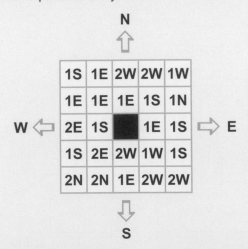

Fill the grid so that every horizontal row and vertical column contains the numbers 1-5. The 'greater than' or 'less than' signs indicate where a number is larger or smaller than that in the neighbouring square.

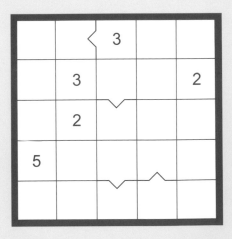

16

Each of the eight segments of the spider's web should be filled with a different number from 1 to 8, in such a way that every ring also contains a different number from 1 to 8.

The segments run from the outside of the spider's web to the centre, and the rings run all the way around.

Some numbers are already in place. Can you fill in the rest?

27

Every oval shape in this diagram contains a different letter of the alphabet from A to K inclusive. Use the clues to determine their locations. Reference in the clues to 'due' means in any location along the same horizontal or vertical line.

1 The A is further south than the B, further east than the F, further north than the G, and further west than the E.

2 The B is further south than the D, but further north than the H.

3 The C is next to and south of the H, which is further east than the I, which is next to and south of the J.

4 The D is next to and north of the K, which is next to and east of the J.

5 The G is next to and south of the E.

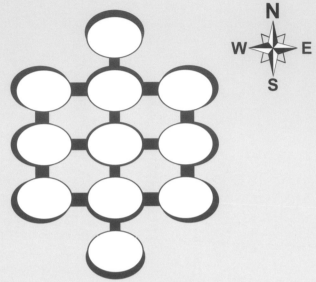

28

Fill the three empty circles with the symbols +, – and x in some order, to make a sum which totals the number in the centre. Each symbol must be used once and calculations are made in the direction of travel (clockwise).

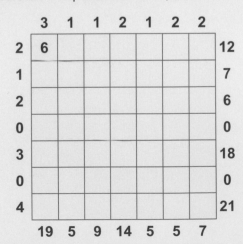

29

The numbers at the top and on the left side show the quantity of single-digit numbers (1-9) used in that row and column. The numbers at the bottom and on the right show the sum of the digits. A number may appear more than once in a row or column, but no numbers are in squares that touch, even at a corner.

	3	1	1	2	1	2	2	
2	6							12
1								7
2								6
0								0
3								18
0								0
4								21
	19	5	9	14	5	5	7	

Using the numbers below, complete these six equations (three reading across and three reading downwards). Every number is used once.

1	2	3	4	5
6	7	8	9	

	+		x		=	117
−		−		x		
	x		+		=	5
+		x		+		
	+		−		=	3
=		=		=		
13		12		34		

In the grid below, which number should replace the question mark?

23	25	9	4	22	23	30
16	18	3	8	6	22	12
8	7	8	4	18	13	6
33	10	13	11	4	15	5
12	2	13	29	12	1	4
1	15	26	31	19	16	14
5	21	26	11	?	8	27

When the box below is folded to form a cube, just one of the five options (A, B, C, D or E) can be produced. Which?

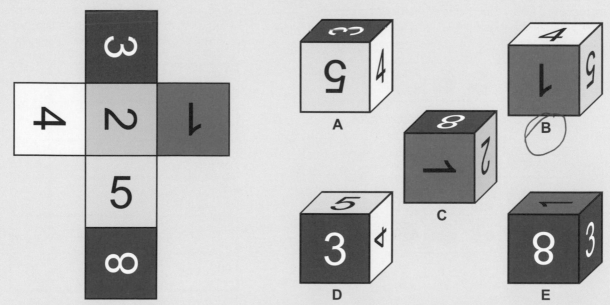

33

In this puzzle, an amateur coin collector has been out with his metal detector, searching for booty. He didn't have time to dig up all the coins he found, so has made a grid map, showing their locations, in the hope that if he loses the map, at least no-one else will understand it…

Those squares containing numbers are empty, but where a number appears in a square, it indicates how many coins are located in the squares (up to a maximum of eight) surrounding the numbered one, touching it at any corner or side. There is only one coin in any individual square.

Place a circle into every square containing a coin.

				1					
2		1				0			2
	0				1			4	
		1							3
2				3	2	2	3		
			3			2		3	
		1							1
	0			2					1
1						6	4		1
		2		2					

34

Each symbol stands for a different number. In order to reach the correct total at the end of each row and column, what is the value of the circle, cross, pentagon, square and star?

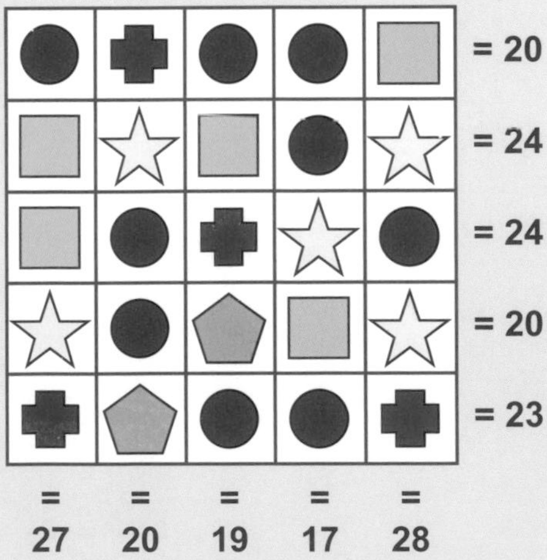
= 20
= 24
= 24
= 20
= 23
= 27
= 20
= 19
= 17
= 28

35

Every row and column of this grid should contain one each of the letters A, B, C, D, E and F. Each of the six shapes (marked by thicker lines) should also contain one each of the letters A, B, C, D, E and F. Can you complete the grid?

	B			A	
					C
	F		E		D

A standard set of 28 dominoes has been laid out as shown. Can you draw in the edges of them all? The checkbox is provided as an aid and the domino already placed will help.

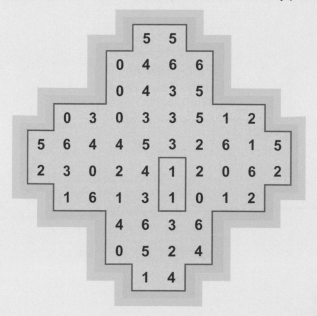

0-0	0-1	0-2	0-3	0-4	0-5	0-6

1-1	1-2	1-3	1-4	1-5	1-6	2-2
✔						

2-3	2-4	2-5	2-6	3-3	3-4	3-5

3-6	4-4	4-5	4-6	5-5	5-6	6-6

Each of the small squares in the grid below contains either A, B or C. Each row, column, and diagonal line of six squares has exactly two of each letter. Can you tell the letter in each square?

Across
1 The Bs are between the As
2 Each B is directly next to and right of a C
3 Each B is directly next to and right of an A
4 The As are next to each other
5 No two letters the same are directly next to each other
6 No two letters the same are directly next to each other

Down
1 The Cs are between the As
2 The Cs are next to each other
3 No two letters the same are directly next to each other
4 The Bs are lower than the As
5 The Bs are next to each other
6 The As are next to each other

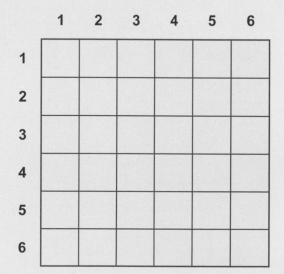

38

Every row and column in this grid originally contained one heart, one club, one diamond, one spade and two blank squares, although not necessarily in that order.

Every symbol with a black arrow refers to the first of the four symbols encountered when travelling in the direction of the arrow. Every symbol with a white arrow refers to the second of the four symbols encountered in the direction of the arrow.

Can you complete the original grid?

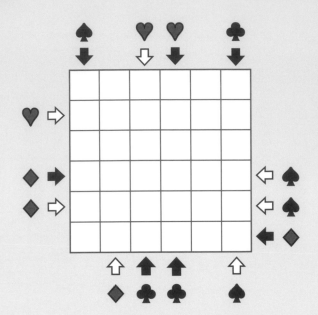

39

The blank squares below should be filled with whole numbers between 1 and 30 inclusive, any of which may occur more than once, or not at all.

The numbers in every horizontal row add up to the totals on the right, as do the two long diagonal lines; whilst those in every vertical column add up to the totals along the bottom.

								101
	25	7	17	20	16			119
30	22			15	24			128
4		18			13	9		92
21			2	16	27	20		108
12	19	25			14	26		128
	18	10	22	9		24		86
17	13		14	26	23	12		124
107	116	122	84	149	95	112	105	

40

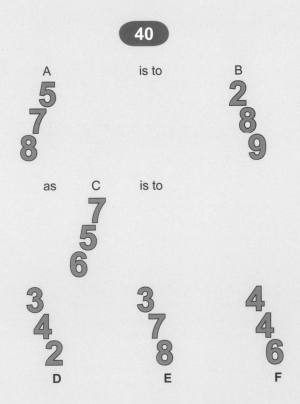

A   is to   B

as   C   is to

D   E   F

Can you place the hexagons into the grid, so that where any hexagon touches another along a straight line, the number in both triangles is the same? No rotation of any hexagon is allowed!

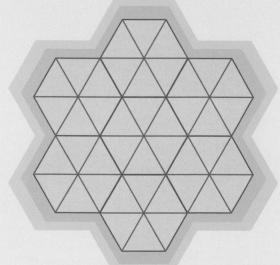

Twelve L-shapes like the ones here need to be inserted in the grid and each L has one hole in it.

There are three pieces of each of the four kinds shown here and any piece may be turned or flipped over before being put in the grid. No pieces of the same kind touch, even at a corner.

The pieces fit together so well that you cannot see any spaces between them; only the holes show.

Can you tell where the Ls are?

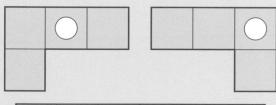

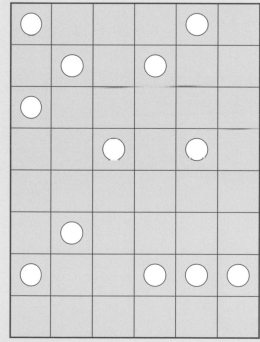

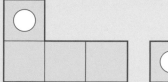

Which of the four lettered alternatives (A, B, C or D) fits most logically into the empty square?

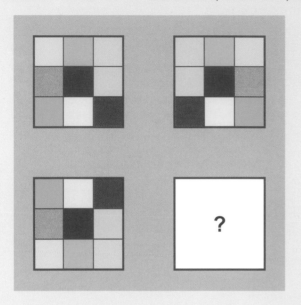

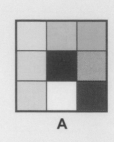

A

B

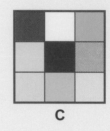

?

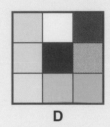

C

D

Which four pieces can be fitted together to form an exact copy of this shape?

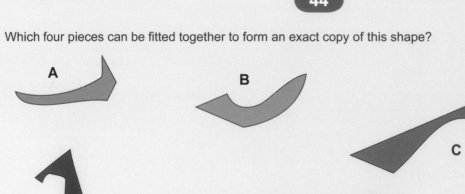

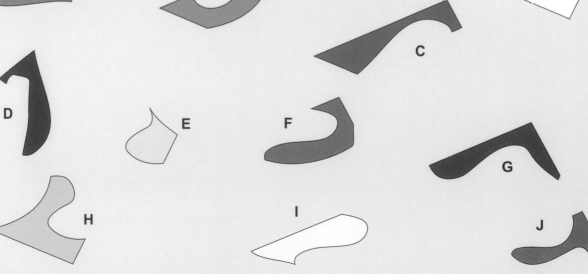

A

B

C

D

E

F

G

H

I

J

Can you place the vessels into the diagram? Some parts of vessels or sea squares have already been filled in. A number to the right or below a row or column refers to the number of occupied squares in that row or column.

Any vessel may be positioned horizontally or vertically, but no part of a vessel touches part of any other vessel, either horizontally, vertically or diagonally.

Empty Area of Sea: ≈

Aircraft Carrier:

Battleships:

Cruisers:

Submarines:

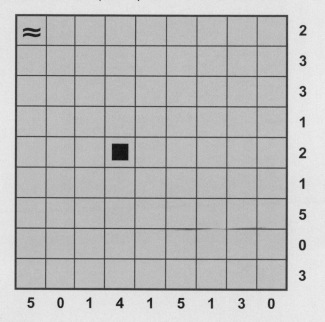

Grid row totals (top to bottom): 2, 3, 3, 1, 2, 1, 5, 0, 3

Grid column totals (left to right): 5, 0, 1, 4, 1, 5, 1, 3, 0

Can you fill each square in the bottom line with the correct digit?

Every square in the solution contains only one digit from each of the lines above, although two or more squares in the solution may contain the same digit.

At the end of every row is a score, which shows:

  a the number of digits placed in the correct finishing position on the bottom line, as indicated by a tick; and

  b the number of digits which appear on the bottom line, but in a different position, as indicated by a cross.

SCORE

9	4	7	3	✔
5	5	5	7	✔
1	7	3	2	✘
2	3	9	1	✔✔
6	6	3	1	✔
				✔✔✔✔

47

The grid should be filled with numbers from 1 to 6, so that each number appears just once in every row and column. The clues refer to the digit totals in the squares, eg A 1 2 3 = 6 means that the numbers in squares A1, A2 and A3 add up to 6.

1 C D 5 = 7

2 D E 6 = 5

3 A 3 4 = 10

4 B 3 4 5 = 6

5 C 1 2 = 3

6 D 1 2 = 11

7 E 2 3 = 4

8 F 1 2 3 = 14

9 A B 1 = 8

10 A B 2 = 7

11 C D 3 = 7

	A	B	C	D	E	F
1						
2						
3						
4						
5						
6						

48

The object of this puzzle is to trace a single path from the top left corner to the bottom right corner of the grid, travelling through all of the cells in either a horizontal, vertical or diagonal direction.

Every cell must be entered once only and your path should take you through the numbers in the sequence 1-2-3-4-5-6-1-2-3-4-5-6, etc.

Can you find the way?

1	2	4	5	6	1
1	6	3	6	5	2
2	5	2	1	4	3
3	4	1	3	5	4
4	2	3	6	4	5
5	6	1	2	3	6

49

Draw a single continuous loop, by connecting the dots. No line may cross the path of another.

The figure inside each set of any four surrounding dots indicates the total number of surrounding lines.

```
    1   1   1               1
    0   1   2           1   1       2
        2           3           0   1
1   1   2   2   1       2
2               1               2       1
1       1   2   2
    1                       3
2   1   2   1                   3
    1   3           0
    1       1       1       2   1
1           2   1   1       1   2
        1   1       3       1   2
```

50

Each horizontal row and vertical column should contain different shapes and different numbers.

Every square will contain one number and one shape and no combination may be repeated anywhere else in the puzzle.

1   2   3   4   5

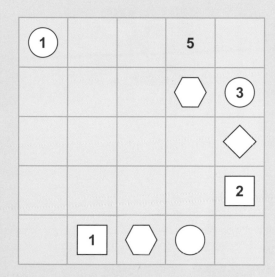

51

Given that the letters are valued 1-26 according to their places in the alphabet, can you crack the mystery code to reveal the missing letter?

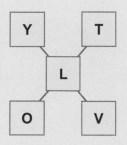
Y   T
  L
O   V

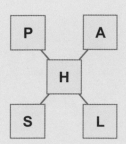
P   A
  H
S   L

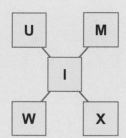
U   M
  I
W   X

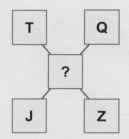
T   Q
  ?
J   Z

52

Which is the odd one out?

A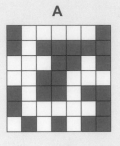

B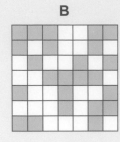

C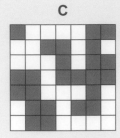

D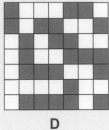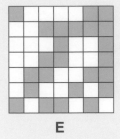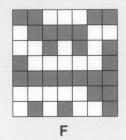

D

E

F

53

Which of the alternatives (A, B, C or D) comes next in this sequence?

?

A

B

C

D

Place the eight tiles into the puzzle grid so that all adjacent numbers on each tile match up. Tiles may be rotated through 360 degrees, but none may be flipped over.

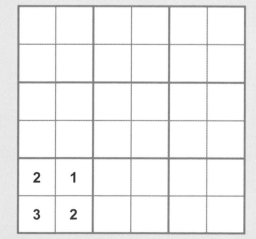

Place all twelve of the pieces into the grid. Any may be rotated or flipped over, but none may touch another, not even diagonally. The numbers outside the grid refer to the number of consecutive black squares; and each block is separated from the others by at least one white square. For instance, '3 2' could refer to a row with none, one or more white squares, then three black squares, then at least one white square, then two more black squares, followed by any number of white squares.

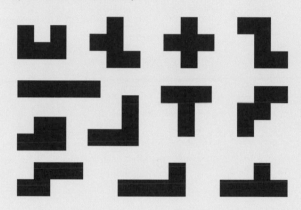

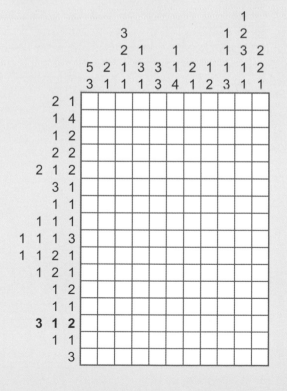

56

What number should replace the question mark?

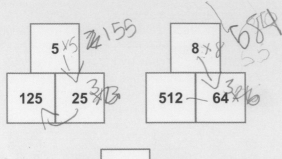

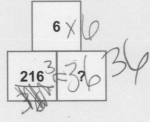

57

In the square below, change the positions of six numbers, one per horizontal row, vertical column and long diagonal line of six smaller squares, in such a way that the numbers in each row, column and long diagonal line total exactly 130. Any number may appear more than once in a row, column or line.

25	8	10	28	43	21
30	21	25	15	25	21
27	32	3	17	10	23
18	34	25	25	21	16
15	27	23	32	11	12
22	13	26	20	29	27

58

Every brick in this pyramid contains a number which is the sum of the two numbers below it, so that F=A+B, etc. Just work out the missing numbers!

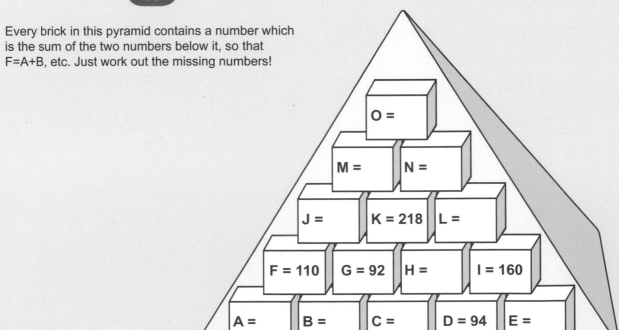

With the starter already given, can you fit all of the remaining listed numbers into this grid? Take care, this puzzle may not be as easy as it looks!

135	625	3388	35545	76129
163	678	5550	40557	76591
251	786	6759	44373	93413
269	836	6939	46222	194215
302	887	7392	49423	274106
428	941	7401	53321	599098
429	945	9972	57164	656152
448	966	11775	61106	666444
500	969	19964	66025	933310
520	1082	25486	70036	8362246
580	2044	31231	71549	9959949
603	2337	34172 ✓	73973	

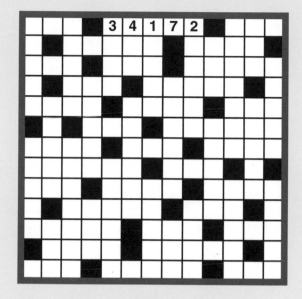

The chart gives directions to a hidden treasure behind the centre black square in the grid. Move the indicated number of spaces north, south, east and west (eg 4N means move four squares north) stopping at every square once only to arrive there. At which square should you start?

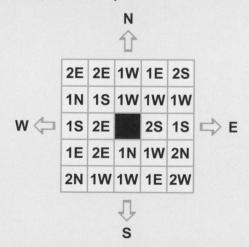

Fill the grid so that every horizontal row and vertical column contains the numbers 1-5. The 'greater than' or 'less than' signs indicate where a number is larger or smaller than that in the neighbouring square.

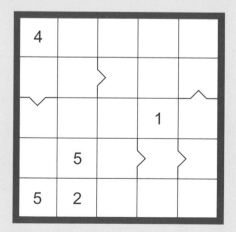

Each of the eight segments of the spider's web should be filled with a different number from 1 to 8, in such a way that every ring also contains a different number from 1 to 8.

The segments run from the outside of the spider's web to the centre, and the rings run all the way around.

Some numbers are already in place. Can you fill in the rest?

Every oval shape in this diagram contains a different letter of the alphabet from A to K inclusive. Use the clues to determine their locations. Reference in the clues to 'due' means in any location along the same horizontal or vertical line.

1 The A is next to and west of the H, which is next to and north of the C.

2 The B is due west of the C, which is next to and north of the F.

3 The E is further north than the J, which is due north of the A.

4 The K is next to and west of the G, which is next to and north of the I, which is next to and north of the D.

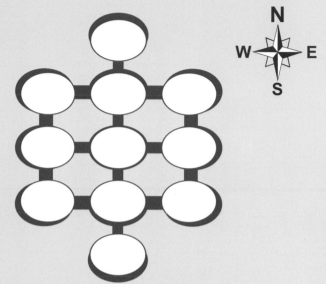

Fill the three empty circles with the symbols +, – and x in some order, to make a sum which totals the number in the centre. Each symbol must be used once and calculations are made in the direction of travel (clockwise).

```
        =        22

  6                   

         46

                 2

     2        
```

The numbers at the top and on the left side show the quantity of single-digit numbers (1-9) used in that row and column. The numbers at the bottom and on the right side show the sum of the digits. A number may appear more than once in a row or column, but no numbers are in squares that touch, even at a corner.

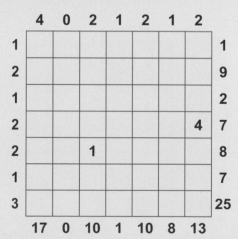

	4	0	2	1	2	1	2	
1								1
2								9
1								2
2							4	7
2			1					8
1								7
3								25
	17	0	10	1	10	8	13	

66

Using the numbers below, complete these six equations (three reading across and three reading downwards). Every number is used once.

1 2 3 4 5
6 7 8 9

	x	5	−	7	=	23
+		+		+		
3	−		x		=	6
−		x		x		
	x	8	x		=	24
=		=		=		
8		30		7		

67

In the grid below, which number should replace the question mark?

17	2	43	52	4	1	3
7	21	22	11	7	15	49
12	16	32	9	18	15	40
27	11	?	5	31	51	9
5	42	5	3	11	16	80
36	17	10	4	65	28	15
23	25	30	37	11	28	28

68

When the box below is folded to form a cube, just one of the five options (A, B, C, D or E) can be produced. Which?

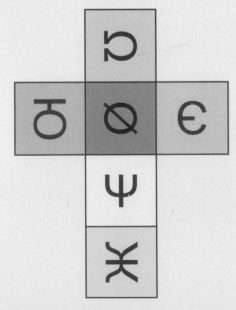

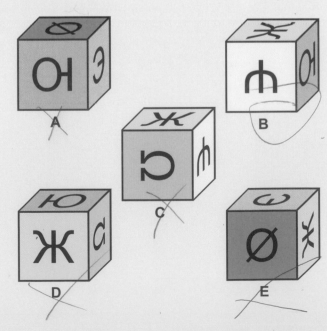

A

B

C

D

E

69

In this puzzle, an amateur coin collector has been out with his metal detector, searching for booty. He didn't have time to dig up all the coins he found, so has made a grid map, showing their locations, in the hope that if he loses the map, at least no-one else will understand it…

Those squares containing numbers are empty, but where a number appears in a square, it indicates how many coins are located in the squares (up to a maximum of eight) surrounding the numbered one, touching it at any corner or side. There is only one coin in any individual square.

Place a circle into every square containing a coin.

				1	3			2	1
1		1							
1			2	1			3		
	1		1		2		4	4	
0									
					0				1
		6					0	1	
2				3		1	2		
1		4			2				2
	0	2		2			3		

70

Every row and column of this grid should contain one each of the letters A, B, C, D, E and F. Each of the six shapes (marked by thicker lines) should also contain one each of the letters A, B, C, D, E and F. Can you complete the grid?

				B	A
					C
			D		
		E			
			F		

71

Each symbol stands for a different number. In order to reach the correct total at the end of each row and column, what is the value of the circle, cross, pentagon, square and star?

cross	circle	pentagon	circle	cross	= 26
pentagon	square	circle	square	cross	= 20
square	cross	star	star	circle	= 14
cross	pentagon	star	pentagon	square	= 18
square	square	square	star	square	= 9
= 16	= 20	= 17	= 17	= 17	

SECTION 1

35

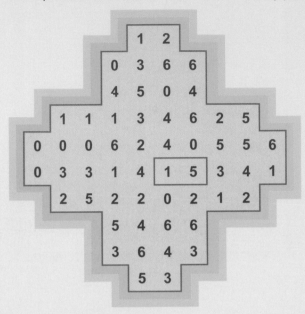

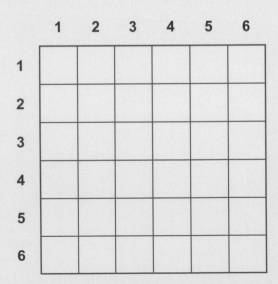

A standard set of 28 dominoes has been laid out as shown. Can you draw in the edges of them all? The check-box is provided as an aid and the domino already placed will help.

0-0	0-1	0-2	0-3	0-4	0-5	0-6

1-1	1-2	1-3	1-4	1-5	1-6	2-2
				✔		

2-3	2-4	2-5	2-6	3-3	3-4	3-5

3-6	4-4	4-5	4-6	5-5	5-6	6-6

73

Each of the small squares in the grid below contains either A, B or C. Each row, column, and diagonal line of six squares has exactly two of each letter. Can you tell the letter in each square?

Across
1. The Cs are next to each other
2. The Bs are further right than the As
3. Each A is directly next to and right of a C
4. The Bs are between the Cs
5. The Cs are next to each other
6. No two letters the same are directly next to each other

Down
1. The Cs are lower than the As
2. No two letters the same are directly next to each other
3. The Cs are lower than the As
4. The As are lower than the Bs
5. No two letters the same are directly next to each other
6. No two letters the same are directly next to each other

Every row and column in this grid originally contained one heart, one club, one diamond, one spade and two blank squares, although not necessarily in that order.

Every symbol with a black arrow refers to the first of the four symbols encountered when travelling in the direction of the arrow. Every symbol with a white arrow refers to the second of the four symbols encountered in the direction of the arrow.

Can you complete the original grid?

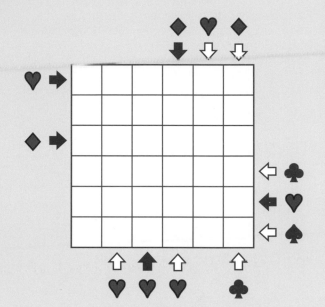

The blank squares below should be filled with whole numbers between 1 and 30 inclusive, any of which may occur more than once, or not at all.

The numbers in every horizontal row add up to the totals on the right, as do the two long diagonal lines; whilst those in every vertical column add up to the totals along the bottom.

							125
	14	3	13	7	12		103
20	28	2		21		17	119
4		6	11	21	10		98
6	17	28			13	27	127
	29	4	9	5	15	23	115
19		16	24		13	20	121
21	13		30		11	22	136
129	138	73	125	105	89	160	12

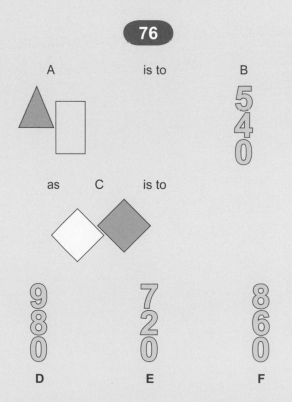

A   is to   B

as   C   is to

D   E   F

77

Can you place the hexagons into the grid, so that where any hexagon touches another along a straight line, the number in both triangles is the same? No rotation of any hexagon is allowed!

78

Twelve L-shapes like the ones here need to be inserted in the grid and each L has one hole in it.

There are three pieces of each of the four kinds shown here and any piece may be turned or flipped over before being put in the grid. No pieces of the same kind touch, even at a corner.

The pieces fit together so well that you cannot see any spaces between them; only the holes show.

Can you tell where the Ls are?

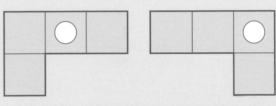

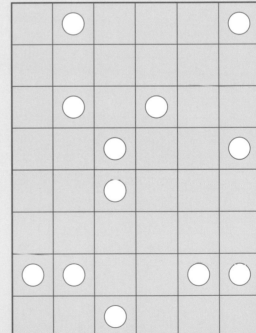

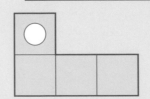

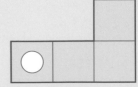

Draw walls to partition the grid into areas (some walls are already drawn in for you). Each area must contain two circles, area sizes must match those numbers shown next to the grid and each '+' must be linked to at least two walls.

3, 3, 3, 5, 5, 6

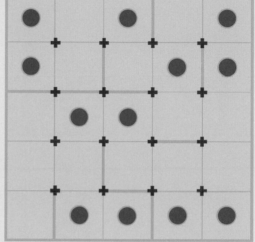

80

Which of the four lettered alternatives (A, B, C or D) fits most logically into the empty square?

13	6	9
11	12	8
27	4	18

27	18	23
25	24	20
41	16	30

55	42	51
53	48	44
69	40	54

A

55	42	51
53	46	44
69	40	54

B

41	30	37
39	36	32
55	28	42

?

55	43	50
53	48	44
69	40	54

C

55	42	51
54	48	42
69	40	54

D

SECTION

1

39

81

The object of this puzzle is to trace a single path from the top left corner to the bottom right corner of the grid, travelling through all of the cells in either a horizontal, vertical or diagonal direction.

Every cell must be entered once only and your path should take you through the numbers in the sequence 1-2-3-4-5-6-1-2-3-4-5-6, etc.

Can you find the way?

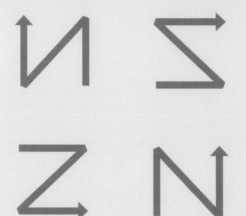

1	4	3	2	6	5
2	4	5	1	3	4
5	3	6	1	3	2
2	6	1	2	1	4
3	1	6	2	6	5
4	5	3	4	5	6

82

The grid should be filled with numbers from 1 to 6, so that each number appears just once in every row and column. The clues refer to the digit totals in the squares, eg A 1 2 3 = 6 means that the numbers in squares A1, A2 and A3 add up to 6.

1 D E F 5 = 12

2 D E F 6 = 11

3 A 2 3 = 10

4 B 2 3 = 9

5 C 1 2 = 3

6 D 1 2 = 8

7 E 3 4 = 6

8 F 3 4 = 8

9 E F 1 = 5

10 E F 2 = 9

11 C D 3 = 6

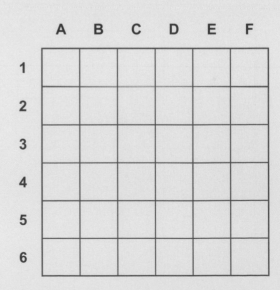

Can you fill each square in the bottom line with the correct digit?

Every square in the solution contains only one digit from each of the lines above, although two or more squares in the solution may contain the same digit.

At the end of every row is a score, which shows:

a the number of digits placed in the correct finishing position on the bottom line, as indicated by a tick; and

b the number of digits which appear on the bottom line, but in a different position, as indicated by a cross.

SCORE

5	6	4	8	✗
4	8	4	5	✗
3	5	4	2	✗
3	2	7	3	✗
1	1	5	7	✓✓
				✓✓✓✓

Can you place the vessels into the diagram? Some parts of vessels or sea squares have already been filled in. A number to the right or below a row or column refers to the number of occupied squares in that row or column.

Any vessel may be positioned horizontally or vertically, but no part of a vessel touches part of any other vessel, either horizontally, vertically or diagonally.

Empty Area of Sea: ≈

Aircraft Carrier: ◀■■▶

Battleships: ◀■▶ ◀■▶

Cruisers: ◀▶ ◀▶ ◀▶

Submarines: ● ● ● ●

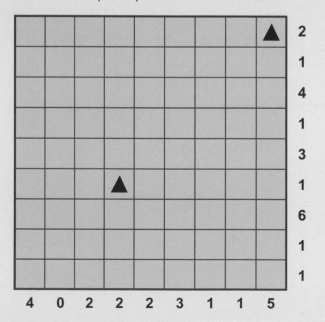

2
1
4
1
3
1
6
1
1

4 0 2 2 2 3 1 1 5

S
E
C
T
I
O
N

1

41

85

Draw a single continuous loop, by connecting the dots. No line may cross the path of another.

The figure inside each set of any four surrounding dots indicates the total number of surrounding lines.

```
2        3        3     1
1  1  1     2     1     1
1     3              2  1
            1  0        2
      3     1     0     0
2           2     0     1
3  1     1  1  3     2
   1     3        1  2     3
   0        0     0  2
2  1  3  1     0  2     1
3                 1  1  1
      1        2  0
```

86

Each horizontal row and vertical column should contain different shapes and different numbers.

Every square will contain one number and one shape and no combination may be repeated anywhere else in the puzzle.

1   2   3   4   5

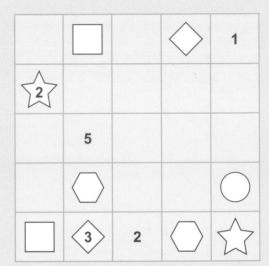

87

Given that the letters are valued 1-26 according to their places in the alphabet, can you crack the mystery code to reveal the missing letter?

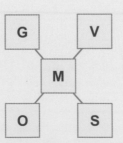

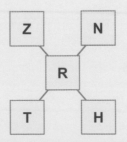

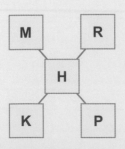

A set of dominoes is to be placed in four rows as shown below. The numbers indicate which values are shown on all the dominoes in each column and the relevant half of the domino in every row. Find out where each domino is placed by carefully comparing rows and columns to determine the possible positions of certain dominoes: for instance, if any column contains only one 6, then the domino 6/6 isn't in that column.

A set of dominoes consists of:

0/0, 0/1, 0/2, 0/3, 0/4, 0/5, 0/6, 1/1, 1/2, 1/3, 1/4, 1/5, 1/6, 2/2,

2/3, 2/4, 2/5, 2/6, 3/3, 3/4, 3/5, 3/6, 4/4, 4/5, 4/6, 5/5, 5/6, 6/6.

0, 1, 2, 2, 3, 4, 4, 4.	0, 1, 3, 3, 4, 4, 5, 6.	1, 4, 4, 5, 5, 5, 6, 6.	0, 0, 1, 2, 2, 6, 6, 6.	0, 2, 3, 3, 3, 3, 5, 6.	0, 0, 0, 1, 1, 2, 2, 3.	1, 1, 2, 4, 5, 5, 5, 6.

0, 2, 3, 4, 5, 6, 6.							
0, 1, 3, 3, 4, 6, 6.							
0, 1, 1, 1, 3, 5, 5.							
0, 0, 1, 2, 2, 2, 3.							
2, 2, 2, 3, 4, 4, 5.							
2, 3, 4, 4, 5, 6, 6.							
0, 1, 5, 5, 5, 6, 6.							
0, 0, 1, 1, 3, 4, 4.							

Place the eight tiles into the puzzle grid so that all adjacent numbers on each tile match up. Tiles may be rotated through 360 degrees, but none may be flipped over.

Place all twelve of the pieces into the grid. Any may be rotated or flipped over, but none may touch another, not even diagonally. The numbers outside the grid refer to the number of consecutive black squares; and each block is separated from the others by at least one white square. For instance, '3 2' could refer to a row with none, one or more white squares, then three black squares, then at least one white square, then two more black squares, followed by any number of white squares.

Tiles:

1	2
4	1

1	3
2	3

2	3
3	1

3	2
1	4

1	1
3	2

4	3
3	2

4	2
1	3

4	3
3	1

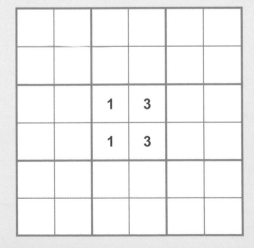

(grid with central cells: 1 3 / 1 3)

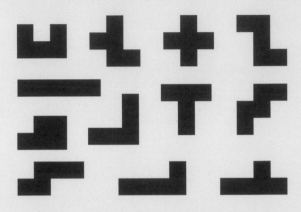

91

In the diagram below, which number should replace the question mark?

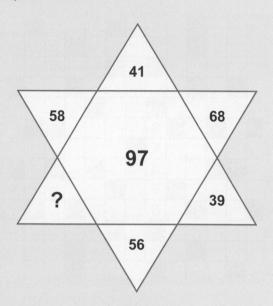

92

In the square below, change the positions of six numbers, one per horizontal row, vertical column and long diagonal line of six smaller squares, in such a way that the numbers in each row, column and long diagonal line total exactly 144. Any number may appear more than once in a row, column or line.

25	31	20	35	11	25
12	17	36	15	34	5
31	20	14	40	36	11
42	15	22	26	31	38
39	6	21	26	12	12
25	30	34	10	32	25

93

Every brick in this pyramid contains a number which is the sum of the two numbers below it, so that F=A+B, etc. Just work out the missing numbers!

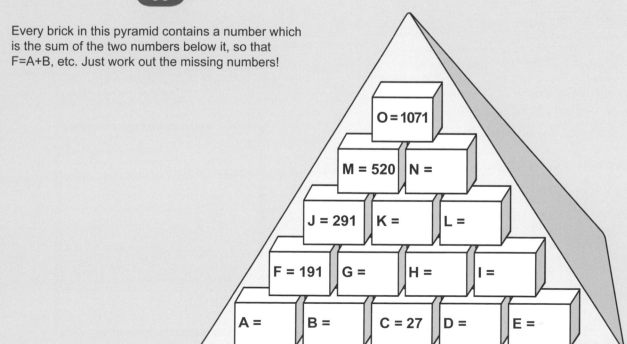

With the starter already given, can you fit all of the remaining listed numbers into this grid? Take care, this puzzle may not be as easy as it looks!

15	206	787	23010	89590
37	252	789	28839	94290
40	288	1691	28850	94909
55	388	2820	29038	95870
60	389	8509	30517	96404
85	390	8988	30680	97076
90	405	8992	33430	98874
96	470	9028	35966	99650
108	570	10731	76864	154885
147	585	16933	80004	160746
161	606	17669	81456 ✓	285611
202	694	20851	85417	897749

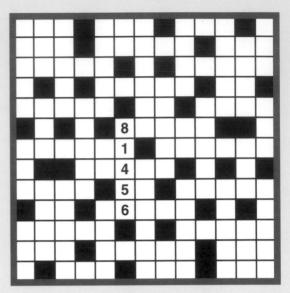

The chart gives directions to a hidden treasure behind the centre black square in the grid. Move the indicated number of spaces north, south, east and west (eg 4N means move four squares north) stopping at every square once only to arrive there. At which square should you start?

N

1S	1W	1E	1S	2S
2S	1S	1N	2W	1N
2E	1W	■	2S	1W
1E	1S	2N	1W	2N
2E	1W	2E	1N	1N

W ⇦   ⇨ E

S

Fill the grid so that every horizontal row and vertical column contains the numbers 1-5. The 'greater than' or 'less than' signs indicate where a number is larger or smaller than that in the neighbouring square.

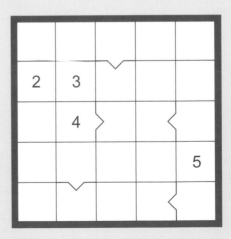

Each of the eight segments of the spider's web should be filled with a different number from 1 to 8, in such a way that every ring also contains a different number from 1 to 8.

The segments run from the outside of the spider's web to the centre, and the rings run all the way around.

Some numbers are already in place. Can you fill in the rest?

A standard set of 28 dominoes has been laid out as shown. Can you draw in the edges of them all? The check-box is provided as an aid and the domino already placed will help.

0-0	0-1	0-2	0-3	0-4	0-5	0-6
✗	✗	✓	--	✓		

1-1	1-2	1-3	1-4	1-5	1-6	2-2
						✓

2-3	2-4	2-5	2-6	3-3	3-4	3-5

3-6	4-4	4-5	4-6	5-5	5-6	6-6

2

Draw walls to partition the grid into areas (some walls are already drawn in for you). Each area must contain two circles, area sizes must match those numbers shown next to the grid and each '+' must be linked to at least two walls.

2, 3, 4, 4, 5, 7

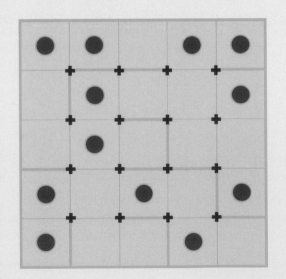

Every row and column in this grid originally contained one heart, one club, one diamond, one spade and two blank squares, although not necessarily in that order.

Every symbol with a black arrow refers to the first of the four symbols encountered when travelling in the direction of the arrow. Every symbol with a white arrow refers to the second of the four symbols encountered in the direction of the arrow.

Can you complete the original grid?

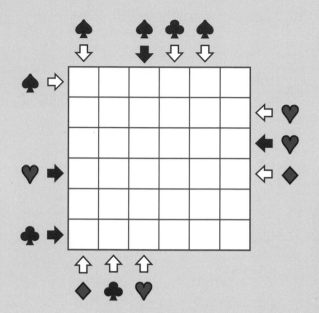

4

The blank squares below should be filled with whole numbers between 1 and 30 inclusive, any of which may occur more than once, or not at all.

The numbers in every horizontal row add up to the totals on the right, as do the two long diagonal lines; whilst those in every vertical column add up to the totals along the bottom.

								101
8	13	17	2			28	7	105
21			10	4	9	3		89
	22	15		16	18	13		128
	23	2		19	9			106
5	14	25	15			21		139
16		28	2	11	6			97
1	12		8	16		25		92
80	127	125	88	125	110	101	131	

5

Draw in the missing hands on the final clock.

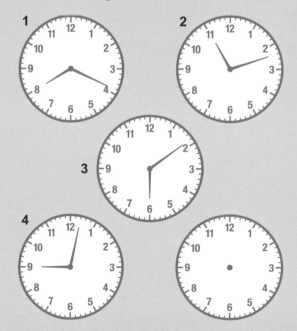

6

Can you place the hexagons into the grid, so that where any hexagon touches another along a straight line, the number in both triangles is the same? No rotation of any hexagon is allowed!

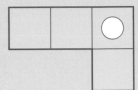

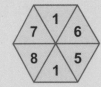

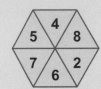

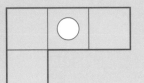

7

Twelve L-shapes like the ones here need to be inserted in the grid and each L has one hole in it.

There are three pieces of each of the four kinds shown here and any piece may be turned or flipped over before being put in the grid. No pieces of the same kind touch, even at a corner.

The pieces fit together so well that you cannot see any spaces between them; only the holes show.

Can you tell where the Ls are?

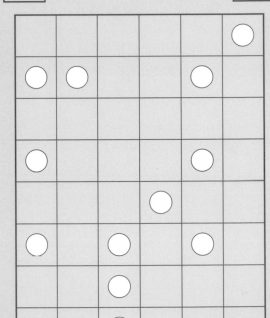

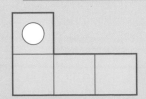

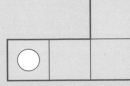

8

In this puzzle, an amateur coin collector has been out with his metal detector, searching for booty. He didn't have time to dig up all the coins he found, so has made a grid map, showing their locations, in the hope that if he loses the map, at least no-one else will understand it…

Those squares containing numbers are empty, but where a number appears in a square, it indicates how many coins are located in the squares (up to a maximum of eight) surrounding the numbered one, touching it at any corner or side. There is only one coin in any individual square.

Place a circle into every square containing a coin.

					1			1	
	0	2	2			1	0		
								2	2
3							1	1	
			3			1		1	
3			4	3					
2		4							
1		3			6		1	1	
	3		5				0	0	
1					2				

9

The grid should be filled with numbers from 1 to 6, so that each number appears just once in every row and column. The clues refer to the digit totals in the squares, eg A 1 2 3 = 6 means that the numbers in squares A1, A2 and A3 add up to 6.

1 E F 6 = 11

2 A 4 5 6 = 8

3 B 4 5 = 8

4 C 4 5 6 = 10

5 D 5 6 = 10

6 E 1 2 = 9

7 F 1 2 = 3

8 A B 1 = 11

9 A B 2 = 9

10 B C 3 = 9

11 E F 4 = 6

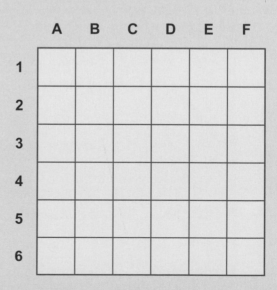

Each of the small squares in the grid below contains either A, B or C. Each row, column, and diagonal line of six squares has exactly two of each letter. Can you tell the letter in each square?

Across

1 The Cs are between the Bs
2 The Bs are further right than the As
3 The As are between the Bs
4 The Bs are further right than the Cs
5 The Cs are further right than the Bs
6 The As are between the Bs

Down

1 The Cs are lower than the Bs
2 The Bs are next to each other
3 Each B is directly next to and below a C
4 Each C is directly next to and below a B
5 The Cs are between the Bs
6 The Bs are between the Cs

	1	2	3	4	5	6
1						
2						
3						
4						
5						
6						

The object of this puzzle is to trace a single path from the top left corner to the bottom right corner of the grid, travelling through all of the cells in either a horizontal, vertical or diagonal direction.

Every cell must be entered once only and your path should take you through the numbers in the sequence 1-2-3-4-5-6-1-2-3-4-5-6, etc.

Can you find the way?

1	2	6	1	6	5
4	5	3	1	2	4
3	6	5	4	2	3
2	1	4	3	6	2
1	2	4	5	3	1
6	5	3	4	5	6

Can you place the vessels into the diagram? Some parts of vessels or sea squares have already been filled in. A number to the right or below a row or column refers to the number of occupied squares in that row or column.

Any vessel may be positioned horizontally or vertically, but no part of a vessel touches part of any other vessel, either horizontally, vertically or diagonally.

Empty Area of Sea:

Aircraft Carrier:

Battleships:

Cruisers:

Submarines:

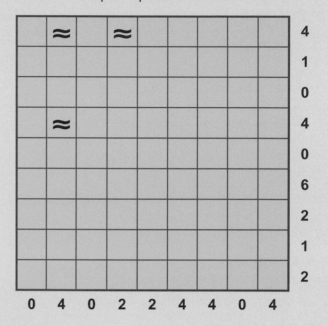

Rows (top to bottom): 4, 1, 0, 4, 0, 6, 2, 1, 2

Columns (left to right): 0, 4, 0, 2, 2, 4, 4, 0, 4

Can you fill each square in the bottom line with the correct digit?

Every square in the solution contains only one digit from each of the lines above, although two or more squares in the solution may contain the same digit.

At the end of every row is a score, which shows:

a the number of digits placed in the correct finishing position on the bottom line, as indicated by a tick; and

b the number of digits which appear on the bottom line, but in a different position, as indicated by a cross.

SCORE

2	8	5	2	✓ ✗ ✗
1	1	8	2	✗ ✗ ✗
1	8	7	4	✗ ✗
8	3	4	2	✗ ✗
7	5	6	2	✗
				✓ ✓ ✓ ✓

S
E
C
T
I
O
N

2

53

14

Draw a single continuous loop, by connecting the dots. No line may cross the path of another.

The figure inside each set of any four surrounding dots indicates the total number of surrounding lines.

```
.   .   .   .   .   .   .   .   .   .
      1   2       1   2
.   .   .   .   .   .   .   .   .   .
  2     1               0   1   2
.   .   .   .   .   .   .   .   .   .
  2   1   1     3   0               1
.   .   .   .   .   .   .   .   .   .
  2   0                 1       2
.   .   .   .   .   .   .   .   .   .
    1   1                   1   2
.   .   .   .   .   .   .   .   .   .
      3   2       1       2   2
.   .   .   .   .   .   .   .   .   .
  3                 3   2   1
.   .   .   .   .   .   .   .   .   .
    0       3           0           2
.   .   .   .   .   .   .   .   .   .
      2   2   0               2   3
.   .   .   .   .   .   .   .   .   .
  0                 1   3   2   2
.   .   .   .   .   .   .   .   .   .
                    1               2
.   .   .   .   .   .   .   .   .   .
  1   2       2   1   3       1   1   2
.   .   .   .   .   .   .   .   .   .
```

15

Each horizontal row and vertical column should contain different shapes and different numbers.

Every square will contain one number and one shape and no combination may be repeated anywhere else in the puzzle.

| 1 | 2 | 3 | 4 | 5 |

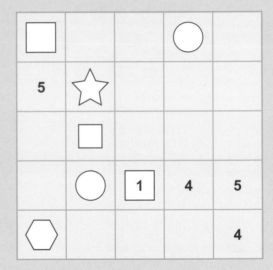

16

Given that the letters are valued 1-26 according to their places in the alphabet, can you crack the mystery code to reveal the missing letter?

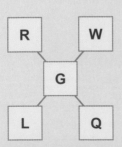

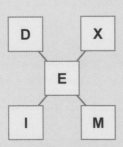

A set of dominoes is to be placed in four rows as shown below. The numbers indicate which values are shown on all the dominoes in each column and the relevant half of the domino in every row. Find out where each domino is placed by carefully comparing rows and columns to determine the possible positions of certain dominoes: for instance, if any column contains only one 6, then the domino 6/6 isn't in that column.

A set of dominoes consists of:

0/0, 0/1, 0/2, 0/3, 0/4, 0/5, 0/6, 1/1, 1/2, 1/3, 1/4, 1/5, 1/6, 2/2,

2/3, 2/4, 2/5, 2/6, 3/3, 3/4, 3/5, 3/6, 4/4, 4/5, 4/6, 5/5, 5/6, 6/6.

	1, 2, 2, 2, 4, 5, 6, 6.	1, 1, 1, 1, 2, 3, 5, 6.	0, 3, 3, 3, 3, 3, 4, 6.	0, 1, 3, 3, 4, 4, 5, 6.	0, 0, 4, 5, 5, 5, 5, 6.	0, 1, 1, 2, 4, 4, 4, 6.	0, 0, 0, 2, 2, 2, 5, 6.
1, 3, 4, 4, 6, 6, 6.							
0, 1, 1, 2, 3, 3, 5.							
0, 2, 3, 3, 4, 5, 6.							
0, 0, 1, 2, 2, 5, 6.							
1, 2, 2, 3, 4, 4, 5.							
0, 0, 4, 5, 5, 6, 6.							
0, 1, 1, 3, 3, 4, 6.							
0, 1, 2, 2, 4, 5, 5.							

18

Place the eight tiles into the puzzle grid so that all adjacent numbers on each tile match up. Tiles may be rotated through 360 degrees, but none may be flipped over.

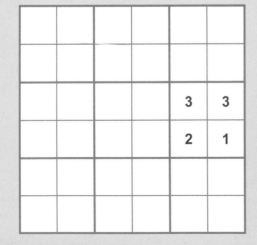

19

Place all twelve of the pieces into the grid. Any may be rotated or flipped over, but none may touch another, not even diagonally. The numbers outside the grid refer to the number of consecutive black squares; and each block is separated from the others by at least one white square. For instance, '3 2' could refer to a row with none, one or more white squares, then three black squares, then at least one white square, then two more black squares, followed by any number of white squares.

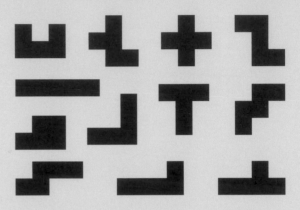

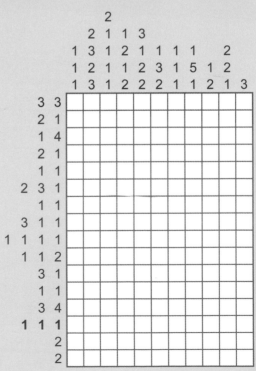

20

In the diagram below, which letter should replace the question mark?

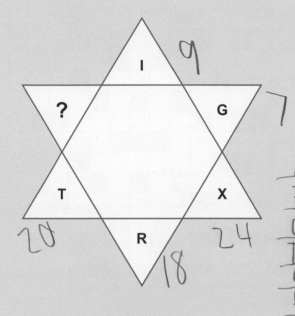

21

In the square below, change the positions of six numbers, one per horizontal row, vertical column and long diagonal line of six smaller squares, in such a way that the numbers in each row, column and long diagonal line total exactly 177. Any number may appear more than once in a row, column or line.

53	29	14	36	42	21
14	31	34	50	26	16
34	36	32	29	27	22
11	47	58	3	9	27
33	27	2	33	26	33
10	25	40	56	41	35

22

Every brick in this pyramid contains a number which is the sum of the two numbers below it, so that F=A+B, etc. Just work out the missing numbers!

O =

M =   N = 723

J =   K =   L =

F = 153   G =   H = 196   I = 189

A =   B =   C = 75   D =   E =

With the starter already given, can you fit all of the remaining listed numbers into this grid? Take care, this puzzle may not be as easy as it looks!

23	260	732	5147	62370
32	308	753	5661	65612
40	376	829	6238	66235 ✓
51	379	896	6325	72758
62	403	926	7731	83079
77	432	981	8913	92631
127	493	1891	14946	94154
177	575	2073	29630	96507
189	582	2337	30073	195092
217	635	2485	38472	592747
240	649	3327	50491	771926
256	683	4564	62066	793421

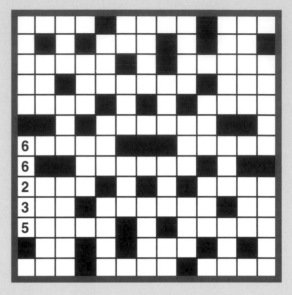

The chart gives directions to a hidden treasure behind the centre black square in the grid. Move the indicated number of spaces north, south, east and west (eg 4N means move four squares north) stopping at every square once only to arrive there. At which square should you start?

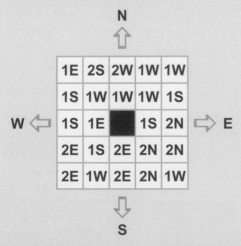

Fill the grid so that every horizontal row and vertical column contains the numbers 1-5. The 'greater than' or 'less than' signs indicate where a number is larger or smaller than that in the neighbouring square.

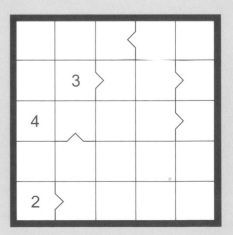

58

Each of the eight segments of the spider's web should be filled with a different number from 1 to 8, in such a way that every ring also contains a different number from 1 to 8.

The segments run from the outside of the spider's web to the centre, and the rings run all the way around.

Some numbers are already in place. Can you fill in the rest?

Every oval shape in this diagram contains a different letter of the alphabet from A to K inclusive. Use the clues to determine their locations. Reference in the clues to 'due' means in any location along the same horizontal or vertical line.

1 The A is next to and north of the D, which is next to and north of the G, which is due west of the C, which is due north of the I.

2 The B is due north of the F, which is next to and west of the E, which is further west than the I.

3 The J is further west and further south than the H, which is due east of the D.

4 The K is further south than the F.

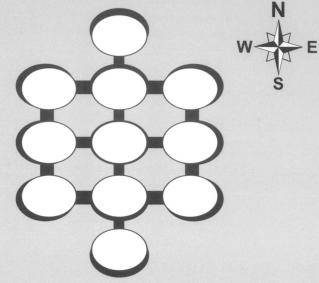

Fill the three empty circles with the symbols +, − and x in some order, to make a sum which totals the number in the centre. Each symbol must be used once and calculations are made in the direction of travel (clockwise).

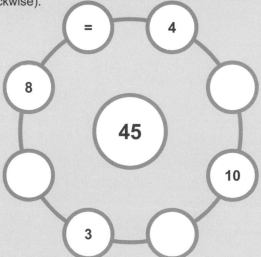

The numbers at the top and on the left side show the quantity of single-digit numbers (1-9) used in that row and column. The numbers at the bottom and on the right side show the sum of the digits. A number may appear more than once in a row or column, but no numbers are in squares that touch, even at a corner.

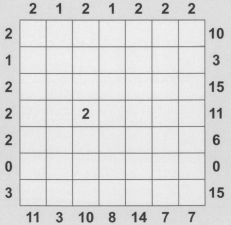

Using the numbers below, complete these six equations (three reading across and three reading downwards). Every number is used once.

1   2   3   4   5
  6   7   8   9

	+		−		=	4
−	■	+	■	+		
	x		+		=	11
x	■	−	■	−		
	x		−		=	21
=		=		=		
16		10		7		

In the grid below, which number should replace the question mark?

183	120	68	69	86	81	153
171	109	58	60	78	74	147
159	98	48	51	70	67	141
147	87	38	42	62	60	135
135	76	28	33	54	53	129
123	65	18	24	?	46	123
111	54	8	15	38	39	117

When the box below is folded to form a cube, just one of the five options (A, B, C, D or E) can be produced. Which?

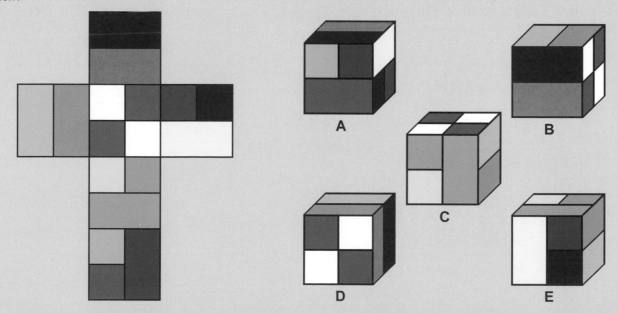

A

B

C

D

E

33

In this puzzle, an amateur coin collector has been out with his metal detector, searching for booty. He didn't have time to dig up all the coins he found, so has made a grid map, showing their locations, in the hope that if he loses the map, at least no-one else will understand it…

Those squares containing numbers are empty, but where a number appears in a square, it indicates how many coins are located in the squares (up to a maximum of eight) surrounding the numbered one, touching it at any corner or side. There is only one coin in any individual square.

Place a circle into every square containing a coin.

		2							
2			1			3		2	0
	2			5		3			
	2	2				2		2	1
	4						0	2	
		2		3	3	1			
2		1				3			
							4		1
0			0					1	
					3				

34

Each symbol stands for a different number. In order to reach the correct total at the end of each row and column, what is the value of the circle, cross, pentagon, square and star?

●	☆	●	✚	⬠	= 21
●	✚	◻	●	☆	= 29
◻	☆	⬠	✚	●	= 23
☆	⬠	●	●	☆	= 23
☆	☆	●	●	☆	= 26
=	=	=	=	=	
31	15	31	25	20	

35

Every row and column of this grid should contain one each of the letters A, B, C, D, E and F. Each of the six shapes (marked by thicker lines) should also contain one each of the letters A, B, C, D, E and F. Can you complete the grid?

			B		A
D				C	
E					
F					

A standard set of 28 dominoes has been laid out as shown. Can you draw in the edges of them all? The check-box is provided as an aid and the domino already placed will help.

0-0	0-1	0-2	0-3	0-4	0-5	0-6
				✔		

1-1	1-2	1-3	1-4	1-5	1-6	2-2

2-3	2-4	2-5	2-6	3-3	3-4	3-5

3-6	4-4	4-5	4-6	5-5	5-6	6-6

Each of the small squares in the grid below contains either A, B or C. Each row, column, and diagonal line of six squares has exactly two of each letter. Can you tell the letter in each square?

Across
1 The As are next to each other
2 Each B is directly next to and right of an A
3 The Cs are next to each other
4 The As are next to each other
5 No two letters the same are directly next to each other
6 The As are further right than the Bs

Down
1 The Bs are lower than the As
2 No two letters the same are directly next to each other
3 Each C is directly next to and below a B
4 The Cs are next to each other
5 The Cs are next to each other
6 Each A is directly next to and below a B

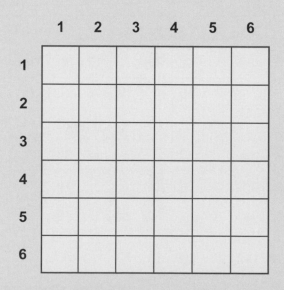

38

Every row and column in this grid originally contained one heart, one club, one diamond, one spade and two blank squares, although not necessarily in that order.

Every symbol with a black arrow refers to the first of the four symbols encountered when travelling in the direction of the arrow. Every symbol with a white arrow refers to the second of the four symbols encountered in the direction of the arrow.

Can you complete the original grid?

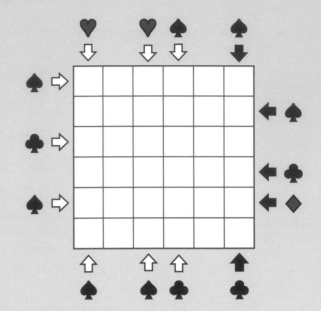

39

The blank squares below should be filled with whole numbers between 1 and 30 inclusive, any of which may occur more than once, or not at all.

The numbers in every horizontal row add up to the totals on the right, as do the two long diagonal lines; whilst those in every vertical column add up to the totals along the bottom.

40

							117
19	8	10	14	6			101
25		2	26		17	7	116
	3	25	2	12	16		90
	15		18	8	7	20	112
13		23		6	14	28	101
21		20	24	5		14	133
4	8			24	9	19	99
126	99	129	98	70	113	117	147

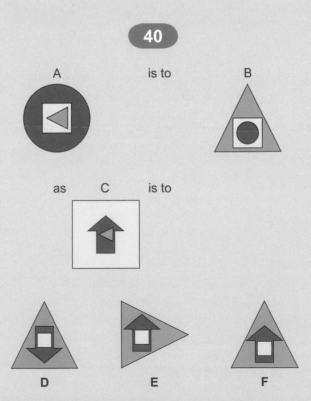

A   is to   B

as   C   is to

D   E   F

Can you place the hexagons into the grid, so that where any hexagon touches another along a straight line, the number in both triangles is the same? No rotation of any hexagon is allowed!

Twelve L-shapes like the ones here need to be inserted in the grid and each L has one hole in it.

There are three pieces of each of the four kinds shown here and any piece may be turned or flipped over before being put in the grid. No pieces of the same kind touch, even at a corner.

The pieces fit together so well that you cannot see any spaces between them; only the holes show.

Can you tell where the Ls are?

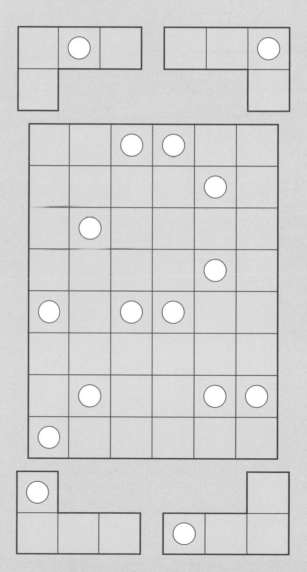

43

Which of the four lettered alternatives (A, B, C or D) fits most logically into the empty square?

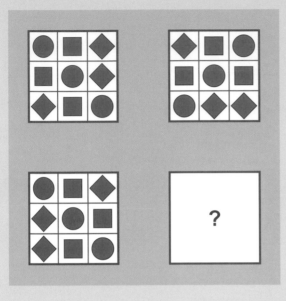

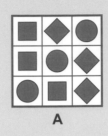

?

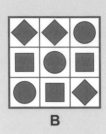

A

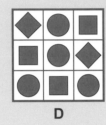

B

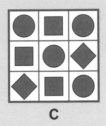

C

D

44

Which four pieces can be fitted together to form an exact copy of this shape?

A

B

C

E

D

F

G

H

I

J

Can you place the vessels into the diagram? Some parts of vessels or sea squares have already been filled in. A number to the right or below a row or column refers to the number of occupied squares in that row or column.

Any vessel may be positioned horizontally or vertically, but no part of a vessel touches part of any other vessel, either horizontally, vertically or diagonally.

Empty Area of Sea:

Aircraft Carrier:

Battleships:

Cruisers:

Submarines:

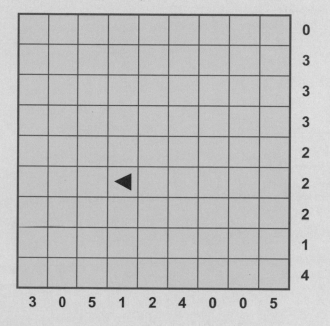

0
3
3
3
2
2
2
1
4

3 0 5 1 2 4 0 0 5

46

Can you fill each square in the bottom line with the correct digit?

Every square in the solution contains only one digit from each of the lines above, although two or more squares in the solution may contain the same digit.

At the end of every row is a score, which shows:

a the number of digits placed in the correct finishing position on the bottom line, as indicated by a tick; and

b the number of digits which appear on the bottom line, but in a different position, as indicated by a cross.

SCORE

2	9	9	7	✔ ✗
2	3	6	5	✔
7	3	2	2	✔ ✗
6	3	6	9	✔
5	4	2	1	✔
				✔✔✔✔

The grid should be filled with numbers from 1 to 6, so that each number appears just once in every row and column. The clues refer to the digit totals in the squares, eg A 1 2 3 = 6 means that the numbers in squares A1, A2 and A3 add up to 6.

1   B C 4 = 9

2   A B 5 = 4

3   E F 6 = 7

4   A 1 2 = 10

5   B 1 2 = 8

6   C 5 6 = 9

7   D 2 3 = 8

8   E 3 4 = 10

9   F 3 4 5 = 9

10   C D E 1 = 12

11   E F 2 = 8

	A	B	C	D	E	F
1						
2						
3						
4						
5						
6						

The object of this puzzle is to trace a single path from the top left corner to the bottom right corner of the grid, travelling through all of the cells in either a horizontal, vertical or diagonal direction.

Every cell must be entered once only and your path should take you through the numbers in the sequence 1-2-3-4-5-6-1-2-3-4-5-6, etc.

Can you find the way?

1	6	5	6	2	3
2	4	1	1	5	4
3	2	1	6	5	4
1	3	4	2	3	3
2	6	5	4	5	2
3	4	5	6	1	6

SECTION 2

49

Draw a single continuous loop, by connecting the dots. No line may cross the path of another.

The figure inside each set of any four surrounding dots indicates the total number of surrounding lines.

```
2           1         0
  3     1 0     1     3 3
      2 2             0
    2 2                 1
  1     2 2 1 3     3
      2 1 2 2     3     1
  2     3
  2 1             2 3     2
  1     3 1 3 2         3
  1 0 1     1       1     2
            0     2 3 3
      1     1     2 0     1
```

50

Each horizontal row and vertical column should contain different shapes and different numbers.

Every square will contain one number and one shape and no combination may be repeated anywhere else in the puzzle.

| 1 | 2 | 3 | 4 | 5 |

	5	○	□	3
		5		
	◇			
◇		⬡	2	
		1	◇	

51

Given that the letters are valued 1-26 according to their places in the alphabet, can you crack the mystery code to reveal the missing letter?

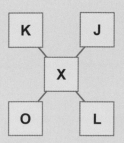

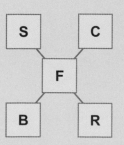

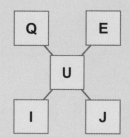

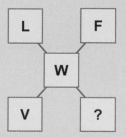

Which is the odd one out?

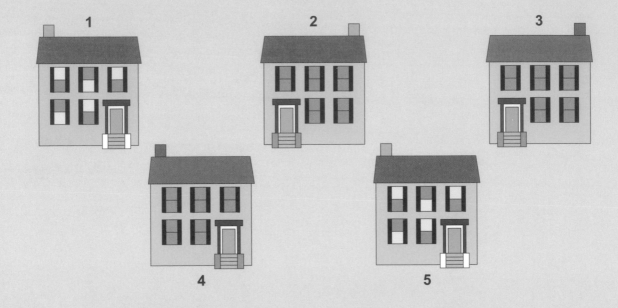

53

Which of the alternatives (A, B, C or D) comes next in this sequence?

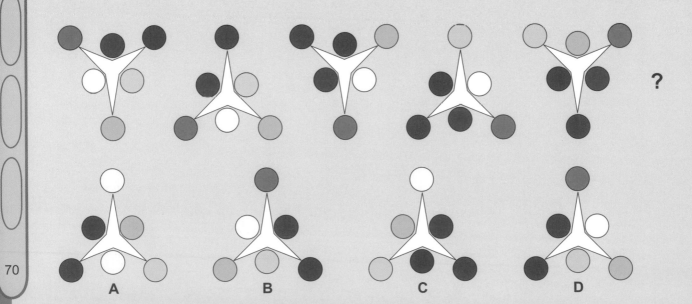

Place the eight tiles into the puzzle grid so that all adjacent numbers on each tile match up. Tiles may be rotated through 360 degrees, but none may be flipped over.

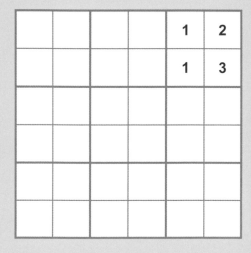

Place all twelve of the pieces into the grid. Any may be rotated or flipped over, but none may touch another, not even diagonally. The numbers outside the grid refer to the number of consecutive black squares; and each block is separated from the others by at least one white square. For instance, '3 2' could refer to a row with none, one or more white squares, then three black squares, then at least one white square, then two more black squares, followed by any number of white squares.

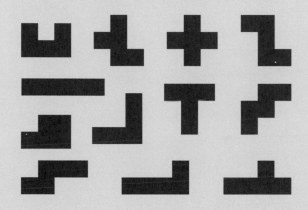

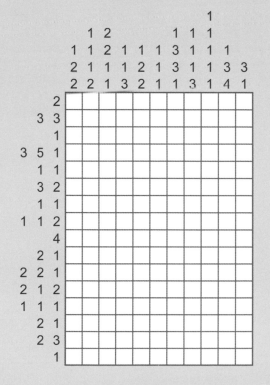

56

What number should replace the question mark?

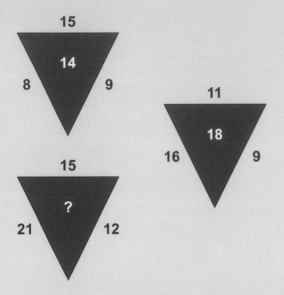

15
14
8   9

11
18
16   9

15
?
21   12

57

In the square below, change the positions of six numbers, one per horizontal row, vertical column and long diagonal line of six smaller squares, in such a way that the numbers in each row, column and long diagonal line total exactly 163. Any number may appear more than once in a row, column or line.

32	16	21	25	38	32
34	36	29	15	28	30
40	32	27	30	12	31
20	48	28	33	17	28
15	21	32	33	32	27
33	19	27	36	9	12

58

Every brick in this pyramid contains a number which is the sum of the two numbers below it, so that F=A+B, etc. Just work out the missing numbers!

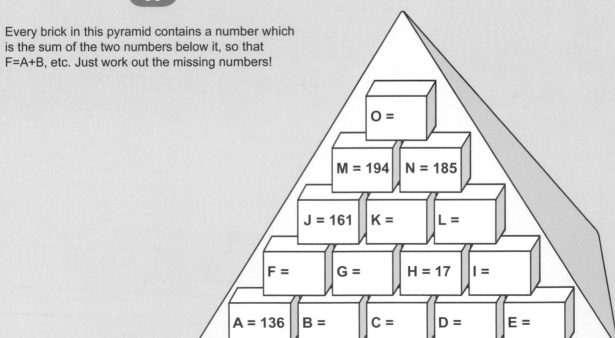

O =

M = 194   N = 185

J = 161   K =   L =

F =   G =   H = 17   I =

A = 136   B =   C =   D =   E =

With the starter already given, can you fit all of the remaining listed numbers into this grid? Take care, this puzzle may not be as easy as it looks!

21	143	3447	22090	60395
25	176	3759	24417	62575
32	327	4776	34276	72400
44	470	5034	34559	75046
50	594	6035	35780	360037
64	656	7000	38954	510262
71	1018	8656	40603	948819
73	1031	9953	41067	968096
76	1259	10062	48916	7950460
83	2514	13432	50038	8046635
85	2804	17557	57687	8131735
92	2833	20316	59688 ✓	9010028

The chart gives directions to a hidden treasure behind the centre black square in the grid. Move the indicated number of spaces north, south, east and west (eg 4N means move four squares north) stopping at every square once only to arrive there. At which square should you start?

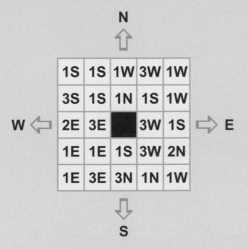

Fill the grid so that every horizontal row and vertical column contains the numbers 1-5. The 'greater than' or 'less than' signs indicate where a number is larger or smaller than that in the neighbouring square.

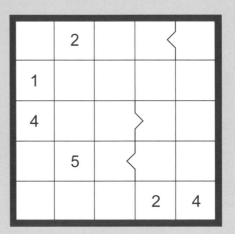

Each of the eight segments of the spider's web should be filled with a different number from 1 to 8, in such a way that every ring also contains a different number from 1 to 8.

The segments run from the outside of the spider's web to the centre, and the rings run all the way around.

Some numbers are already in place. Can you fill in the rest?

Every oval shape in this diagram contains a different letter of the alphabet from A to K inclusive. Use the clues to determine their locations. Reference in the clues to 'due' means in any location along the same horizontal or vertical line.

1   The E is next to and south of the G, which is next to and east of the J.

2   The F is due south of both the B and the K.

3   The J is further south than the C, which is next to and east of the H, which is next to and south of the A.

4   The K is next to and east of the I, which is next to and south of the D, which is further east than the A.

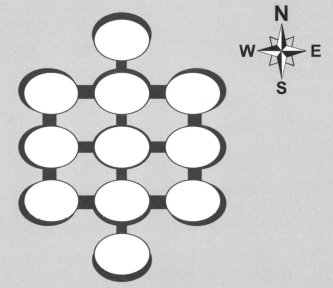

Fill the three empty circles with the symbols +, – and x in some order, to make a sum which totals the number in the centre. Each symbol must be used once and calculations are made in the direction of travel (clockwise).

= 60

6

27

99   2

The numbers at the top and on the left side show the quantity of single-digit numbers (1-9) used in that row and column. The numbers at the bottom and on the right side show the sum of the digits. A number may appear more than once in a row or column, but no numbers are in squares that touch, even at a corner.

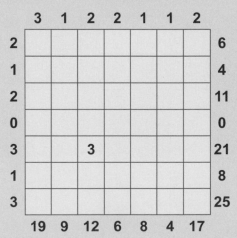

	3	1	2	2	1	1	2	
2								6
1								4
2								11
0								0
3			3					21
1								8
3								25
	19	9	12	6	8	4	17	

66

Using the numbers below, complete these six equations (three reading across and three reading downwards). Every number is used once.

1   2   3   4   5
   6   7   8   9

	x		x		=	12
x	■	+	■	−		
	−		x		=	2
+	■	+	■	+		
	−		x		=	32
=		=		=		
37		12		9		

67

In the grid below, which number should replace the question mark?

48	41	34	27	20	13	6
34	29	24	19	14	9	4
26	23	20	17	14	11	8
?	58	50	42	34	26	18
48	42	36	30	24	18	12
27	23	19	15	11	7	3
21	19	17	15	13	11	9

68

When the box below is folded to form a cube, just one of the five options (A, B, C, D or E) can be produced. Which?

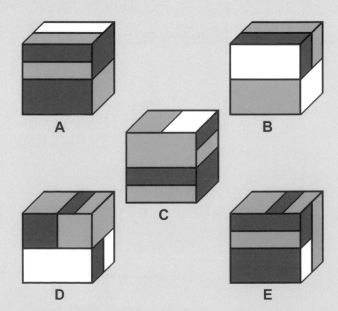

A

B

C

D

E

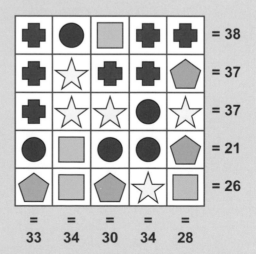

69

In this puzzle, an amateur coin collector has been out with his metal detector, searching for booty. He didn't have time to dig up all the coins he found, so has made a grid map, showing their locations, in the hope that if he loses the map, at least no-one else will understand it…

Those squares containing numbers are empty, but where a number appears in a square, it indicates how many coins are located in the squares (up to a maximum of eight) surrounding the numbered one, touching it at any corner or side. There is only one coin in any individual square.

Place a circle into every square containing a coin.

		1	1	2			2	0	
1					3				
	2				2			1	
1	2		3			1			0
			3				2		1
				4				3	
1		1					2		
	0		2			2		4	4
1		0			4	1			
									3

70

Every row and column of this grid should contain one each of the letters A, B, C, D, E and F. Each of the six shapes (marked by thicker lines) should also contain one each of the letters A, B, C, D, E and F. Can you complete the grid?

	C		B		A
	E				D
		F			

71

Each symbol stands for a different number. In order to reach the correct total at the end of each row and column, what is the value of the circle, cross, pentagon, square and star?

= 38
= 37
= 37
= 21
= 26

= = = = =
33 34 30 34 28

72

A standard set of 28 dominoes has been laid out as shown. Can you draw in the edges of them all? The check-box is provided as an aid and the domino already placed will help.

0-0	0-1	0-2	0-3	0-4	0-5	0-6
						✔

1-1	1-2	1-3	1-4	1-5	1-6	2-2

2-3	2-4	2-5	2-6	3-3	3-4	3-5

3-6	4-4	4-5	4-6	5-5	5-6	6-6

73

Each of the small squares in the grid below contains either A, B or C. Each row, column, and diagonal line of six squares has exactly two of each letter. Can you tell the letter in each square?

Across
1. The As are further right than the Cs
2. The Bs are further right than the As
3. No two letters the same are directly next to each other
4. The Bs are further right than the As
5. The As are further right than the Bs
6. The As are between the Bs

Down
1. The Cs are lower than the Bs
2. The Bs are lower than the As
3. The As are lower than the Cs
4. The Cs are between the As
5. Each A is directly next to and below a C
6. The Bs are between the As

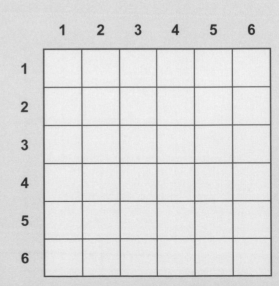

Every row and column in this grid originally contained one heart, one club, one diamond, one spade and two blank squares, although not necessarily in that order.

Every symbol with a black arrow refers to the first of the four symbols encountered when travelling in the direction of the arrow. Every symbol with a white arrow refers to the second of the four symbols encountered in the direction of the arrow.

Can you complete the original grid?

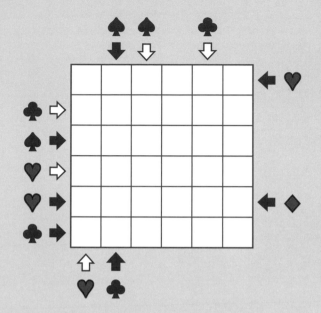

75

The blank squares below should be filled with whole numbers between 1 and 30 inclusive, any of which may occur more than once, or not at all.

The numbers in every horizontal row add up to the totals on the right, as do the two long diagonal lines; whilst those in every vertical column add up to the totals along the bottom.

							95
	18	23		21	2	17	98
		22	11		12	28	102
20	7	29	12	18			140
13		16	5		21	19	92
7	15		6	16	11		105
18	17	23		20		5	121
1		6	14	21	28	3	103
78	110	144	77	115	116	121	88

76

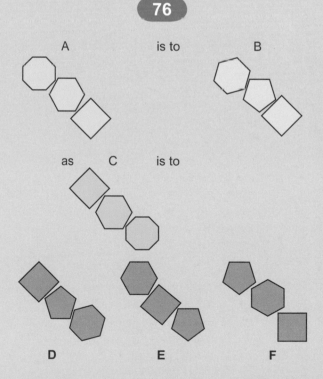

A   is to   B

as   C   is to

D   E   F

Can you place the hexagons into the grid, so that where any hexagon touches another along a straight line, the number in both triangles is the same? No rotation of any hexagon is allowed!

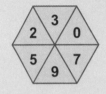

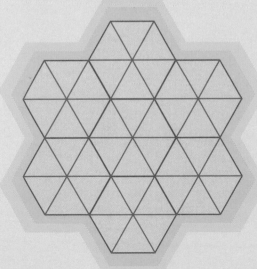

Twelve L-shapes like the ones here need to be inserted in the grid and each L has one hole in it.

There are three pieces of each of the four kinds shown here and any piece may be turned or flipped over before being put in the grid. No pieces of the same kind touch, even at a corner.

The pieces fit together so well that you cannot see any spaces between them; only the holes show.

Can you tell where the Ls are?

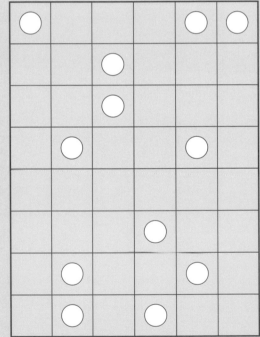

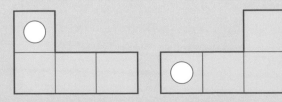

Draw walls to partition the grid into areas (some walls are already drawn in for you). Each area must contain two circles, area sizes must match those numbers shown next to the grid and each '+' must be linked to at least two walls.

2, 3, 3, 4, 6, 7

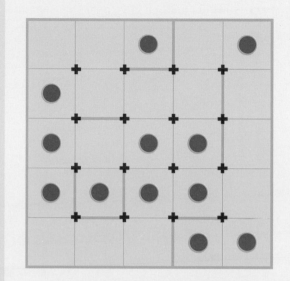

Which of the four lettered alternatives (A, B, C or D) fits most logically into the empty square?

X	C	F
T	Y	M
H	B	S

A

F	X	C
M	Y	T
S	H	B

B

C	T	X
B	Y	S
M	F	H

C

C	X	F
M	Y	T
B	S	H

D

The object of this puzzle is to trace a single path from the top left corner to the bottom right corner of the grid, travelling through all of the cells in either a horizontal, vertical or diagonal direction.

Every cell must be entered once only and your path should take you through the numbers in the sequence 1-2-3-4-5-6-1-2-3-4-5-6, etc.

Can you find the way?

1	3	4	5	6	5
2	2	1	6	1	4
1	6	3	2	3	2
5	4	2	3	3	5
1	5	4	1	6	4
6	2	3	4	5	6

82

The grid should be filled with numbers from 1 to 6, so that each number appears just once in every row and column. The clues refer to the digit totals in the squares, eg A 1 2 3 = 6 means that the numbers in squares A1, A2 and A3 add up to 6.

1 D 4 5 = 6

2 E 5 6 = 5

3 F 1 2 = 6

4 A B C 1 = 6

5 B C 2 = 11

6 C D E 3 = 12

7 E F 4 = 10

8 A B 5 = 6

9 A B 6 = 11

10 A 2 3 = 7

11 B 3 4 = 3

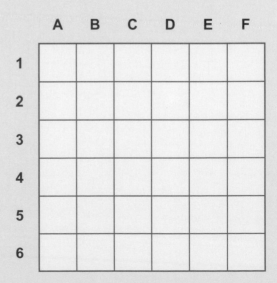

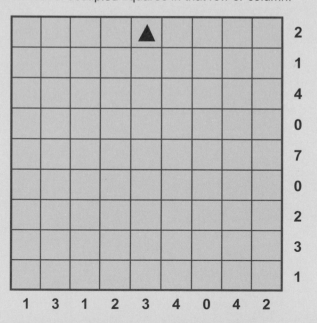

Can you fill each square in the bottom line with the correct digit?

Every square in the solution contains only one digit from each of the lines above, although two or more squares in the solution may contain the same digit.

At the end of every row is a score, which shows:

a the number of digits placed in the correct finishing position on the bottom line, as indicated by a tick; and

b the number of digits which appear on the bottom line, but in a different position, as indicated by a cross.

SCORE

2	6	7	4	✗
2	1	7	2	✗
4	5	8	5	✓
3	2	8	2	✓
3	3	2	6	✗
				✓✓✓✓

84

Can you place the vessels into the diagram? Some parts of vessels or sea squares have already been filled in. A number to the right or below a row or column refers to the number of occupied squares in that row or column.

Any vessel may be positioned horizontally or vertically, but no part of a vessel touches part of any other vessel, either horizontally, vertically or diagonally.

Empty Area of Sea: ≈

Aircraft Carrier: ◀■■▶

Battleships: ◀■▶ ◀■▶

Cruisers: ◀▶ ◀▶ ◀▶

Submarines: ● ● ● ●

Grid column totals: 1 3 1 2 3 4 0 4 2

Grid row totals: 2 1 4 0 7 0 2 3 1

S
E
C
T
I
O
N

2

Draw a single continuous loop, by connecting the dots. No line may cross the path of another.

The figure inside each set of any four surrounding dots indicates the total number of surrounding lines.

```
.   .   .   .   .   .   .   .   .   .   .
    1       3               3   2
.   .   .   .   .   .   .   .   .   .   .
  2                   2   0           2
.   .   .   .   .   .   .   .   .   .   .
  1       2   2           1   2
.   .   .   .   .   .   .   .   .   .   .
              2           1
.   .   .   .   .   .   .   .   .   .   .
  3   1   0       0       1   3       3
.   .   .   .   .   .   .   .   .   .   .
  2   3       1           0       1
.   .   .   .   .   .   .   .   .   .   .
  2       1       1           1       1
.   .   .   .   .   .   .   .   .   .   .
      3   2   1       1
.   .   .   .   .   .   .   .   .   .   .
      2               0       1   2
.   .   .   .   .   .   .   .   .   .   .
              0               2
.   .   .   .   .   .   .   .   .   .   .
  3       2           3   1
.   .   .   .   .   .   .   .   .   .   .
      3           2       2   2
.   .   .   .   .   .   .   .   .   .   .
```

Each horizontal row and vertical column should contain different shapes and different numbers.

Every square will contain one number and one shape and no combination may be repeated anywhere else in the puzzle.

| 1 | 2 | 3 | 4 | 5 |

1	2	3	4	5
	3		5	□
		2		
1				3
◇	⬡		1	5
		③		

87

Given that the letters are valued 1-26 according to their places in the alphabet, can you crack the mystery code to reveal the missing letter?

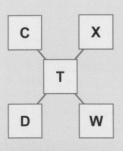

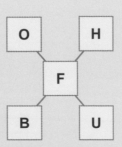

A set of dominoes is to be placed in four rows as shown below. The numbers indicate which values are shown on all the dominoes in each column and the relevant half of the domino in every row. Find out where each domino is placed by carefully comparing rows and columns to determine the possible positions of certain dominoes: for instance, if any column contains only one 6, then the domino 6/6 isn't in that column.

A set of dominoes consists of:

0/0, 0/1, 0/2, 0/3, 0/4, 0/5, 0/6, 1/1, 1/2, 1/3, 1/4, 1/5, 1/6, 2/2,

2/3, 2/4, 2/5, 2/6, 3/3, 3/4, 3/5, 3/6, 4/4, 4/5, 4/6, 5/5, 5/6, 6/6.

	0, 1, 1, 3, 4, 4, 5, 6.	0, 1, 1, 2, 3, 5, 5, 5.	0, 0, 0, 1, 1, 3, 5, 5.	0, 0, 0, 3, 3, 5, 6, 6.	2, 2, 3, 4, 4, 4, 6, 6.	1, 2, 2, 3, 5, 6, 6, 6.	1, 2, 2, 2, 3, 4, 4, 4.
1, 3, 4, 4, 5, 6, 6.							
0, 1, 1, 3, 4, 4, 5.							
0, 1, 1, 1, 2, 5, 6.							
0, 2, 2, 2, 3, 5, 6.							
0, 1, 2, 5, 6, 6, 6.							
0, 3, 4, 4, 5, 5, 6.							
0, 0, 0, 2, 2, 3, 3.							
1, 2, 3, 3, 4, 4, 5.							

**S
E
C
T
I
O
N**

2

Place the eight tiles into the puzzle grid so that all adjacent numbers on each tile match up. Tiles may be rotated through 360 degrees, but none may be flipped over.

Place all twelve of the pieces into the grid. Any may be rotated or flipped over, but none may touch another, not even diagonally. The numbers outside the grid refer to the number of consecutive black squares; and each block is separated from the others by at least one white square. For instance, '3 2' could refer to a row with none, one or more white squares, then three black squares, then at least one white square, then two more black squares, followed by any number of white squares.

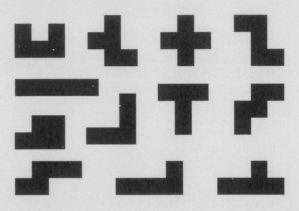

2	1
2	3

1	2
3	4

1	2
1	3

1	2
2	1

4	2
2	3

4	4
1	1

2	2
3	2

3	2
1	3

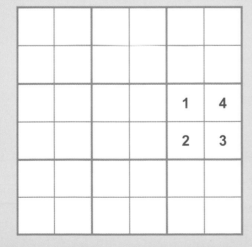

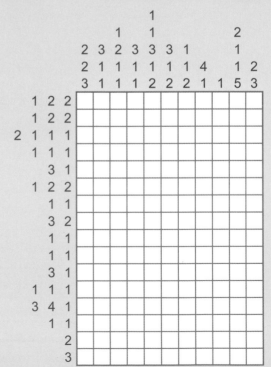

91

In the diagram below, which number should replace the question mark?

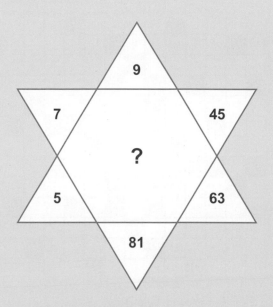

92

In the square below, change the positions of six numbers, one per horizontal row, vertical column and long diagonal line of six smaller squares, in such a way that the numbers in each row, column and long diagonal line total exactly 214. Any number may appear more than once in a row, column or line.

44	18	30	26	52	42
19	35	18	25	39	37
21	50	35	51	25	23
57	43	39	59	17	39
18	27	44	51	39	29
14	32	42	42	60	42

93

Every brick in this pyramid contains a number which is the sum of the two numbers below it, so that F=A+B, etc. Just work out the missing numbers!

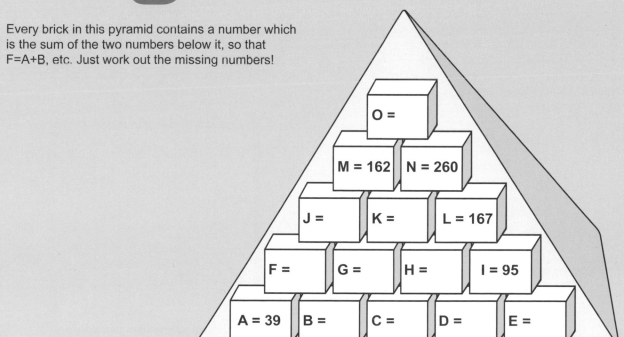

With the starter already given, can you fit all of the remaining listed numbers into this grid? Take care, this puzzle may not be as easy as it looks!

10	497	4821	30918	92859
22	501	4896	34905	101904
33	539	5906 ✓	38705	302016
41	669	6487	46197	309744
67	693	6927	57166	385892
73	835	6930	58391	395835
188	942	7895	59023	417723
232	1197	14060	68061	419788
267	1999	19109	69972	491949
328	2086	25403	71414	744803
349	2142	26975	72982	779592
380	3012	29381	84939	1284909

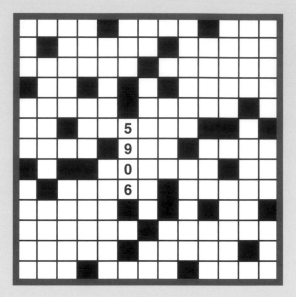

The chart gives directions to a hidden treasure behind the centre black square in the grid. Move the indicated number of spaces north, south, east and west (eg 4N means move four squares north) stopping at every square once only to arrive there. At which square should you start?

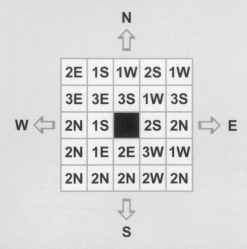

Fill the grid so that every horizontal row and vertical column contains the numbers 1-5. The 'greater than' or 'less than' signs indicate where a number is larger or smaller than that in the neighbouring square.

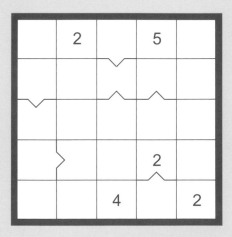

Each of the eight segments of the spider's web should be filled with a different number from 1 to 8, in such a way that every ring also contains a different number from 1 to 8.

The segments run from the outside of the spider's web to the centre, and the rings run all the way around.

Some numbers are already in place. Can you fill in the rest?

A standard set of 28 dominoes has been laid out as shown. Can you draw in the edges of them all? The check-box is provided as an aid and the domino already placed will help.

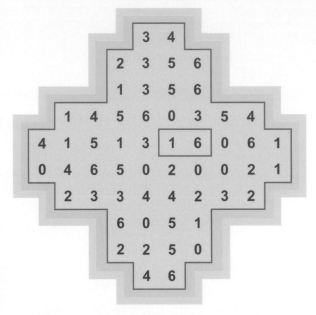

0-0	0-1	0-2	0-3	0-4	0-5	0-6

1-1	1-2	1-3	1-4	1-5	1-6	2-2
					✓	

2-3	2-4	2-5	2-6	3-3	3-4	3-5

3-6	4-4	4-5	4-6	5-5	5-6	6-6

Draw walls to partition the grid into areas (some walls are already drawn in for you). Each area must contain two circles, area sizes must match those numbers shown next to the grid and each '+' must be linked to at least two walls.

3, 4, 5, 6, 7

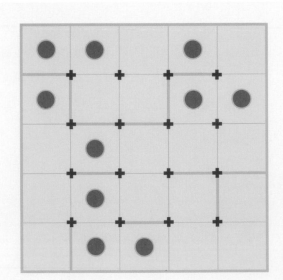

Every row and column in this grid originally contained one heart, one club, one diamond, one spade and two blank squares, although not necessarily in that order.

Every symbol with a black arrow refers to the first of the four symbols encountered when travelling in the direction of the arrow. Every symbol with a white arrow refers to the second of the four symbols encountered in the direction of the arrow.

Can you complete the original grid?

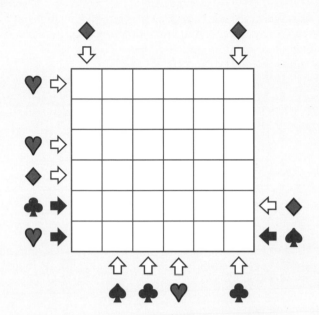

4

The blank squares below should be filled with whole numbers between 1 and 30 inclusive, any of which may occur more than once, or not at all.

The numbers in every horizontal row add up to the totals on the right, as do the two long diagonal lines; whilst those in every vertical column add up to the totals along the bottom.

							120
16	17			9	11	20	100
10		15	7	16		13	99
	5	28		1		26	127
	12	14	22	20	13		108
2	15		17		18		115
25	16	12	20		5	4	106
10	14	26	4		19	13	104
87	93	145	104	96	109	125	106

5

Draw in the missing hands on the final clock.

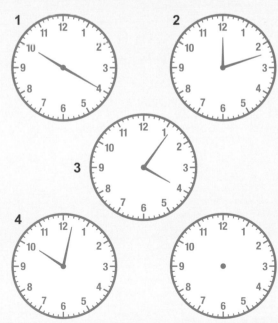

6

Can you place the hexagons into the grid, so that where any hexagon touches another along a straight line, the number in both triangles is the same? No rotation of any hexagon is allowed!

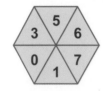

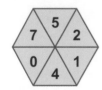

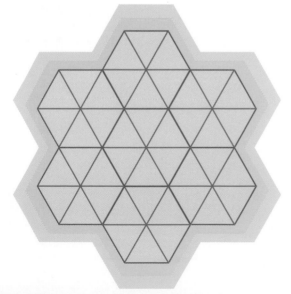

7

Twelve L-shapes like the ones here need to be inserted in the grid and each L has one hole in it.

There are three pieces of each of the four kinds shown here and any piece may be turned or flipped over before being put in the grid. No pieces of the same kind touch, even at a corner.

The pieces fit together so well that you cannot see any spaces between them; only the holes show.

Can you tell where the Ls are?

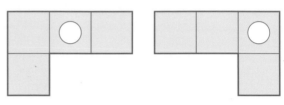

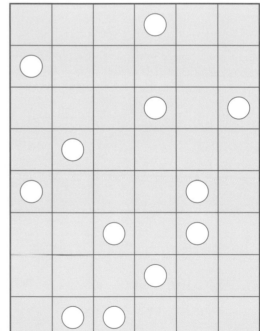

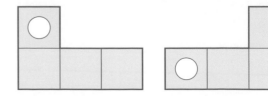

In this puzzle, an amateur coin collector has been out with his metal detector, searching for booty. He didn't have time to dig up all the coins he found, so has made a grid map, showing their locations, in the hope that if he loses the map, at least no-one else will understand it…

Those squares containing numbers are empty, but where a number appears in a square, it indicates how many coins are located in the squares (up to a maximum of eight) surrounding the numbered one, touching it at any corner or side. There is only one coin in any individual square.

Place a circle into every square containing a coin.

	2				2			2	
1				2		1			
2	2		2				3		2
1				2	2				
						2	3		2
		2	2	2			3		
	2		1						2
		0			1		3	3	
2			3			1	2		
	1							1	

The grid should be filled with numbers from 1 to 6, so that each number appears just once in every row and column. The clues refer to the digit totals in the squares, eg A 1 2 3 = 6 means that the numbers in squares A1, A2 and A3 add up to 6.

1   C D 5 = 6

2   D E 6 = 6

3   A 1 2 = 3

4   B 1 2 = 9

5   C 1 2 3 = 8

6   D 2 3 = 9

7   E 3 4 = 11

8   F 3 4 5 = 13

9   D E 1 = 8

10   E F 2 = 5

11   A B 3 = 10

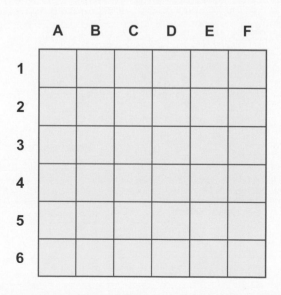

	A	B	C	D	E	F
1						
2						
3						
4						
5						
6						

10

Each of the small squares in the grid below contains either A, B or C. Each row, column, and diagonal line of six squares has exactly two of each letter. Can you tell the letter in each square?

Across

2 The Cs are between the As

4 The As are between the Cs

5 No two letters the same are directly next to each other

Down

2 The Cs are next to each other

3 The Bs are between the Cs

4 The Cs are between the As

5 The Cs are lower than the As

6 The Bs are next to each other

	1	2	3	4	5	6
1						
2						
3						
4						
5						
6						

11

The object of this puzzle is to trace a single path from the top left corner to the bottom right corner of the grid, travelling through all of the cells in either a horizontal, vertical or diagonal direction.

Every cell must be entered once only and your path should take you through the numbers in the sequence 1-2-3-4-1-2-3-4, etc.

Can you find the way?

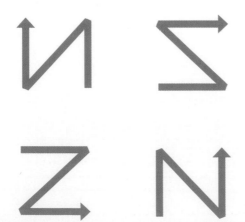

1	4	1	1	2	1	4	3
3	2	4	2	1	3	2	4
1	3	3	4	2	3	1	4
2	4	2	4	4	2	3	1
3	1	3	1	1	2	2	3
2	3	4	4	1	4	3	4
4	2	2	2	3	1	1	2
3	1	1	4	3	2	3	4

12

Can you place the vessels into the diagram? Some parts of vessels or sea squares have already been filled in. A number to the right or below a row or column refers to the number of occupied squares in that row or column.

Any vessel may be positioned horizontally or vertically, but no part of a vessel touches part of any other vessel, either horizontally, vertically or diagonally.

Empty Area of Sea: ≈

Aircraft Carrier:

Battleships:

Cruisers:

Submarines:

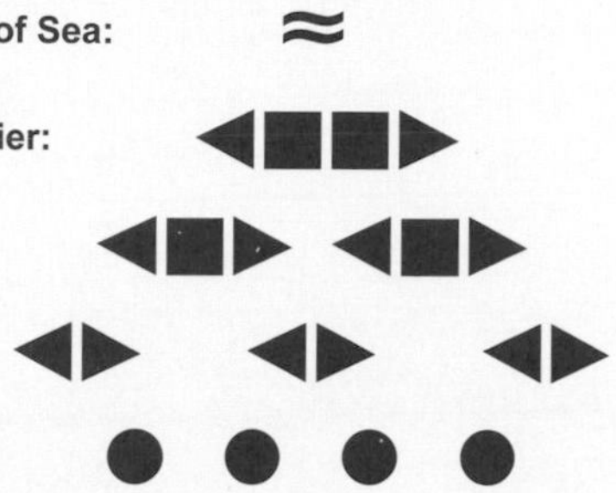

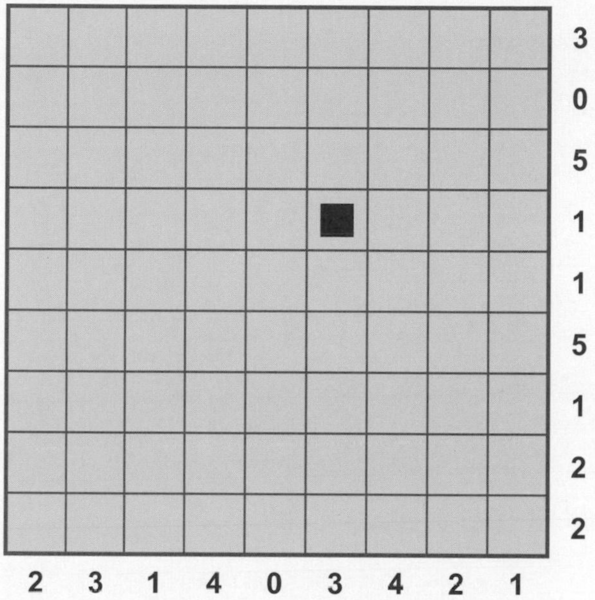
3
0
5
1
1
5
1
2
2
2 3 1 4 0 3 4 2 1

13

Can you fill each square in the bottom line with the correct digit?

Every square in the solution contains only one digit from each of the lines above, although two or more squares in the solution may contain the same digit.

At the end of every row is a score, which shows:

a the number of digits placed in the correct finishing position on the bottom line, as indicated by a tick; and

b the number of digits which appear on the bottom line, but in a different position, as indicated by a cross.

				SCORE
7	7	1	8	✓✓✗
2	7	2	1	✓✓
5	7	4	5	✓
5	3	3	1	✓
3	6	1	6	✗
				✓✓✓✓

Draw a single continuous loop, by connecting the dots. No line may cross the path of another.

The figure inside each set of any four surrounding dots indicates the total number of surrounding lines.

```
  .   .   .   .   .   .   .   .   .   .
    0       1       1   1   2
  .   .   .   .   .   .   .   .   .   .
                  0   1
  .   .   .   .   .   .   .   .   .   .
      2   1       1           2   2
  .   .   .   .   .   .   .   .   .   .
    0       1       0
  .   .   .   .   .   .   .   .   .   .
          2   0       0   2   2   3
  .   .   .   .   .   .   .   .   .   .
  1       2   2               3
  .   .   .   .   .   .   .   .   .   .
  1       2           0       1
  .   .   .   .   .   .   .   .   .   .
    0   0               1   3
  .   .   .   .   .   .   .   .   .   .
    1                           0
  .   .   .   .   .   .   .   .   .   .
          0   1   0
  .   .   .   .   .   .   .   .   .   .
  1           0       1   2
  .   .   .   .   .   .   .   .   .   .
    1   2       2   1       3
  .   .   .   .   .   .   .   .   .   .
```

Each horizontal row and vertical column should contain different shapes and different numbers.

Every square will contain one number and one shape and no combination may be repeated anywhere else in the puzzle.

1   2   3   4   5

			3	
☐1		◇	○	
	◇4		☐5	⬡
	2		1	
	1			

Given that the letters are valued 1-26 according to their places in the alphabet, can you crack the mystery code to reveal the missing letter?

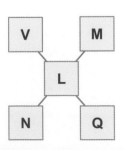

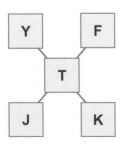

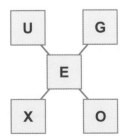

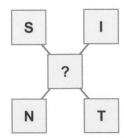

A set of dominoes is to be placed in four rows as shown below. The numbers indicate which values are shown on all the dominoes in each column and the relevant half of the domino in every row. Find out where each domino is placed by carefully comparing rows and columns to determine the possible positions of certain dominoes: for instance, if any column contains only one 6, then the domino 6/6 isn't in that column.

A set of dominoes consists of:

0/0, 0/1, 0/2, 0/3, 0/4, 0/5, 0/6, 1/1, 1/2, 1/3, 1/4, 1/5, 1/6, 2/2,

2/3, 2/4, 2/5, 2/6, 3/3, 3/4, 3/5, 3/6, 4/4, 4/5, 4/6, 5/5, 5/6, 6/6.

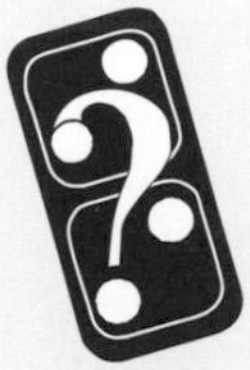

1, 2, 2, 2, 3, 3, 5, 6.	0, 1, 2, 2, 3, 4, 5, 6.	0, 0, 0, 1, 3, 4, 5, 5.	0, 1, 2, 3, 5, 6, 6, 6.	0, 1, 3, 4, 4, 4, 5, 5.	0, 1, 1, 1, 2, 3, 4, 4.	0, 2, 3, 4, 5, 6, 6, 6.

0, 2, 2, 3, 3, 4, 5.							
0, 4, 5, 5, 6, 6, 6.							
1, 2, 3, 4, 4, 5, 6.							
0, 1, 2, 2, 3, 4, 4.							
0, 2, 3, 3, 4, 6, 6.							
0, 0, 4, 5, 5, 6, 6.							
1, 1, 1, 2, 2, 5, 5.							
0, 0, 1, 1, 1, 3, 3.							

Place the eight tiles into the puzzle grid so that all adjacent numbers on each tile match up. Tiles may be rotated through 360 degrees, but none may be flipped over.

Tile 1:
| 4 | 4 |
| 1 | 1 |

Tile 2:
| 2 | 4 |
| 2 | 1 |

Tile 3:
| 3 | 1 |
| 2 | 3 |

Tile 4:
| 4 | 1 |
| 2 | 3 |

Tile 5:
| 2 | 2 |
| 4 | 3 |

Tile 6:
| 4 | 3 |
| 4 | 3 |

Tile 7:
| 1 | 3 |
| 4 | 1 |

Tile 8:
| 4 | 2 |
| 3 | 1 |

Puzzle grid (partially filled):
				2	1
				3	3

Place all twelve of the pieces into the grid. Any may be rotated or flipped over, but none may touch another, not even diagonally. The numbers outside the grid refer to the number of consecutive black squares; and each block is separated from the others by at least one white square. For instance, '3 2' could refer to a row with none, one or more white squares, then three black squares, then at least one white square, then two more black squares, followed by any number of white squares.

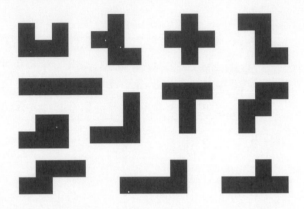

Column clues:
```
        1           2
        1     1     1 1
    1   3 3   1     1 4
    2 1 2 3 1 1 1 3   1 4
    3 1 1 1 5 1 2 2 0 2 3
```

Row clues:
```
1 3 2
2 2 1
  2 1
1 1 1
  3 2
  1 1
    1
    3
    1
1 1 2
1 1 1
3 1 2
  1 1
1 1 1 2
3 2 2
1 2 1
```

SECTION 3

20

In the diagram below, which number should replace the question mark?

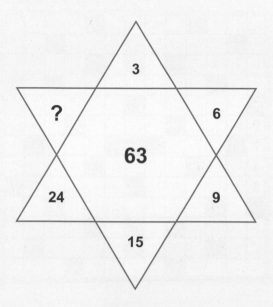

21

In the square below, change the positions of six numbers, one per horizontal row, vertical column and long diagonal line of six smaller squares, in such a way that the numbers in each row, column and long diagonal line total exactly 264. Any number may appear more than once in a row, column or line.

37	52	56	77	51	37
10	66	39	28	20	42
54	20	38	74	61	35
35	19	84	12	46	77
32	30	57	26	68	45
37	69	36	65	12	37

22

Every brick in this pyramid contains a number which is the sum of the two numbers below it, so that F=A+B, etc. Just work out the missing numbers!

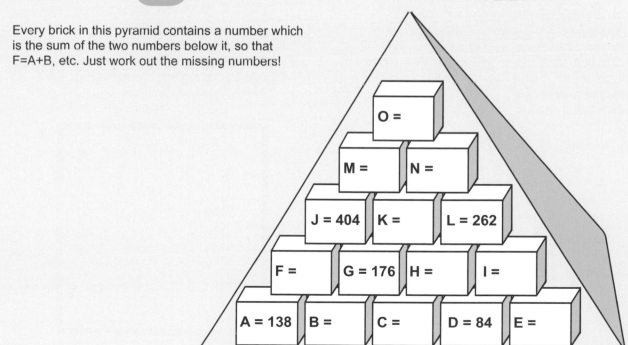

With the starter already given, can you fit all of the remaining listed numbers into this grid? Take care, this puzzle may not be as easy as it looks!

15	484	2544	7090	151089
24	514	3841	8557	297905
30	542	3949	8765	390920
46	608	4309	9460	451915
50	791	4496	9555	460888
62	879	4944	9742 ✓	651286
74	925	5260	14665	705308
80	984	5316	44348	733408
166	1076	6238	46437	853157
280	1827	6766	58148	855602
367	1879	7007	62234	5783296
433	2066	7051	99997	9932109

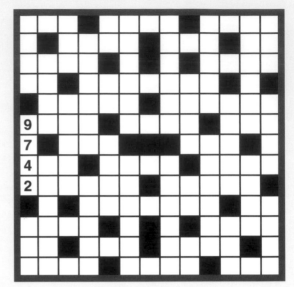

The chart gives directions to a hidden treasure behind the centre black square in the grid. Move the indicated number of spaces north, south, east and west (eg 4N means move four squares north) stopping at every square once only to arrive there. At which square should you start?

N

2E	2S	2E	3S	1W
1N	1E	2E	2W	3S
3E	3E	■	1N	2W
1N	3N	1W	1E	2W
3N	2E	1W	3W	2W

W ⇦   ⇨ E

S

Fill the grid so that every horizontal row and vertical column contains the numbers 1-5. The 'greater than' or 'less than' signs indicate where a number is larger or smaller than that in the neighbouring square.

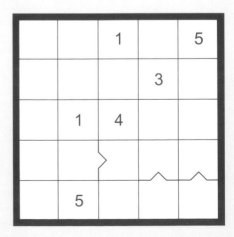

Each of the eight segments of the spider's web should be filled with a different number from 1 to 8, in such a way that every ring also contains a different number from 1 to 8.

The segments run from the outside of the spider's web to the centre, and the rings run all the way around.

Some numbers are already in place. Can you fill in the rest?

Every oval shape in this diagram contains a different letter of the alphabet from A to K inclusive. Use the clues to determine their locations. Reference in the clues to 'due' means in any location along the same horizontal or vertical line.

1 The A is due west of the H, which is next to and north of the F, which is next to and east of the E.

2 The C is due south of the D, which is next to and west of the K, which is next to and south of the B, which is further north than the G.

3 The J is due south of the I, which is next to and west of the H.

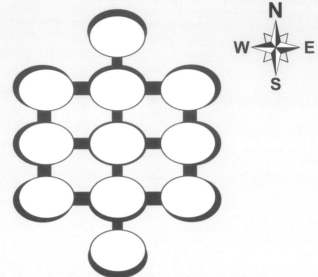

Fill the three empty circles with the symbols +, – and x in some order, to make a sum which totals the number in the centre. Each symbol must be used once and calculations are made in the direction of travel (clockwise).

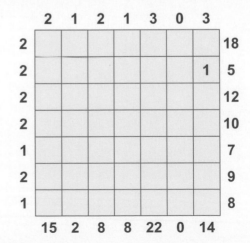

= 17

4

64

6

5

The numbers at the top and on the left side show the quantity of single-digit numbers (1-9) used in that row and column. The numbers at the bottom and on the right side show the sum of the digits. A number may appear more than once in a row or column, but no numbers are in squares that touch, even at a corner.

	2	1	2	1	3	0	3	
2								18
2							1	5
2								12
2								10
1								7
2								9
1								8
	15	2	8	8	22	0	14	

Using the numbers below, complete these six equations (three reading across and three reading downwards). Every number is used once.

```
 1       2       3       4       5
    6       7       8       9

   | x |   | – |   | = | 19
 – |███| x |███| + |
   | x |   | x |   | = | 18
 x |███| + |███| – |
   | + |   | x |   | = | 26
 = |   | = |   | = |
 15    50     10
```

In the grid below, which number should replace the question mark?

3	4	6	18	8	1	2
9	7	5	2	3	4	14
1	3	5	7	22	3	5
19	16	1	2	1	4	5
8	6	13	4	5	11	3
2	4	16	6	9	5	10
6	17	12	3	8	4	?

When the box below is folded to form a cube, just one of the five options (A, B, C, D or E) can be produced. Which?

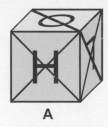

A

B

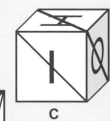

C

D

E

In this puzzle, an amateur coin collector has been out with his metal detector, searching for booty. He didn't have time to dig up all the coins he found, so has made a grid map, showing their locations, in the hope that if he loses the map, at least no-one else will understand it…

Those squares containing numbers are empty, but where a number appears in a square, it indicates how many coins are located in the squares (up to a maximum of eight) surrounding the numbered one, touching it at any corner or side. There is only one coin in any individual square.

Place a circle into every square containing a coin.

1	2		2	2			2	1	1
	2				4			3	
	1		3						
									2
	3				1			2	
		2		0			3		
2		1				3			
		1					1	2	2
2				1				2	
	1						2		

Each symbol stands for a different number. In order to reach the correct total at the end of each row and column, what is the value of the circle, cross, pentagon, square and star?

= 35
= 40
= 30
= 32
= 31

= 30   = 37   = 38   = 34   = 29

Every row and column of this grid should contain one each of the letters A, B, C, D, E and F. Each of the six shapes (marked by thicker lines) should also contain one each of the letters A, B, C, D, E and F. Can you complete the grid?

104

A standard set of 28 dominoes has been laid out as shown. Can you draw in the edges of them all? The checkbox is provided as an aid and the domino already placed will help.

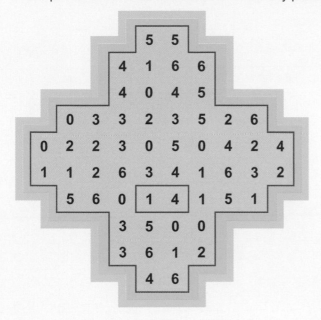

0-0	0-1	0-2	0-3	0-4	0-5	0-6

1-1	1-2	1-3	1-4	1-5	1-6	2-2
			✔			

2-3	2-4	2-5	2-6	3-3	3-4	3-5

3-6	4-4	4-5	4-6	5-5	5-6	6-6

Each of the small squares in the grid below contains either A, B or C. Each row, column, and diagonal line of six squares has exactly two of each letter. Can you tell the letter in each square?

Across

1 The As are next to each other
3 The Bs are between the Cs
4 The As are further right than the Cs
5 No two letters the same are directly next to each other
6 Each B is directly next to and right of an A

Down

1 The As are next to each other
4 The Cs are between the Bs
5 The As are next to each other
6 Each C is directly next to and below an A

Every row and column in this grid originally contained one heart, one club, one diamond, one spade and two blank squares, although not necessarily in that order.

Every symbol with a black arrow refers to the first of the four symbols encountered when travelling in the direction of the arrow. Every symbol with a white arrow refers to the second of the four symbols encountered in the direction of the arrow.

Can you complete the original grid?

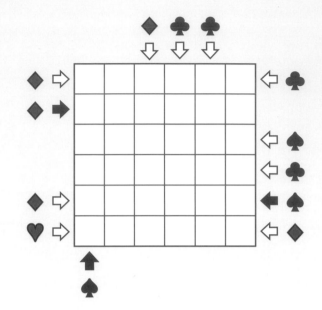

39

The blank squares below should be filled with whole numbers between 1 and 30 inclusive, any of which may occur more than once, or not at all.

The numbers in every horizontal row add up to the totals on the right, as do the two long diagonal lines; whilst those in every vertical column add up to the totals along the bottom.

40

							118
	28	5	2	15	18		107
6			27	24	11	19	117
16	21	23		1	30	12	106
25	30	6		4	14		117
	2		26	8	19	3	107
9		7	5			13	101
21		14	25	17		10	116
123	144	78	103	81	142	100	131

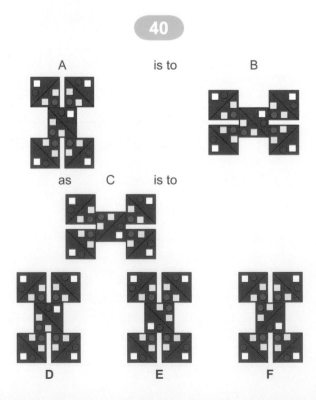

A is to B as C is to

D   E   F

Can you place the hexagons into the grid, so that where any hexagon touches another along a straight line, the number in both triangles is the same? No rotation of any hexagon is allowed!

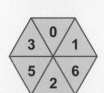

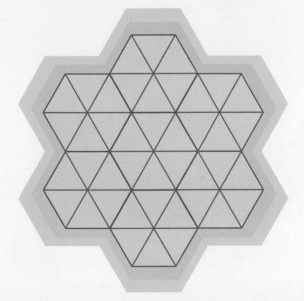

Twelve L-shapes like the ones here need to be inserted in the grid and each L has one hole in it.

There are three pieces of each of the four kinds shown here and any piece may be turned or flipped over before being put in the grid. No pieces of the same kind touch, even at a corner.

The pieces fit together so well that you cannot see any spaces between them; only the holes show.

Can you tell where the Ls are?

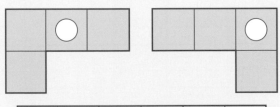

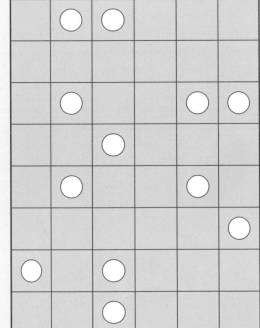

Which of the four lettered alternatives (A, B, C or D) fits most logically into the empty square?

C	3	X
J	10	Q
E	5	V

L	12	O
F	6	U
G	7	T

D	5	W
S	7	I
J	10	Q

A

K	12	P
C	3	Y
E	4	W

B

K	11	P
H	8	S
I	9	R

?

D	4	W
M	13	N
B	2	Y

C

L	13	O
F	6	V
G	7	S

D

Which four pieces can be fitted together to form an exact copy of this shape?

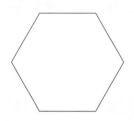

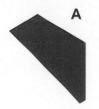
A

B

C

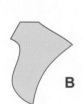
D

E

F

G

H

I

J

Can you place the vessels into the diagram? Some parts of vessels or sea squares have already been filled in. A number to the right or below a row or column refers to the number of occupied squares in that row or column.

Any vessel may be positioned horizontally or vertically, but no part of a vessel touches part of any other vessel, either horizontally, vertically or diagonally.

Empty Area of Sea:

Aircraft Carrier:

Battleships:

Cruisers:

Submarines:

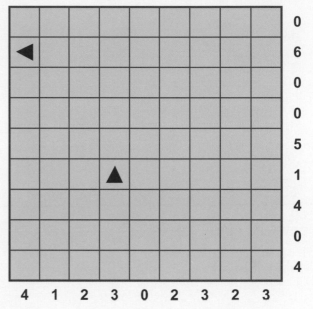

46

Can you fill each square in the bottom line with the correct digit?

Every square in the solution contains only one digit from each of the lines above, although two or more squares in the solution may contain the same digit.

At the end of every row is a score, which shows:

    a the number of digits placed in the correct finishing position on the bottom line, as indicated by a tick; and

    b the number of digits which appear on the bottom line, but in a different position, as indicated by a cross.

SCORE

8	2	8	5	✗ ✗
1	6	4	4	✗ ✗
1	7	7	5	✗
2	8	1	8	✓✓✓
6	8	6	3	✓
				✓✓✓✓

109

The grid should be filled with numbers from 1 to 6, so that each number appears just once in every row and column. The clues refer to the digit totals in the squares, eg A 1 2 3 = 6 means that the numbers in squares A1, A2 and A3 add up to 6.

1 A 4 5 = 4

2 B 5 6 = 3

3 C 1 2 = 8

4 D 3 4 5 = 7

5 E 1 2 3 = 6

6 F 1 2 = 6

7 A B 1 = 7

8 A B 2 = 6

9 A B 3 = 11

10 B C 4 = 6

11 E F 5 = 9

	A	B	C	D	E	F
1						
2						
3						
4						
5						
6						

The object of this puzzle is to trace a single path from the top left corner to the bottom right corner of the grid, travelling through all of the cells in either a horizontal, vertical or diagonal direction.

Every cell must be entered once only and your path should take you through the numbers in the sequence 1-2-3-4-1-2-3-4, etc.

Can you find the way?

1	3	2	1	3	1	4	2
4	2	4	3	4	2	3	1
1	1	3	1	4	4	3	4
2	2	2	3	4	2	1	3
4	3	4	1	1	1	4	2
1	3	2	2	3	4	2	3
4	2	2	1	1	3	3	1
3	1	4	3	2	2	4	4

49

Draw a single continuous loop, by connecting the dots. No line may cross the path of another.

The figure inside each set of any four surrounding dots indicates the total number of surrounding lines.

```
    2  1  1  1  3  2  2
          0                 3
          2  0     2  1  3
  1  3     3     3        1
     3              2
  1  1        1              1
  2        0        2     1  2
  3     0  2        1  0
          2  2           2  1
  1     0        1
  3              1  2  1
     1     1     1  1
```

50

Each horizontal row and vertical column should contain different shapes and different numbers.

Every square will contain one number and one shape and no combination may be repeated anywhere else in the puzzle.

1	2	3	4	5

		□		
	○		4	⬡
2			☆	4
	□			5
			①	

51

Given that the letters are valued 1-26 according to their places in the alphabet, can you crack the mystery code to reveal the missing letter?

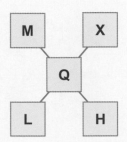

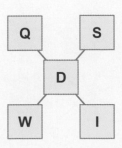

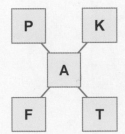

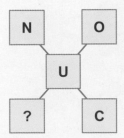

52

Which is the odd one out?

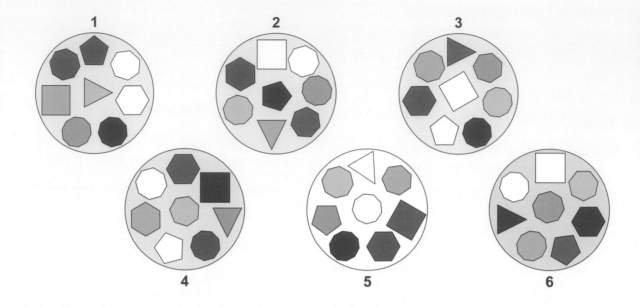

1   2   3

4   5   6

53

Which of the alternatives (A, B, C or D) comes next in this sequence?

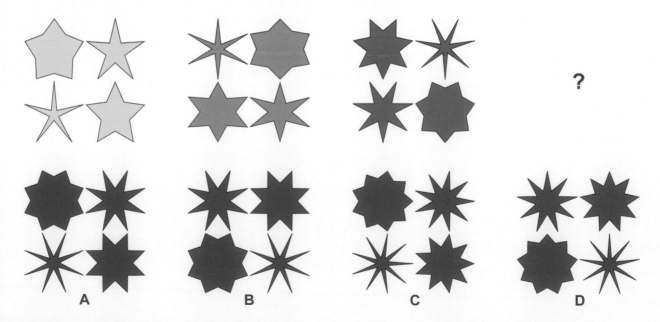

?

A   B   C   D

Place the eight tiles into the puzzle grid so that all adjacent numbers on each tile match up. Tiles may be rotated through 360 degrees, but none may be flipped over.

1	2
4	3

2	1
3	3

4	4
1	1

1	4
1	2

1	3
2	2

2	4
3	3

2	3
1	1

1	2
4	2

		4	3		
		1	3		

Place all twelve of the pieces into the grid. Any may be rotated or flipped over, but none may touch another, not even diagonally. The numbers outside the grid refer to the number of consecutive black squares; and each block is separated from the others by at least one white square. For instance, '3 2' could refer to a row with none, one or more white squares, then three black squares, then at least one white square, then two more black squares, followed by any number of white squares.

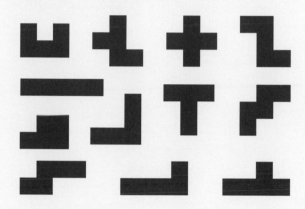

56

What number should replace the question mark?

27	19
6	14

34	31
19	22

29	41
30	18

40	28
?	31

57

In the square below, change the positions of six numbers, one per horizontal row, vertical column and long diagonal line of six smaller squares, in such a way that the numbers in each row, column and long diagonal line total exactly 223. Any number may appear more than once in a row, column or line.

38	8	33	31	68	48
47	37	35	30	38	42
43	56	37	40	27	27
37	58	38	41	33	41
5	43	53	37	30	25
23	24	33	51	52	29

58

Every brick in this pyramid contains a number which is the sum of the two numbers below it, so that F=A+B, etc. Just work out the missing numbers!

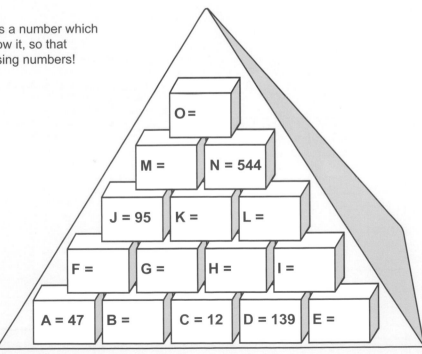

O =
M =   N = 544
J = 95   K =   L =
F =   G =   H =   I =
A = 47   B =   C = 12   D = 139   E =

With the starter already given, can you fit all of the remaining listed numbers into this grid? Take care, this puzzle may not be as easy as it looks!

21	674	4204	12680	252060
38	739	4904	15506	763758
60	842	5206	22409	1846622
78	865	5793	25883	3467409
82	915	6022	30637	3895949
88	936	6699	34848	5237055
168	1050	7398	47332	7150850
286	1203	7593	51203	7227167
373	2000	8555	51432	7594499
408	2776	8644	60628	8802423
485	3374	9289 ✓	66047	9006930
520	3577	9570	93499	9680720

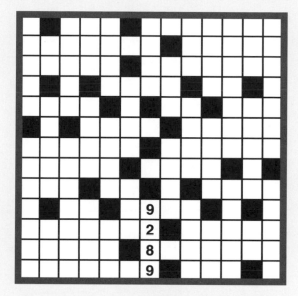

The chart gives directions to a hidden treasure behind the centre black square in the grid. Move the indicated number of spaces north, south, east and west (eg 4N means move four squares north) stopping at every square once only to arrive there. At which square should you start?

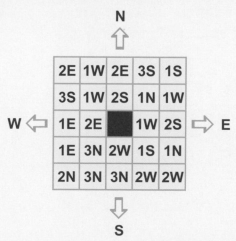

Fill the grid so that every horizontal row and vertical column contains the numbers 1-5. The 'greater than' or 'less than' signs indicate where a number is larger or smaller than that in the neighbouring square.

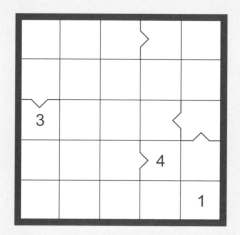

Each of the eight segments of the spider's web should be filled with a different number from 1 to 8, in such a way that every ring also contains a different number from 1 to 8.

The segments run from the outside of the spider's web to the centre, and the rings run all the way around.

Some numbers are already in place. Can you fill in the rest?

Every oval shape in this diagram contains a different letter of the alphabet from A to K inclusive. Use the clues to determine their locations. Reference in the clues to 'due' means in any location along the same horizontal or vertical line.

1 The A is due north of the I, which is next to and east of the G, which is further east than the J.

2 The C is next to and east of the K, which is next to and north of the D.

3 The F is next to and east of the H, which is next to and north of the E, which is further north than the J.

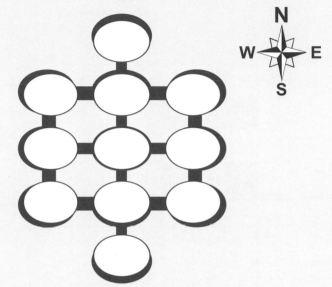

Fill the three empty circles with the symbols +, − and x in some order, to make a sum which totals the number in the centre. Each symbol must be used once and calculations are made in the direction of travel (clockwise).

= 34
21
99
26
2

The numbers at the top and on the left side show the quantity of single-digit numbers (1-9) used in that row and column. The numbers at the bottom and on the right side show the sum of the digits. A number may appear more than once in a row or column, but no numbers are in squares that touch, even at a corner.

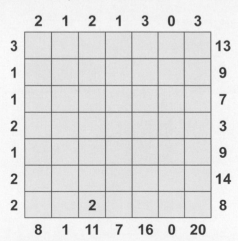

2	1	2	1	3	0	3	
3							13
1							9
1							7
2							3
1							9
2							14
2		2					8
8	1	11	7	16	0	20	

66

Using the numbers below, complete these six equations (three reading across and three reading downwards). Every number is used once.

1   2   3   4   5

6   7   8   9

	+		+		=	9
+		−		+		
	+		x		=	42
x		x		+		
	x		+		=	57
=		=		=		
72		6		17		

67

In the grid below, which number should replace the question mark?

15	24	19	17	29	26	22
14	23	18	16	28	25	21
16	25	20	18	30	27	23
13	22	17	15	27	24	20
17	26	21	19	31	28	24
12	21	16	14	26	23	19
18	27	?	20	32	29	25

68

When the box below is folded to form a cube, just one of the five options (A, B, C, D or E) can be produced. Which?

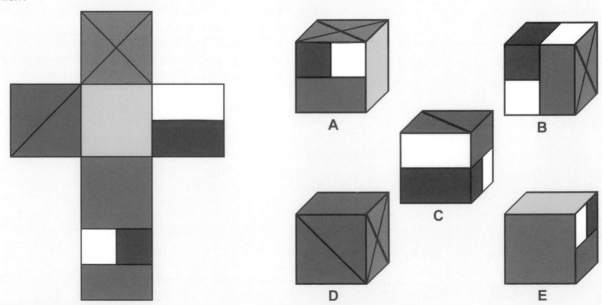

A

B

C

D

E

69

In this puzzle, an amateur coin collector has been out with his metal detector, searching for booty. He didn't have time to dig up all the coins he found, so has made a grid map, showing their locations, in the hope that if he loses the map, at least no-one else will understand it…

Those squares containing numbers are empty, but where a number appears in a square, it indicates how many coins are located in the squares (up to a maximum of eight) surrounding the numbered one, touching it at any corner or side. There is only one coin in any individual square.

Place a circle into every square containing a coin.

1		3		3		3	3		
								3	1
	2	3			3				1
2				2		1			
2		1							1
	2			0					
	2			0			1	1	
		2				3		3	
2			3				4		1
		2			3			1	

70

Every row and column of this grid should contain one each of the letters A, B, C, D, E and F. Each of the six shapes (marked by thicker lines) should also contain one each of the letters A, B, C, D, E and F. Can you complete the grid?

				B	A
	C				
			D		
	E				
		F			

71

Each symbol stands for a different number. In order to reach the correct total at the end of each row and column, what is the value of the circle, cross, pentagon, square and star?

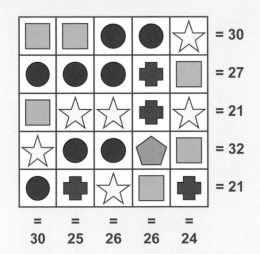

119

A standard set of 28 dominoes has been laid out as shown. Can you draw in the edges of them all? The check-box is provided as an aid and the domino already placed will help.

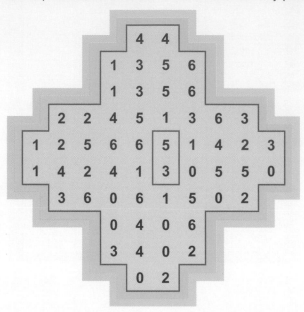

0-0	0-1	0-2	0-3	0-4	0-5	0-6

1-1	1-2	1-3	1-4	1-5	1-6	2-2

2-3	2-4	2-5	2-6	3-3	3-4	3-5
						✔

3-6	4-4	4-5	4-6	5-5	5-6	6-6

Each of the small squares in the grid below contains either A, B or C. Each row, column, and diagonal line of six squares has exactly two of each letter. Can you tell the letter in each square?

Across

1 The As are between the Bs
2 The Bs are further right than the As
3 The As are further right than the Bs
4 The As are further right than the Bs
5 The Cs are further right than the As
6 The Bs are next to each other

Down

1 No two letters the same are directly next to each other
3 The As are between the Cs
6 The As are lower than the Cs

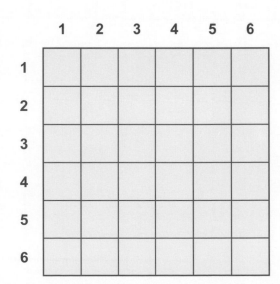

Every row and column in this grid originally contained one heart, one club, one diamond, one spade and two blank squares, although not necessarily in that order.

Every symbol with a black arrow refers to the first of the four symbols encountered when travelling in the direction of the arrow. Every symbol with a white arrow refers to the second of the four symbols encountered in the direction of the arrow.

Can you complete the original grid?

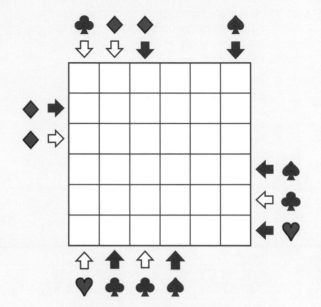

The blank squares below should be filled with whole numbers between 1 and 30 inclusive, any of which may occur more than once, or not at all.

The numbers in every horizontal row add up to the totals on the right, as do the two long diagonal lines; whilst those in every vertical column add up to the totals along the bottom.

							73
21	17	1		25		8	95
	15	19	24	20		7	103
25	10		19		24	9	119
2	23	12		7	16		103
30		19	28		1	4	122
	13	6	24	14		12	94
3	27		2	13	26		87
104	120	98	131	106	92	72	120

A   is to   B

as   C   is to

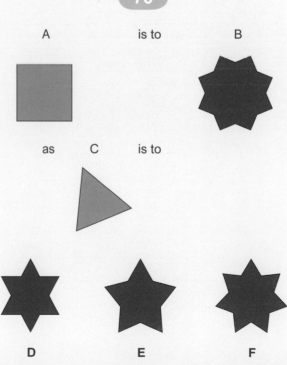

Can you place the hexagons into the grid, so that where any hexagon touches another along a straight line, the number in both triangles is the same? No rotation of any hexagon is allowed!

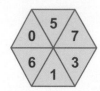

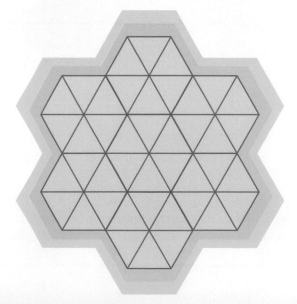

Twelve L-shapes like the ones here need to be inserted in the grid and each L has one hole in it.

There are three pieces of each of the four kinds shown here and any piece may be turned or flipped over before being put in the grid. No pieces of the same kind touch, even at a corner.

The pieces fit together so well that you cannot see any spaces between them; only the holes show.

Can you tell where the Ls are?

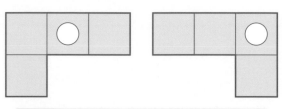

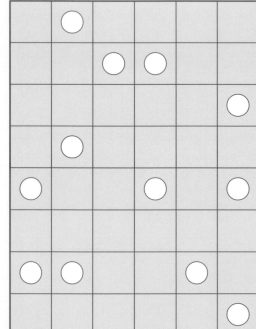

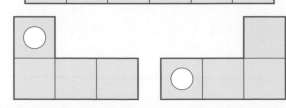

Draw walls to partition the grid into areas (some walls are already drawn in for you). Each area must contain two circles, area sizes must match those numbers shown next to the grid and each '+' must be linked to at least two walls.

3, 3, 5, 7, 7

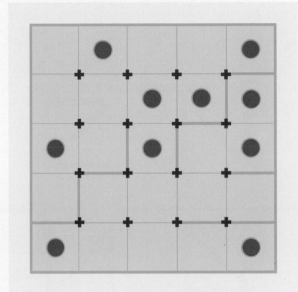

Which of the four lettered alternatives (A, B, C or D) fits most logically into the empty square?

11	12	15
13	17	3
6	2	14

5	12	1
19	7	11
6	12	20

10	10	13
5	20	11
15	1	8

?

5	14	8
16	4	12
9	13	12

A

6	18	15
18	5	12
4	7	4

B

16	3	12
10	9	15
4	17	3

C

11	16	13
5	12	11
13	3	9

D

81

The object of this puzzle is to trace a single path from the top left corner to the bottom right corner of the grid, travelling through all of the cells in either a horizontal, vertical or diagonal direction.

Every cell must be entered once only and your path should take you through the numbers in the sequence 1-2-3-4-1-2-3-4, etc.

Can you find the way?

1	3	4	4	1	4	3	2
1	2	1	2	3	2	1	3
4	2	3	4	1	2	4	2
3	4	4	2	3	1	1	3
2	1	1	3	4	2	4	2
4	2	4	3	3	1	3	1
1	3	2	1	3	4	1	2
2	3	4	1	2	4	3	4

82

The grid should be filled with numbers from 1 to 6, so that each number appears just once in every row and column. The clues refer to the digit totals in the squares, eg A 1 2 3 = 6 means that the numbers in squares A1, A2 and A3 add up to 6.

1   B C 2 = 5

2   A B C 3 = 13

3   E F 4 = 11

4   D E 5 = 5

5   B C D 6 = 11

6   A 4 5 = 9

7   B 4 5 = 4

8   C 4 5 = 6

9   D 1 2 = 11

10   E 2 3 = 10

11   F 5 6 = 7

	A	B	C	D	E	F
1						
2						
3						
4						
5						
6						

Can you fill each square in the bottom line with the correct digit?

Every square in the solution contains only one digit from each of the lines above, although two or more squares in the solution may contain the same digit.

At the end of every row is a score, which shows:

a the number of digits placed in the correct finishing position on the bottom line, as indicated by a tick; and

b the number of digits which appear on the bottom line, but in a different position, as indicated by a cross.

SCORE

3	2	8	7	✓✓
3	7	6	1	✓✓
1	7	2	2	✗✗
1	5	6	2	✗✗
4	6	3	2	✗✗
				✓✓✓✓

84

Can you place the vessels into the diagram? Some parts of vessels or sea squares have already been filled in. A number to the right or below a row or column refers to the number of occupied squares in that row or column.

Any vessel may be positioned horizontally or vertically, but no part of a vessel touches part of any other vessel, either horizontally, vertically or diagonally.

Empty Area of Sea: ≈

Aircraft Carrier: ◀■■▶

Battleships: ◀■▶ ◀■▶

Cruisers: ◀▶ ◀▶ ◀▶

Submarines: ● ● ● ●

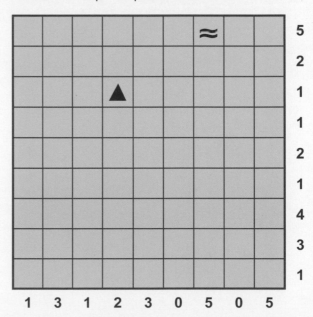

85

Draw a single continuous loop, by connecting the dots. No line may cross the path of another.

The figure inside each set of any four surrounding dots indicates the total number of surrounding lines.

```
3        1 2 2    3 1
   3
2        0 2          1
1 1      1 2    1 1
2    3   3      0 1 0 1
2    3
     3        0 1
  1    1    2 2        2
3 2        2      1    1
  2 1           2      0
              1 0      1
2           2 3    1   3
```

86

Each horizontal row and vertical column should contain different shapes and different numbers.

Every square will contain one number and one shape and no combination may be repeated anywhere else in the puzzle.

1   2   3   4   5

◇			4	
		1		◇
		4		⑤
○	4	2		3
□		3	2	⬡

87

Given that the letters are valued 1-26 according to their places in the alphabet, can you crack the mystery code to reveal the missing letter?

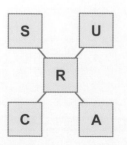

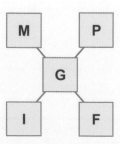

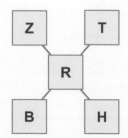

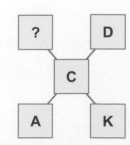

A set of dominoes is to be placed in four rows as shown below. The numbers indicate which values are shown on all the dominoes in each column and the relevant half of the domino in every row. Find out where each domino is placed by carefully comparing rows and columns to determine the possible positions of certain dominoes: for instance, if any column contains only one 6, then the domino 6/6 isn't in that column.

A set of dominoes consists of:

0/0, 0/1, 0/2, 0/3, 0/4, 0/5, 0/6, 1/1, 1/2, 1/3, 1/4, 1/5, 1/6, 2/2,

2/3, 2/4, 2/5, 2/6, 3/3, 3/4, 3/5, 3/6, 4/4, 4/5, 4/6, 5/5, 5/6, 6/6.

	0, 0, 3, 3, 6, 6, 6, 6.	0, 2, 2, 4, 4, 4, 5, 5.	0, 0, 1, 2, 2, 2, 2, 3.	0, 1, 1, 1, 3, 3, 3, 6.	1, 1, 2, 3, 5, 5, 5, 6.	1, 2, 3, 4, 4, 4, 5, 6.	0, 0, 1, 4, 4, 5, 5, 6.
0, 3, 4, 5, 5, 5, 6.							
0, 1, 3, 3, 3, 4, 6.							
0, 0, 2, 3, 4, 5, 5.							
0, 1, 2, 4, 6, 6, 6.							
0, 1, 1, 1, 2, 2, 4.							
0, 1, 1, 3, 4, 6, 6.							
1, 2, 2, 4, 4, 5, 6.							
0, 2, 2, 3, 3, 5, 5.							

Place the eight tiles into the puzzle grid so that all adjacent numbers on each tile match up. Tiles may be rotated through 360 degrees, but none may be flipped over.

2	1
3	2

4	1
1	3

3	3
1	4

1	3
3	2

1	3
1	1

4	1
4	3

2	3
1	3

4	3
2	1

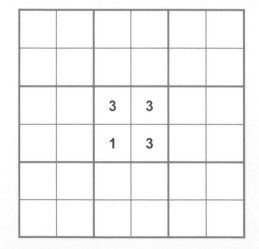

Place all twelve of the pieces into the grid. Any may be rotated or flipped over, but none may touch another, not even diagonally. The numbers outside the grid refer to the number of consecutive black squares; and each block is separated from the others by at least one white square. For instance, '3 2' could refer to a row with none, one or more white squares, then three black squares, then at least one white square, then two more black squares, followed by any number of white squares.

	1		1	2							
	2	2	4	1	1	2	1	3			
	1	2	2	1	1	1	2	3	2	1	2
	5	2	1	3	1	2	1	1	3	2	1
1 1 1											
3 3											
1 1											
4 2											
1 1											
1 1											
1 1											
2 3											
1 1 1											
3											
1 2 3											
1 2 2											
1 1 1											
1 3 1											
1 1 1											
1 3											

91

In the diagram below, which number should replace the question mark?

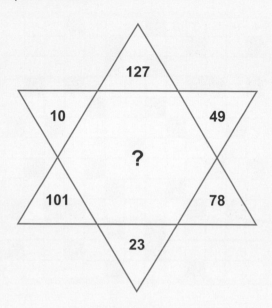

92

In the square below, change the positions of six numbers, one per horizontal row, vertical column and long diagonal line of six smaller squares, in such a way that the numbers in each row, column and long diagonal line total exactly 239. Any number may appear more than once in a row, column or line.

37	13	22	44	84	52
46	39	42	45	44	44
50	77	39	7	18	46
18	32	44	71	16	40
22	41	47	48	24	49
64	19	39	45	45	21

93

Every brick in this pyramid contains a number which is the sum of the two numbers below it, so that F=A+B, etc. Just work out the missing numbers!

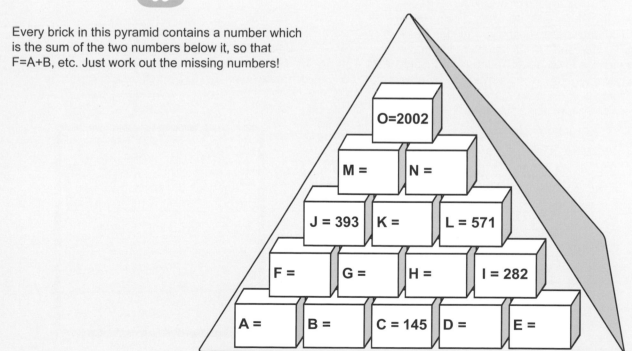

With the starter already given, can you fit all of the remaining listed numbers into this grid? Take care, this puzzle may not be as easy as it looks!

17	367	963	49638 ✓	78928
28	456	977	52199	79389
38	477	1660	52894	86066
43	497	4658	54108	87639
51	501	5268	56507	88063
54	516	7652	58834	89630
66	534	26973	61230	94976
67	636	33562	61632	97505
90	703	38124	65101	143098
92	813	41073	71288	200944
192	839	41676	77052	533222
221	941	49057	77147	981419

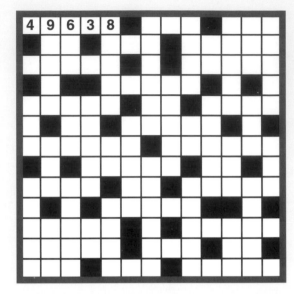

The chart gives directions to a hidden treasure behind the centre black square in the grid. Move the indicated number of spaces north, south, east and west (eg 4N means move four squares north) stopping at every square once only to arrive there. At which square should you start?

N

3S	2E	3S	3W	2W
1S	1S	1W	3W	2W
3E	2N	■	1E	2N
1S	2E	1N	1S	2N
1E	1N	2E	3N	1N

W ⇐   ⇒ E

S

Fill the grid so that every horizontal row and vertical column contains the numbers 1-5. The 'greater than' or 'less than' signs indicate where a number is larger or smaller than that in the neighbouring square.

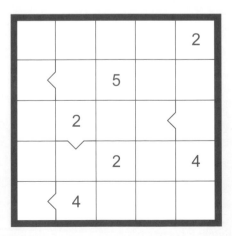

SECTION 3

Each of the eight segments of the spider's web should be filled with a different number from 1 to 8, in such a way that every ring also contains a different number from 1 to 8.

The segments run from the outside of the spider's web to the centre, and the rings run all the way around.

Some numbers are already in place. Can you fill in the rest?

1

A standard set of 28 dominoes has been laid out as shown. Can you draw in the edges of them all? The check-box is provided as an aid and the domino already placed will help.

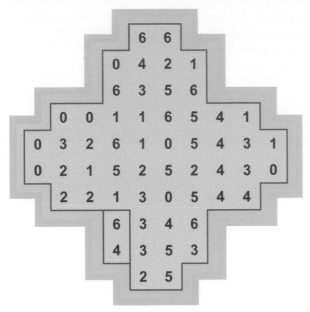

0-0	0-1	0-2	0-3	0-4	0-5	0-6

1-1	1-2	1-3	1-4	1-5	1-6	2-2

2-3	2-4	2-5	2-6	3-3	3-4	3-5

3-6	4-4	4-5	4-6	5-5	5-6	6-6
			✔			

2

Draw walls to partition the grid into areas (some walls are already drawn in for you). Each area must contain two circles, area sizes must match those numbers shown next to the grid and each '+' must be linked to at least two walls.

2, 3, 3, 3, 3, 4, 7

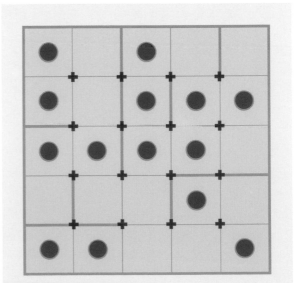

Every row and column in this grid originally contained one heart, one club, one diamond, one spade and two blank squares, although not necessarily in that order.

Every symbol with a black arrow refers to the first of the four symbols encountered when travelling in the direction of the arrow. Every symbol with a white arrow refers to the second of the four symbols encountered in the direction of the arrow.

Can you complete the original grid?

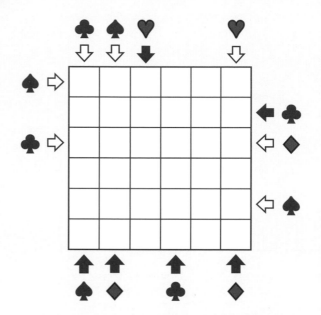

4

The blank squares below should be filled with whole numbers between 1 and 30 inclusive, any of which may occur more than once, or not at all.

The numbers in every horizontal row add up to the totals on the right, as do the two long diagonal lines; whilst those in every vertical column add up to the totals along the bottom.

							70
	16	2		21		5	114
6	14	17	20		1		86
23	12	2			15	30	106
22	8		18	17		8	112
2	4			21	25	18	106
5		26	3	12	14		98
	22	21	1	17		9	104
102	86	102	100	110	109	117	106

5

Draw in the missing hands on the final clock.

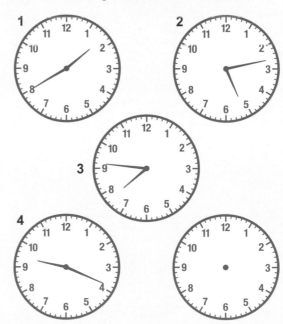

6

Can you place the hexagons into the grid, so that where any hexagon touches another along a straight line, the number in both triangles is the same? No rotation of any hexagon is allowed!

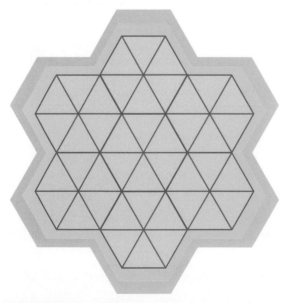

7

Twelve L-shapes like the ones here need to be inserted in the grid and each L has one hole in it.

There are three pieces of each of the four kinds shown here and any piece may be turned or flipped over before being put in the grid. No pieces of the same kind touch, even at a corner.

The pieces fit together so well that you cannot see any spaces between them; only the holes show.

Can you tell where the Ls are?

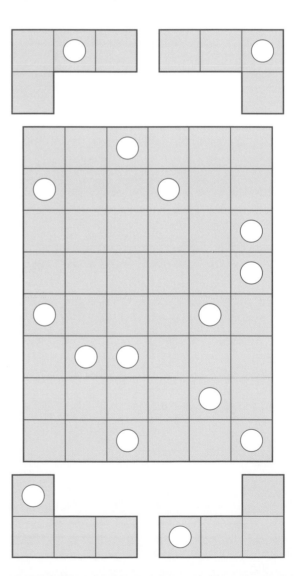

8

In this puzzle, an amateur coin collector has been out with his metal detector, searching for booty. He didn't have time to dig up all the coins he found, so has made a grid map, showing their locations, in the hope that if he loses the map, at least no-one else will understand it…

Those squares containing numbers are empty, but where a number appears in a square, it indicates how many coins are located in the squares (up to a maximum of eight) surrounding the numbered one, touching it at any corner or side. There is only one coin in any individual square.

Place a circle into every square containing a coin.

		1							
1	3		3			1	2	1	
2					2				1
3			4		3			4	
								4	
2		0		3					1
			3			0			
				2					
2						2	2	1	
	0			1	1				

9

The grid should be filled with numbers from 1 to 6, so that each number appears just once in every row and column. The clues refer to the digit totals in the squares, eg A 1 2 3 = 6 means that the numbers in squares A1, A2 and A3 add up to 6.

1 D E F 2 = 7

2 C D 3 = 7

3 B C 4 = 10

4 A B C 5 = 10

5 E F 6 = 4

6 A 1 2 = 7

7 B 1 2 = 5

8 C 1 2 = 9

9 D 4 5 = 6

10 E 4 5 = 9

11 F 3 4 = 9

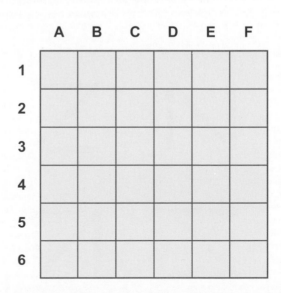

Each of the small squares in the grid below contains either A, B or C. Each row, column, and diagonal line of six squares has exactly two of each letter. Can you tell the letter in each square?

Across

   1 The Cs are between the As

   2 The As are further right than the Bs

   4 No two letters the same are directly next to each other

   5 The Cs are between the As

   6 The Bs are between the Cs

Down

   2 The As are between the Cs

   4 Each A is directly next to and below a C

   5 The As are next to each other

	1	2	3	4	5	6
1						
2						
3						
4						
5						
6						

11

The object of this puzzle is to trace a single path from the top left corner to the bottom right corner of the grid, travelling through all of the cells in either a horizontal, vertical or diagonal direction.

Every cell must be entered once only and your path should take you through the numbers in the sequence 1-2-3-4-1-2-3-4, etc.

Can you find the way?

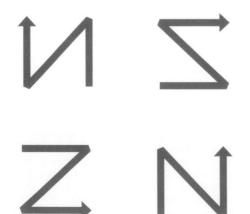

1	2	2	1	4	1	3	2
4	3	3	3	2	4	4	1
1	4	1	3	3	1	3	2
2	4	4	2	2	4	3	1
3	1	2	1	4	1	2	4
4	1	3	1	2	3	4	3
3	2	4	2	1	2	3	2
2	1	3	4	3	4	1	4

Can you place the vessels into the diagram? Some parts of vessels or sea squares have already been filled in. A number to the right or below a row or column refers to the number of occupied squares in that row or column.

Any vessel may be positioned horizontally or vertically, but no part of a vessel touches part of any other vessel, either horizontally, vertically or diagonally.

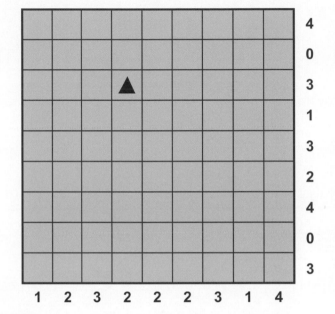

Empty Area of Sea: ≈

Aircraft Carrier:

Battleships:

Cruisers:

Submarines:

13

Can you fill each square in the bottom line with the correct digit?

Every square in the solution contains only one digit from each of the lines above, although two or more squares in the solution may contain the same digit.

At the end of every row is a score, which shows:

   a the number of digits placed in the correct finishing position on the bottom line, as indicated by a tick; and

   b the number of digits which appear on the bottom line, but in a different position, as indicated by a cross.

SCORE

8	5	7	2	✓ ✗
8	2	4	5	✓
7	2	1	2	✗
6	6	7	2	✗ ✗ ✗
5	3	1	7	✗
				✓ ✓ ✓ ✓

Draw a single continuous loop, by connecting the dots. No line may cross the path of another.

The figure inside each set of any four surrounding dots indicates the total number of surrounding lines.

```
    1       2   2                   1
  3   2         2                 1
      1   3   2   2   3           3
  1   0         1         1       1
      1   3   2   1             2
      0   2         2   2       3       2
  1                 1       2   1       3
                                  0
      2   2   1         3           1   2
                  0                 1
      3   1                 0           2
          1   1   1   1   2   2       3
```

Each horizontal row and vertical column should contain different shapes and different numbers.

Every square will contain one number and one shape and no combination may be repeated anywhere else in the puzzle.

| 1 | 2 | 3 | 4 | 5 |

★	⬡5	4		◇3
		★2		
4				
○				
▢				2

Given that the letters are valued 1-26 according to their places in the alphabet, can you crack the mystery code to reveal the missing letter?

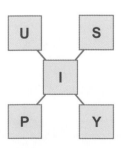

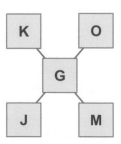

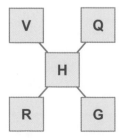

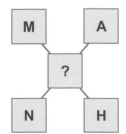

138

A set of dominoes is to be placed in four rows as shown below. The numbers indicate which values are shown on all the dominoes in each column and the relevant half of the domino in every row. Find out where each domino is placed by carefully comparing rows and columns to determine the possible positions of certain dominoes: for instance, if any column contains only one 6, then the domino 6/6 isn't in that column.

A set of dominoes consists of:

0/0, 0/1, 0/2, 0/3, 0/4, 0/5, 0/6, 1/1, 1/2, 1/3, 1/4, 1/5, 1/6, 2/2,

2/3, 2/4, 2/5, 2/6, 3/3, 3/4, 3/5, 3/6, 4/4, 4/5, 4/6, 5/5, 5/6, 6/6.

?	1, 2, 3, 3, 3, 3, 4, 6.	0, 1, 1, 2, 3, 4, 4, 6.	0, 1, 3, 4, 5, 5, 5, 6.	1, 2, 4, 4, 4, 6, 6, 6.	0, 0, 0, 1, 2, 5, 5, 6.	0, 0, 0, 2, 4, 5, 5, 5.	1, 1, 2, 2, 2, 3, 3, 6.
1, 1, 3, 4, 5, 5, 5.							
1, 2, 2, 2, 4, 5, 6.							
0, 0, 2, 3, 3, 4, 6.							
0, 1, 3, 4, 6, 6, 6.							
0, 0, 2, 2, 5, 6, 6.							
0, 1, 2, 2, 4, 5, 6.							
0, 1, 1, 4, 4, 5, 5.							
0, 1, 3, 3, 3, 3, 4.							

Place the eight tiles into the puzzle grid so that all adjacent numbers on each tile match up. Tiles may be rotated through 360 degrees, but none may be flipped over.

1	3
4	4

1	1
4	3

4	3
3	2

4	3
2	1

1	2
1	1

4	4
3	2

1	1
3	4

1	4
2	3

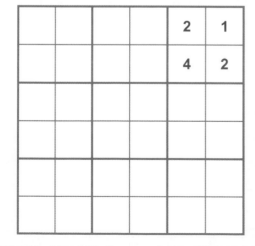

				2	1
				4	2

Place all twelve of the pieces into the grid. Any may be rotated or flipped over, but none may touch another, not even diagonally. The numbers outside the grid refer to the number of consecutive black squares; and each block is separated from the others by at least one white square. For instance, '3 2' could refer to a row with none, one or more white squares, then three black squares, then at least one white square, then two more black squares, followed by any number of white squares.

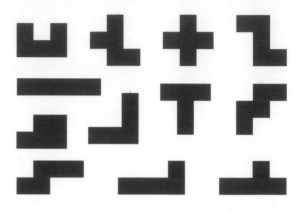

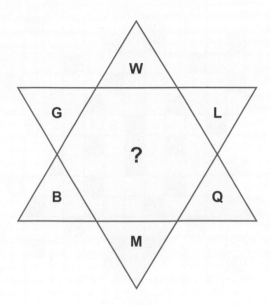

20

In the diagram below, which letter should replace the question mark?

21

In the square below, change the positions of six numbers, one per horizontal row, vertical column and long diagonal line of six smaller squares, in such a way that the numbers in each row, column and long diagonal line total exactly 262. Any number may appear more than once in a row, column or line.

56	8	44	72	84	24
61	43	36	64	47	50
71	55	43	21	27	52
12	67	47	65	18	44
17	27	54	61	11	48
52	18	64	18	66	25

22

Every brick in this pyramid contains a number which is the sum of the two numbers below it, so that F=A+B, etc. Just work out the missing numbers!

O =

M =   N =

J =   K =   L = 455

F =   G = 141   H =   I =

A = 29   B = 72   C =   D = 138   E =

With the starter already given, can you fit all of the remaining listed numbers into this grid? Take care, this puzzle may not be as easy as it looks!

25	732	2644	8869	69456
33	783	3233	9353	73369
47	793	4334	9422 ✓	75418
49	822	4715	9448	83433
73	836	4885	16046	90120
99	870	5122	16875	97956
122	893	6338	27428	1927322
160	910	6408	28653	3224209
260	936	7119	35611	5792441
263	972	7383	37213	6614610
333	1325	7676	44346	6922003
651	1377	8721	60623	8432323

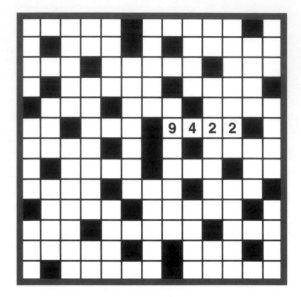

The chart gives directions to a hidden treasure behind the centre black square in the grid. Move the indicated number of spaces north, south, east and west (eg 4N means move four squares north) stopping at every square once only to arrive there. At which square should you start?

N

3S	3E	1E	3W	1S
3S	1W	1N	2S	1W
2E	1N	■	3W	3W
1E	3N	2E	1W	1S
2E	2E	3N	2N	3W

W ⇦   ⇨ E

S

Fill the grid so that every horizontal row and vertical column contains the numbers 1-5. The 'greater than' or 'less than' signs indicate where a number is larger or smaller than that in the neighbouring square.

2			5	
	1		∧	
	2			
3		5		
			∨	

142

Each of the eight segments of the spider's web should be filled with a different number from 1 to 8, in such a way that every ring also contains a different number from 1 to 8.

The segments run from the outside of the spider's web to the centre, and the rings run all the way around.

Some numbers are already in place. Can you fill in the rest?

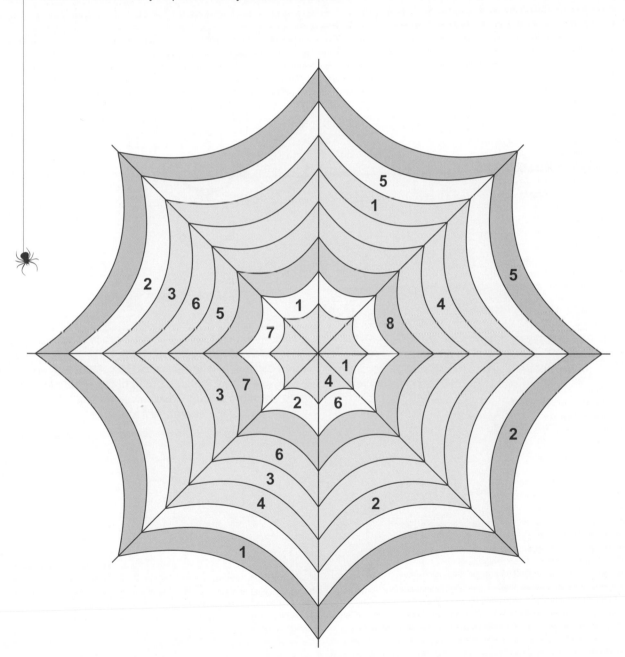

Every oval shape in this diagram contains a different letter of the alphabet from A to K inclusive. Use the clues to determine their locations. Reference in the clues to 'due' means in any location along the same horizontal or vertical line.

1   The F is due east of the I, which is further north than the E, which is due east of the J.

2   The H is due north of the A, which is next to and east of the K, which is next to and north of the B, which is next to and north of the G.

3   The J is next to and south of the D, which is further west than the F, which is next to and south of the C.

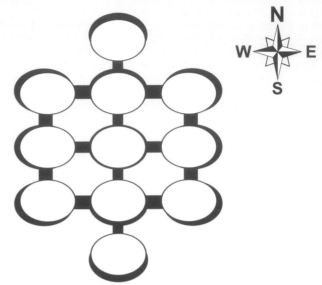

Fill the three empty circles with the symbols +, − and x in some order, to make a sum which totals the number in the centre. Each symbol must be used once and calculations are made in the direction of travel (clockwise).

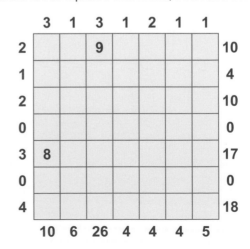

The numbers at the top and on the left side show the quantity of single-digit numbers (1-9) used in that row and column. The numbers at the bottom and on the right side show the sum of the digits. A number may appear more than once in a row or column, but no numbers are in squares that touch, even at a corner.

	3	1	3	1	2	1	1	
2			9					10
1								4
2								10
0								0
3	8							17
0								0
4								18
	10	6	26	4	4	4	5	

144

S
E
C
T
I
O
N

4

30

Using the numbers below, complete these six equations (three reading across and three reading downwards). Every number is used once.

1   2   3   4   5
  6   7   8   9

	+		+		=	21
+	■	−	■	×		
	+		×		=	20
×	■	×	■	−		
	+		+		=	15
=		=		=		
72		6		33		

31

In the grid below, which numbers should replace the question marks?

51	28	39	42	34	19	67
45	22	33	36	28	13	61
39	16	27	30	22	7	55
33	10	21	?	16	1	49
40	17	28	31	23	8	56
47	24	35	38	30	15	63
54	31	42	45	37	22	70

32

When the box below is folded to form a cube, just one of the five options (A, B, C, D or E) can be produced. Which?

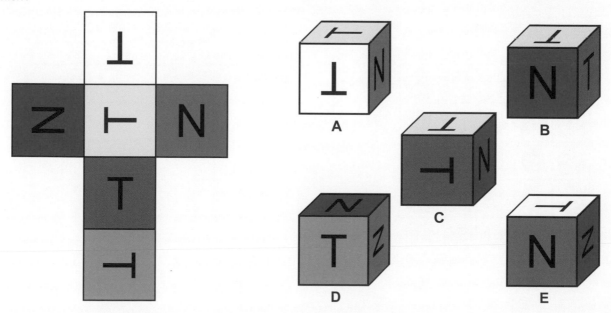

145

33

In this puzzle, an amateur coin collector has been out with his metal detector, searching for booty. He didn't have time to dig up all the coins he found, so has made a grid map, showing their locations, in the hope that if he loses the map, at least no-one else will understand it...

Those squares containing numbers are empty, but where a number appears in a square, it indicates how many coins are located in the squares (up to a maximum of eight) surrounding the numbered one, touching it at any corner or side. There is only one coin in any individual square.

Place a circle into every square containing a coin.

1	3				3	3			0
	4			2				3	
		3						3	
4			0			1			
							2		
3		1	1			1			0
	4		2		2		1		0
			4					1	
	3						1		1
			2		2				

34

Each symbol stands for a different number. In order to reach the correct total at the end of each row and column, what is the value of the circle, cross, pentagon, square and star?

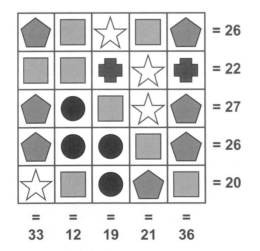

= 26
= 22
= 27
= 26
= 20

= 33 = 12 = 19 = 21 = 36

35

Every row and column of this grid should contain one each of the letters A, B, C, D, E and F. Each of the six shapes (marked by thicker lines) should also contain one each of the letters A, B, C, D, E and F. Can you complete the grid?

				B	A
			E	D	C
					F

A standard set of 28 dominoes has been laid out as shown. Can you draw in the edges of them all? The checkbox is provided as an aid and the domino already placed will help.

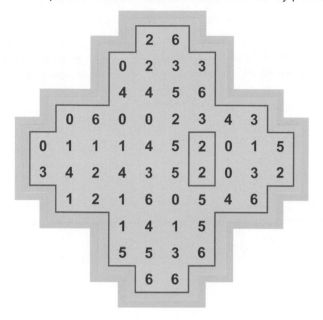

0-0	0-1	0-2	0-3	0-4	0-5	0-6

1-1	1-2	1-3	1-4	1-5	1-6	2-2
						✔

2-3	2-4	2-5	2-6	3-3	3-4	3-5

3-6	4-4	4-5	4-6	5-5	5-6	6-6

Each of the small squares in the grid below contains either A, B or C. Each row, column, and diagonal line of six squares has exactly two of each letter. Can you tell the letter in each square?

Across
- **3** The Cs are between the Bs
- **4** The Bs are between the Cs
- **5** The Bs are between the As
- **6** The As are further left than the Cs

Down
- **2** The Cs are higher than the As
- **3** The Cs are lower than the Bs
- **4** The Cs are lower than the As
- **5** No two letters the same are directly next to each other
- **6** Each B is directly next to and below a C

Every row and column in this grid originally contained one heart, one club, one diamond, one spade and two blank squares, although not necessarily in that order.

Every symbol with a black arrow refers to the first of the four symbols encountered when travelling in the direction of the arrow. Every symbol with a white arrow refers to the second of the four symbols encountered in the direction of the arrow.

Can you complete the original grid?

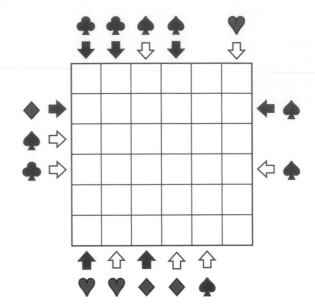

39

The blank squares below should be filled with whole numbers between 1 and 30 inclusive, any of which may occur more than once, or not at all.

The numbers in every horizontal row add up to the totals on the right, as do the two long diagonal lines; whilst those in every vertical column add up to the totals along the bottom.

							135
12	25	5			4	11	99
13		1	10	17		27	104
	7		15	30	18		142
8	9	6			28	16	106
17	22	12	14			13	105
20		2	30	4	11	10	92
24	3			21	17	6	93
115	97	56	120	121	120	112	95

40

A   is to   B

C   is to

as

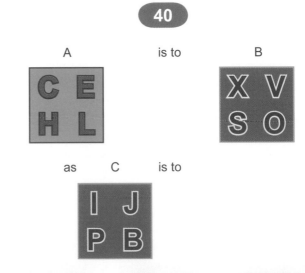

Can you place the hexagons into the grid, so that where any hexagon touches another along a straight line, the number in both triangles is the same? No rotation of any hexagon is allowed!

Twelve L-shapes like the ones here need to be inserted in the grid and each L has one hole in it.

There are three pieces of each of the four kinds shown here and any piece may be turned or flipped over before being put in the grid. No pieces of the same kind touch, even at a corner.

The pieces fit together so well that you cannot see any spaces between them; only the holes show.

Can you tell where the Ls are?

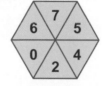

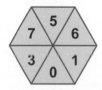
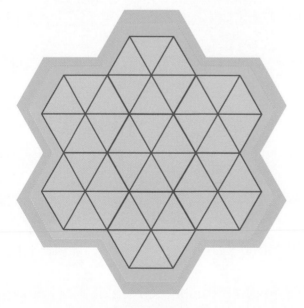

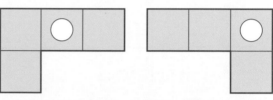
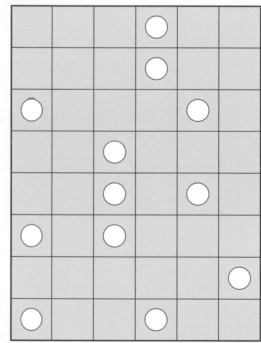
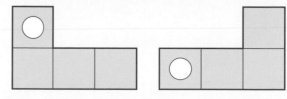

43

Which of the four lettered alternatives (A, B, C or D) fits most logically into the empty square?

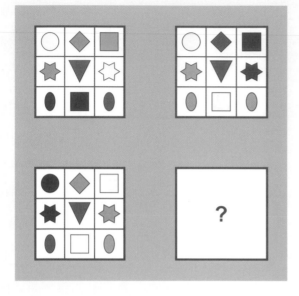

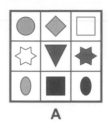
A

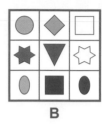
B

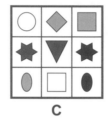
C

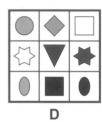
D

44

Which four pieces can be fitted together to form an exact copy of this shape?

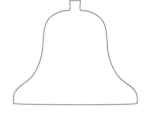

A

B

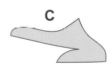
C

D

E

F

G

H

I

J

Can you place the vessels into the diagram? Some parts of vessels or sea squares have already been filled in. A number to the right or below a row or column refers to the number of occupied squares in that row or column.

Any vessel may be positioned horizontally or vertically, but no part of a vessel touches part of any other vessel, either horizontally, vertically or diagonally.

Empty Area of Sea: ≈

Aircraft Carrier: ◀■■▶

Battleships: ◀■▶ ◀■▶

Cruisers: ◀▶ ◀▶ ◀▶

Submarines: ● ● ● ●

Grid row clues (right side, top to bottom): 4, 2, 2, 2, 1, 2, 3, 3, 1

Grid column clues (bottom, left to right): 4, 2, 2, 0, 4, 1, 2, 3, 2

46

Can you fill each square in the bottom line with the correct digit?

Every square in the solution contains only one digit from each of the lines above, although two or more squares in the solution may contain the same digit.

At the end of every row is a score, which shows:

  a the number of digits placed in the correct finishing position on the bottom line, as indicated by a tick; and

  b the number of digits which appear on the bottom line, but in a different position, as indicated by a cross.

				SCORE
6	1	8	4	✓ ✗ ✗
6	1	7	6	✓ ✗ ✗
3	6	5	6	✗ ✗
3	8	5	1	✓ ✓
3	2	6	5	✓
				✓ ✓ ✓ ✓

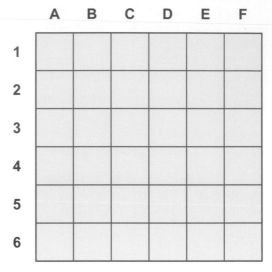

47

The grid should be filled with numbers from 1 to 6, so that each number appears just once in every row and column. The clues refer to the digit totals in the squares, eg A 1 2 3 = 6 means that the numbers in squares A1, A2 and A3 add up to 6.

	A	B	C	D	E	F
1						
2						
3						
4						
5						
6						

1 C 4 5 = 8

2 D 5 6 = 7

3 E 1 2 = 7

4 F 1 2 = 8

5 A B C 1 = 10

6 A B C 2 = 6

7 C D 3 = 8

8 A B 4 = 6

9 E F 5 = 6

10 B C 6 = 8

11 A 5 6 = 9

48

The object of this puzzle is to trace a single path from the top left corner to the bottom right corner of the grid, travelling through all of the cells in either a horizontal, vertical or diagonal direction.

Every cell must be entered once only and your path should take you through the numbers in the sequence 1-2-3-4-1-2-3-4, etc.

Can you find the way?

1	3	4	1	2	1	4	3
2	2	3	4	3	2	2	1
1	2	4	1	4	3	4	2
4	3	1	1	2	3	1	3
1	2	3	2	1	4	3	4
3	4	4	1	3	2	1	4
2	3	1	4	2	2	2	3
4	1	2	3	4	1	3	4

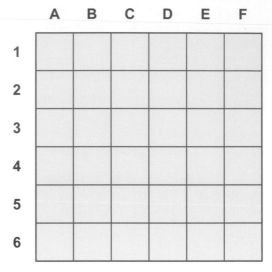

S E C T I O N

4

49

Draw a single continuous loop, by connecting the dots. No line may cross the path of another.

The figure inside each set of any four surrounding dots indicates the total number of surrounding lines.

```
2  1     1     2  2  3  2
2  0                 1  1
      0           1  3
3           2              1
            2     2  1
   0  2  2        1     2
1     1  2              3
1        1  2  2  1  0
3     0  2     1  0
                       3
1              1     0
3     1     3     2  1
```

50

Each horizontal row and vertical column should contain different shapes and different numbers.

Every square will contain one number and one shape and no combination may be repeated anywhere else in the puzzle.

1   2   3   4   5

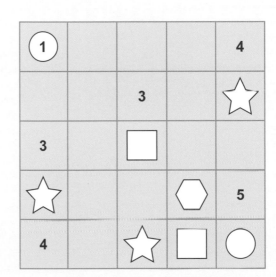

51

Given that the letters are valued 1-26 according to their places in the alphabet, can you crack the mystery code to reveal the missing letter?

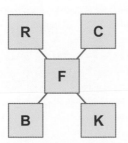

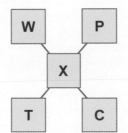

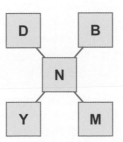

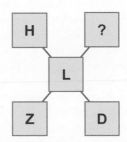

Which is the odd one out?

A

5	8	7	6
7	4	6	1
2	8	3	2
1	3	4	5

B

2	4	5	1
3	5	8	8
6	4	6	3
7	2	7	1

C

1	3	4	5
8	7	6	8
2	5	7	6
3	2	1	4

2	1	1	8
3	5	6	2
8	4	5	3
1	6	4	1

D

6	7	4	3
4	5	7	5
6	3	8	8
1	2	2	1

E

1	8	7	4
4	5	6	3
1	2	8	6
3	5	7	2

F

Which of the alternatives (1, 2, 3 or 4) comes next in this sequence?

15　A　21　G　19　E　30　?

Q	P	O	R
1	**2**	**3**	**4**

Place the eight tiles into the puzzle grid so that all adjacent numbers on each tile match up. Tiles may be rotated through 360 degrees, but none may be flipped over.

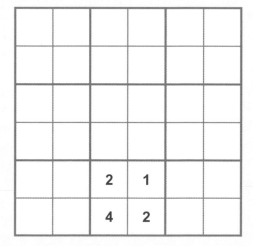

Place all twelve of the pieces into the grid. Any may be rotated or flipped over, but none may touch another, not even diagonally. The numbers outside the grid refer to the number of consecutive black squares; and each block is separated from the others by at least one white square. For instance, '3 2' could refer to a row with none, one or more white squares, then three black squares, then at least one white square, then two more black squares, followed by any number of white squares.

Column clues (top to bottom):
```
          3                 1 3 1
          1       1 2       2 1 1
3 1 2 2 2 2 3 1 1 2 2
3 1 1 1 1 4 2 5 1 3 1
```

Row clues (left):
```
    1 1
    1 3
  1 2 1
    2 1
    2 4
  1 1 1
    3 3
  1 1 2
  1 1 2
  3 1 1
      1
      1
  3 1 1
1 1 1 2
  1 1 1
    2 2
```

56

In the diagram below, what number should replace the question mark?

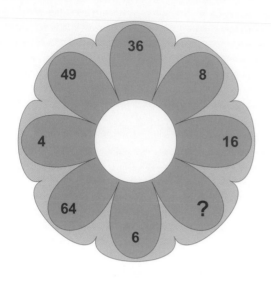

57

In the square below, change the positions of six numbers, one per horizontal row, vertical column and long diagonal line of six smaller squares, in such a way that the numbers in each row, column and long diagonal line total exactly 260. Any number may appear more than once in a row, column or line.

63	2	30	37	44	29
75	43	35	18	45	17
42	99	43	55	24	43
43	72	45	53	25	44
20	69	31	67	15	35
54	21	53	52	52	65

58

Every brick in this pyramid contains a number which is the sum of the two numbers below it, so that F=A+B, etc. Just work out the missing numbers!

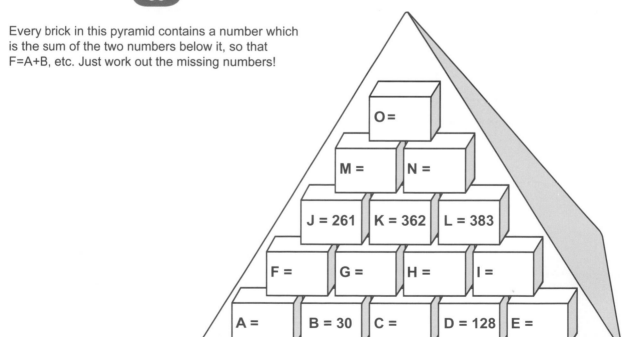

With the starter already given, can you fit all of the remaining listed numbers into this grid? Take care, this puzzle may not be as easy as it looks!

11	102	888	23215	79303
13	112	910	24234	94355
24	265	1348	31486	96216
36	370	1595	37205	98515
42	373	1638	40409	114566
47	415	2357	59226	164064
50	450	3739	59483	203251
68	480	5681	61250	297940
79	524	6366	61569	302404
81	568	7977	67948 ✓	484680
88	594	8721	72743	753261
89	680	9330	74929	821244

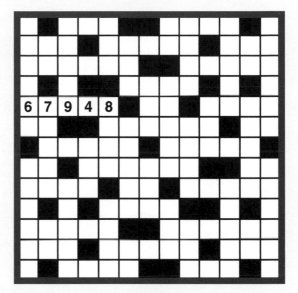

The chart gives directions to a hidden treasure behind the centre black square in the grid. Move the indicated number of spaces north, south, east and west (eg 4N means move four squares north) stopping at every square once only to arrive there. At which square should you start?

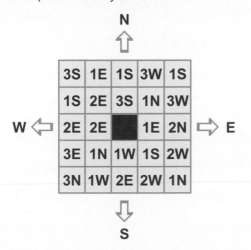

Fill the grid so that every horizontal row and vertical column contains the numbers 1-5. The 'greater than' or 'less than' signs indicate where a number is larger or smaller than that in the neighbouring square.

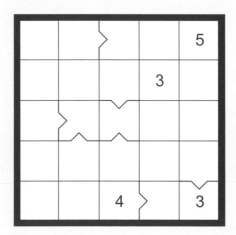

Each of the eight segments of the spider's web should be filled with a different number from 1 to 8, in such a way that every ring also contains a different number from 1 to 8.

The segments run from the outside of the spider's web to the centre, and the rings run all the way around.

Some numbers are already in place. Can you fill in the rest?

Every oval shape in this diagram contains a different letter of the alphabet from A to K inclusive. Use the clues to determine their locations. Reference in the clues to 'due' means in any location along the same horizontal or vertical line.

1   The A is due south of the F, which is further south than the J.

2   The B is further is further south than the A.

3   The C is next to and north of the I, which is next to and east of the F, which is due south of the K.

4   The D is next to and west of the G, which is next to and south of the E.

5   The K is due west of the H, which is further north than the E.

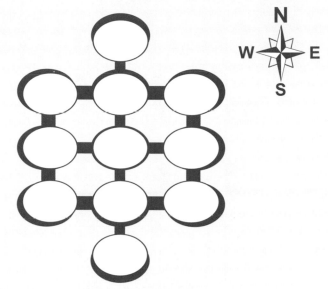

64

Fill the three empty circles with the symbols +, – and x in some order, to make a sum which totals the number in the centre. Each symbol must be used once and calculations are made in the direction of travel (clockwise).

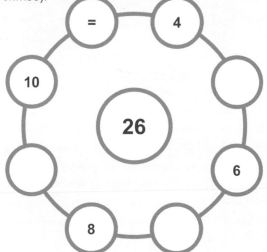

65

The numbers at the top and on the left side show the quantity of single-digit numbers (1-9) used in that row and column. The numbers at the bottom and on the right side show the sum of the digits. A number may appear more than once in a row or column, but no numbers are in squares that touch, even at a corner.

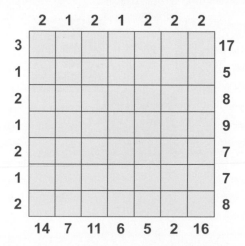

	2	1	2	1	2	2	2	
3								17
1								5
2								8
1								9
2								7
1								7
2								8
	14	7	11	6	5	2	16	

66

Using the numbers below, complete these six equations (three reading across and three reading downwards). Every number is used once.

1   2   3   4   5
6   7   8   9

	x		+		=	29
x		+		x		
	x		−		=	19
+		−		x		
	x		+		=	55
=		=		=		
21		5		14		

67

In the grid below, which number should replace the question mark?

173	107	66	41	25	16	9
101	61	40	21	19	2	17
271	168	103	65	38	27	11
153	93	60	33	27	?	21
219	135	84	51	33	18	15
70	43	27	16	11	5	6
159	99	60	39	21	18	3

68

When the box below is folded to form a cube, just one of the five options (A, B, C, D or E) can be produced. Which?

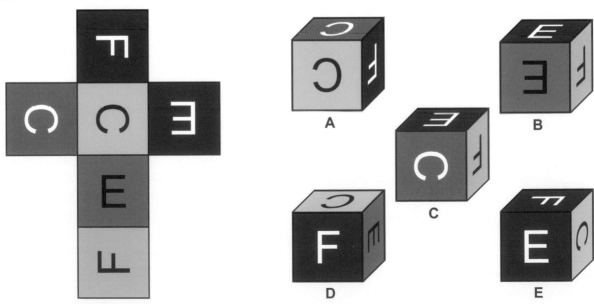

A

B

C

D

E

In this puzzle, an amateur coin collector has been out with his metal detector, searching for booty. He didn't have time to dig up all the coins he found, so has made a grid map, showing their locations, in the hope that if he loses the map, at least no-one else will understand it…

Those squares containing numbers are empty, but where a number appears in a square, it indicates how many coins are located in the squares (up to a maximum of eight) surrounding the numbered one, touching it at any corner or side. There is only one coin in any individual square.

Place a circle into every square containing a coin.

1		0	2				1	
				3		3	3	
		2				1		
0		2		3				
	1						0	
			3	2		0		
		3	2					2
2						3	5	
					2		4	
	3		2				3	

Every row and column of this grid should contain one each of the letters A, B, C, D, E and F. Each of the six shapes (marked by thicker lines) should also contain one each of the letters A, B, C, D, E and F. Can you complete the grid?

	C		B		A
			D		
		E			
					F

Each symbol stands for a different number. In order to reach the correct total at the end of each row and column, what is the value of the circle, cross, pentagon, square and star?

☆	✚	✚	⬠	☆	= 25
●	●	☆	■	●	= 15
☆	✚	■	■	✚	= 19
☆	⬠	●	✚	●	= 21
●	☆	☆	⬠	⬠	= 30
= 19	= 22	= 19	= 29	= 21	

A standard set of 28 dominoes has been laid out as shown. Can you draw in the edges of them all? The check-box is provided as an aid and the domino already placed will help.

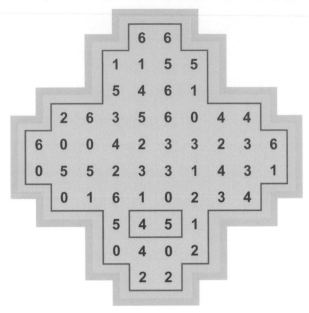

0-0	0-1	0-2	0-3	0-4	0-5	0-6

1-1	1-2	1-3	1-4	1-5	1-6	2-2

2-3	2-4	2-5	2-6	3-3	3-4	3-5

3-6	4-4	4-5	4-6	5-5	5-6	6-6
		✔				

73

Each of the small squares in the grid below contains either A, B or C. Each row, column, and diagonal line of six squares has exactly two of each letter. Can you tell the letter in each square?

Across

2 The Cs are further right than the As

4 Each C is directly next to and right of an A

5 The As are between the Bs

6 The Bs are between the As

Down

1 The As are between the Bs

2 The As are lower than the Bs

4 The Cs are next to each other

5 The Cs are between the As

6 The Bs are between the Cs

Every row and column in this grid originally contained one heart, one club, one diamond, one spade and two blank squares, although not necessarily in that order.

Every symbol with a black arrow refers to the first of the four symbols encountered when travelling in the direction of the arrow. Every symbol with a white arrow refers to the second of the four symbols encountered in the direction of the arrow.

Can you complete the original grid?

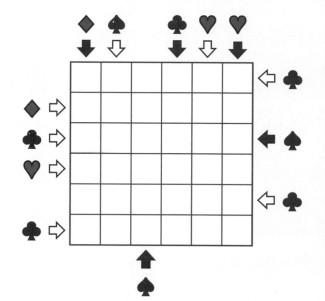

75

The blank squares below should be filled with whole numbers between 1 and 30 inclusive, any of which may occur more than once, or not at all.

The numbers in every horizontal row add up to the totals on the right, as do the two long diagonal lines; whilst those in every vertical column add up to the totals along the bottom.

76

							103
8		27	19	4	5		95
11		12	26	30		1	118
29	15	13		16		4	119
18	23			12		8	114
25	2			3	19	20	117
	14	7	24		6	25	116
	9	13	20	26	1		88
123	**102**	**115**	**137**	**101**	**104**	**85**	**77**

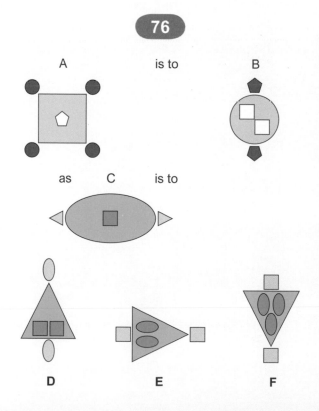

Can you place the hexagons into the grid, so that where any hexagon touches another along a straight line, the number in both triangles is the same? No rotation of any hexagon is allowed!

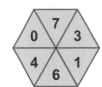

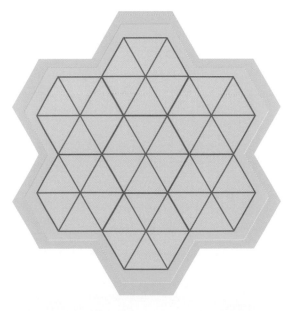

Twelve L-shapes like the ones here need to be inserted in the grid and each L has one hole in it.

There are three pieces of each of the four kinds shown here and any piece may be turned or flipped over before being put in the grid. No pieces of the same kind touch, even at a corner.

The pieces fit together so well that you cannot see any spaces between them; only the holes show.

Can you tell where the Ls are?

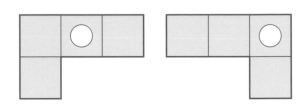
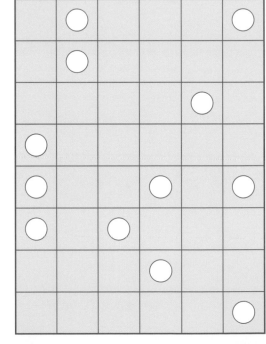

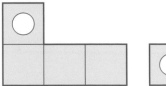

Draw walls to partition the grid into areas (some walls are already drawn in for you). Each area must contain two circles, area sizes must match those numbers shown next to the grid and each '+' must be linked to at least two walls.

2, 3, 3, 3, 7, 7

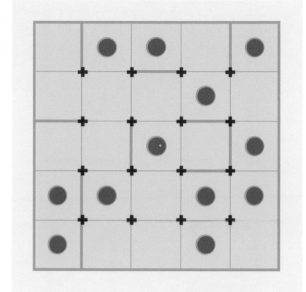

What number should replace the question mark?

37	52	43
70	61	58
55	64	49

23	38	29
56	47	44
41	50	35

14	29	20
47	38	35
32	41	26

?

49	64	55
80	71	68
65	72	59

A

28	43	34
61	52	49
46	54	40

B

19	34	25
52	43	40
37	46	31

C

33	48	39
67	58	54
53	62	47

D

The object of this puzzle is to trace a single path from the top left corner to the bottom right corner of the grid, travelling through all of the cells in either a horizontal, vertical or diagonal direction.

Every cell must be entered once only and your path should take you through the numbers in the sequence 1-2-3-4-1-2-3-4, etc.

Can you find the way?

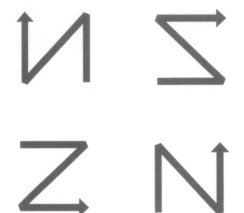

1	2	3	4	1	4	2	1
2	3	1	2	4	3	3	4
3	1	4	3	2	1	1	2
2	4	2	4	1	3	3	4
1	3	4	3	4	2	4	1
3	2	1	2	3	1	2	3
1	4	1	4	2	4	2	3
2	3	4	1	3	2	1	4

The grid should be filled with numbers from 1 to 6, so that each number appears just once in every row and column. The clues refer to the digit totals in the squares, eg A 1 2 3 = 6 means that the numbers in squares A1, A2 and A3 add up to 6.

1 E 2 3 4 = 9

2 C D 4 = 4

3 C 5 6 = 11

4 D E 6 = 9

5 D 1 2 3 = 10

6 A B 2 = 6

7 A B 3 = 9

8 F 1 2 = 8

9 A 4 5 = 5

10 E F 5 = 5

11 B 5 6 = 6

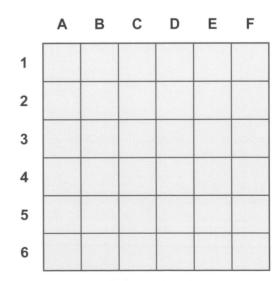

166

Can you fill each square in the bottom line with the correct digit?

Every square in the solution contains only one digit from each of the lines above, although two or more squares in the solution may contain the same digit.

SCORE

At the end of every row is a score, which shows:

  a the number of digits placed in the correct finishing position on the bottom line, as indicated by a tick; and

  b the number of digits which appear on the bottom line, but in a different position, as indicated by a cross.

8	5	7	1	✓ ✗
8	2	4	4	✓
8	3	3	4	✓
6	5	8	4	✓ ✗
6	4	1	4	✓
				✓✓✓✓

Can you place the vessels into the diagram? Some parts of vessels or sea squares have already been filled in. A number to the right or below a row or column refers to the number of occupied squares in that row or column.

Any vessel may be positioned horizontally or vertically, but no part of a vessel touches part of any other vessel, either horizontally, vertically or diagonally.

Empty Area of Sea: ≈

Aircraft Carrier: ◀■■▶

Battleships: ◀■▶ ◀■▶

Cruisers: ◀▶ ◀▶ ◀▶

Submarines: ● ● ● ●

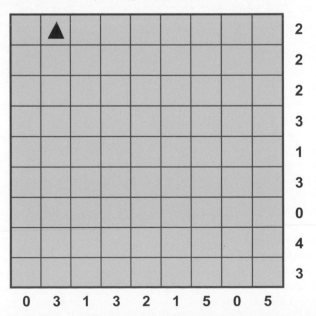

							2
							2
							2
							3
							1
							3
							0
							4
							3

0 3 1 3 2 1 5 0 5

85

Draw a single continuous loop, by connecting the dots. No line may cross the path of another.

The figure inside each set of any four surrounding dots indicates the total number of surrounding lines.

```
.   .   .   .   .   .   .   .   .   .   .
        1               0
.   .   .   .   .   .   .   .   .   .   .
  3   3   1           3   2   1   3
.   .   .   .   .   .   .   .   .   .   .
  2       1           1
.   .   .   .   .   .   .   .   .   .   .
        2   1       1   1   2   3
.   .   .   .   .   .   .   .   .   .   .
            2   2   2   2
.   .   .   .   .   .   .   .   .   .   .
    1                   2   1
.   .   .   .   .   .   .   .   .   .   .
        0       0   2       3
.   .   .   .   .   .   .   .   .   .   .
  1       1   3           0
.   .   .   .   .   .   .   .   .   .   .
    3           1           0
.   .   .   .   .   .   .   .   .   .   .
        2           0
.   .   .   .   .   .   .   .   .   .   .
  3   1   1       0       2   1   2
.   .   .   .   .   .   .   .   .   .   .
        1           1   2
.   .   .   .   .   .   .   .   .   .   .
```

86

Each horizontal row and vertical column should contain different shapes and different numbers.

Every square will contain one number and one shape and no combination may be repeated anywhere else in the puzzle.

1   2   3   4   5

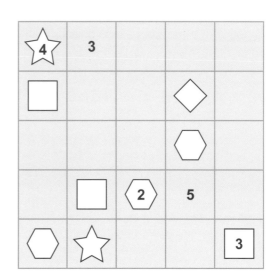

87

Given that the letters are valued 1-26 according to their places in the alphabet, can you crack the mystery code to reveal the missing letter?

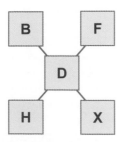

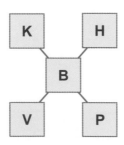

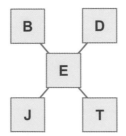

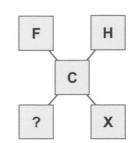

A set of dominoes is to be placed in four rows as shown below. The numbers indicate which values are shown on all the dominoes in each column and the relevant half of the domino in every row. Find out where each domino is placed by carefully comparing rows and columns to determine the possible positions of certain dominoes: for instance, if any column contains only one 6, then the domino 6/6 isn't in that column.

A set of dominoes consists of:

0/0, 0/1, 0/2, 0/3, 0/4, 0/5, 0/6, 1/1, 1/2, 1/3, 1/4, 1/5, 1/6, 2/2,

2/3, 2/4, 2/5, 2/6, 3/3, 3/4, 3/5, 3/6, 4/4, 4/5, 4/6, 5/5, 5/6, 6/6.

	2, 3, 5, 6, 6, 6, 6, 6.	0, 0, 0, 0, 2, 4, 5, 5.	0, 0, 1, 1, 1, 3, 3, 4.	1, 1, 2, 2, 2, 4, 4, 4.	3, 3, 4, 4, 4, 5, 5, 6.	0, 1, 2, 2, 2, 3, 5, 6.	0, 1, 1, 3, 3, 5, 5, 6.
0, 0, 1, 2, 2, 5, 6.							
2, 2, 3, 3, 5, 5, 5.							
0, 2, 2, 4, 4, 6, 6.							
0, 1, 1, 3, 4, 4, 6.							
0, 1, 1, 1, 1, 4, 6.							
0, 0, 1, 2, 5, 6, 6.							
2, 3, 3, 4, 4, 5, 6.							
0, 3, 3, 3, 4, 5, 5.							

Place the eight tiles into the puzzle grid so that all adjacent numbers on each tile match up. Tiles may be rotated through 360 degrees, but none may be flipped over.

1	1
2	2

2	1
3	2

2	4
3	4

3	1
2	4

2	2
1	4

3	4
1	2

2	4
4	2

2	3
1	4

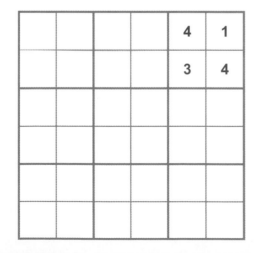

Place all twelve of the pieces into the grid. Any may be rotated or flipped over, but none may touch another, not even diagonally. The numbers outside the grid refer to the number of consecutive black squares; and each block is separated from the others by at least one white square. For instance, '3 2' could refer to a row with none, one or more white squares, then three black squares, then at least one white square, then two more black squares, followed by any number of white squares.

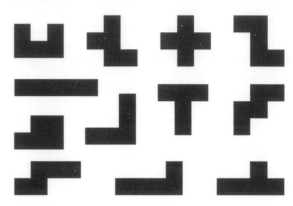

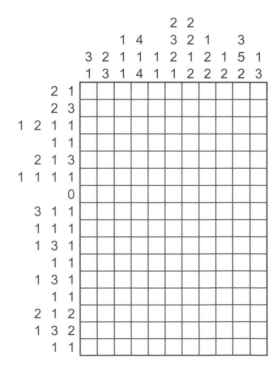

91

In the diagram below, which number should replace the question mark?

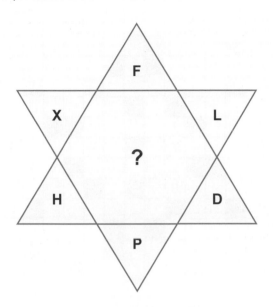

92

In the square below, change the positions of six numbers, one per horizontal row, vertical column and long diagonal line of six smaller squares, in such a way that the numbers in each row, column and long diagonal line total exactly 265. Any number may appear more than once in a row, column or line.

35	15	26	44	58	79
72	44	51	31	52	22
79	48	53	8	34	52
45	56	45	80	39	20
30	64	46	49	23	38
24	25	53	45	66	39

93

Every brick in this pyramid contains a number which is the sum of the two numbers below it, so that F=A+B, etc. Just work out the missing numbers!

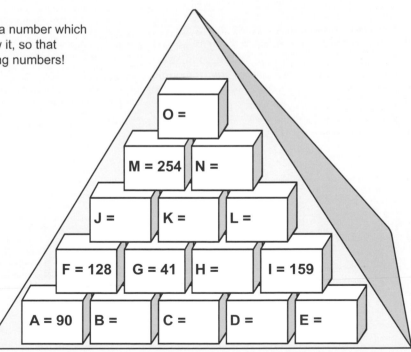

With the starter already given, can you fit all of the remaining listed numbers into this grid? Take care, this puzzle may not be as easy as it looks!

16	542	5742	41606	225559
35	621	6650	45737	341812
39	746	7236	55226	463896
44	764	7597	56364	856281
46	833	7956	60766	859765
62	869	8209	64720	872441
142	1362	8330	66273	1229349
169	1506	17089	67324	2333498
216	1729 ✓	22476	86105	2545621
302	3310	30455	173353	3778326
422	4469	34696	214116	5885733
536		36126		7073261

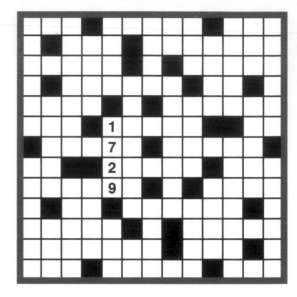

The chart gives directions to a hidden treasure behind the centre black square in the grid. Move the indicated number of spaces north, south, east and west (eg 4N means move four squares north) stopping at every square once only to arrive there. At which square should you start?

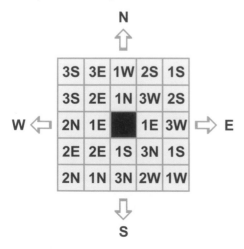

Fill the grid so that every horizontal row and vertical column contains the numbers 1-5. The 'greater than' or 'less than' signs indicate where a number is larger or smaller than that in the neighbouring square.

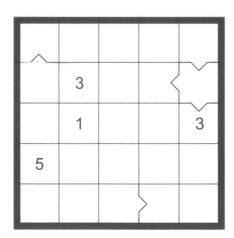

S
E
C
T
I
O
N

4

Each of the eight segments of the spider's web should be filled with a different number from 1 to 8, in such a way that every ring also contains a different number from 1 to 8.

The segments run from the outside of the spider's web to the centre, and the rings run all the way around.

Some numbers are already in place. Can you fill in the rest?

1

A standard set of 28 dominoes has been laid out as shown. Can you draw in the edges of them all? The check-box is provided as an aid and the domino already placed will help.

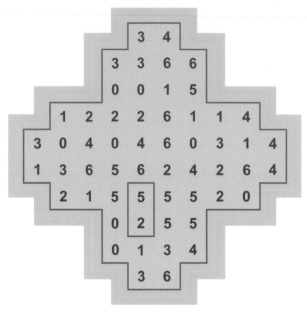

0-0	0-1	0-2	0-3	0-4	0-5	0-6

1-1	1-2	1-3	1-4	1-5	1-6	2-2

2-3	2-4	2-5	2-6	3-3	3-4	3-5
		✓				

3-6	4-4	4-5	4-6	5-5	5-6	6-6

2

Draw walls to partition the grid into areas (some walls are already drawn in for you). Each area must contain two circles, area sizes must match those numbers shown next to the grid and each '+' must be linked to at least two walls.

2, 3, 6, 7, 7

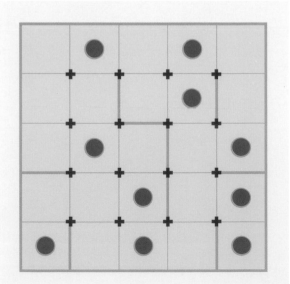

Every row and column in this grid originally contained one heart, one club, one diamond, one spade and two blank squares, although not necessarily in that order.

Every symbol with a black arrow refers to the first of the four symbols encountered when travelling in the direction of the arrow. Every symbol with a white arrow refers to the second of the four symbols encountered in the direction of the arrow.

Can you complete the original grid?

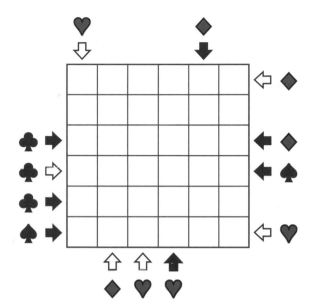

4

The blank squares below should be filled with whole numbers between 1 and 30 inclusive, any of which may occur more than once, or not at all.

The numbers in every horizontal row add up to the totals on the right, as do the two long diagonal lines; whilst those in every vertical column add up to the totals along the bottom.

							128
25			20	12	19	7	101
15	10	16		21	8		102
22	13	26	1				111
20	5	14	25			12	100
		12	22	24	8	19	119
11	29			7	19	23	122
	1	28	10	15	17		110
144	85	127	107	114	79	109	138

5

Draw in the missing hands on the final clock.

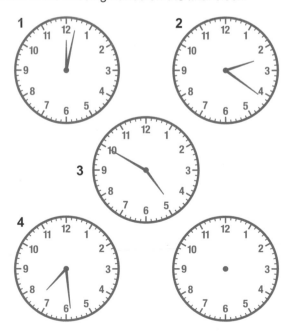

6

Can you place the hexagons into the grid, so that where any hexagon touches another along a straight line, the number in both triangles is the same? No rotation of any hexagon is allowed!

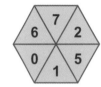

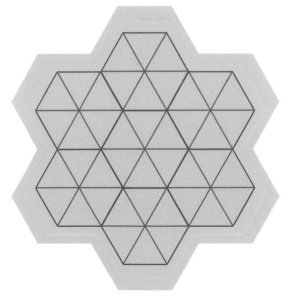

7

Twelve L-shapes like the ones here need to be inserted in the grid and each L has one hole in it.

There are three pieces of each of the four kinds shown here and any piece may be turned or flipped over before being put in the grid. No pieces of the same kind touch, even at a corner.

The pieces fit together so well that you cannot see any spaces between them; only the holes show.

Can you tell where the Ls are?

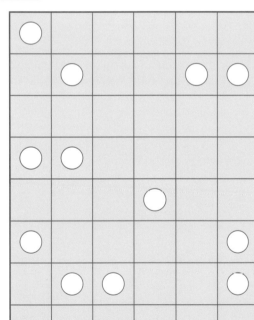

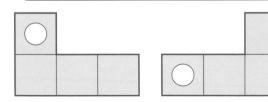

8

In this puzzle, an amateur coin collector has been out with his metal detector, searching for booty. He didn't have time to dig up all the coins he found, so has made a grid map, showing their locations, in the hope that if he loses the map, at least no-one else will understand it…

Those squares containing numbers are empty, but where a number appears in a square, it indicates how many coins are located in the squares (up to a maximum of eight) surrounding the numbered one, touching it at any corner or side. There is only one coin in any individual square.

Place a circle into every square containing a coin.

1						0			2
	3		3			1	2		
2		3		0					2
				2	2				
	3		2				1	1	1
1	2							0	
			4		3		0		
	2	2			2				
							4		2
1		2	1		1				

9

The grid should be filled with numbers from 1 to 6, so that each number appears just once in every row and column. The clues refer to the digit totals in the squares, eg A 1 2 3 = 6 means that the numbers in squares A1, A2 and A3 add up to 6.

1 B C D 2 = 6

2 B 3 4 5 = 15

3 E F 3 = 7

4 E 5 6 = 6

5 C D 5 = 11

6 C 3 4 = 8

7 D 3 4 = 5

8 A B 6 = 6

9 E F 4 = 3

10 F 5 6 = 5

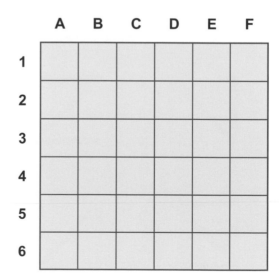

Each of the small squares in the grid below contains either A, B or C. Each row, column, and diagonal line of six squares has exactly two of each letter. Can you tell the letter in each square?

Across
1 The Cs are between the Bs
2 The As are further right than the Bs
4 The As are between the Cs
5 The Bs are between the As
6 The Bs are between the Cs

Down
1 The Bs are between the Cs
2 The Bs are higher than the As
3 The Bs are between the As
4 The Cs are higher than the **B**s
5 The As are lower than the Cs

	1	2	3	4	5	6
1						
2						
3						
4						
5						
6						

The object of this puzzle is to trace a single path from the top left corner to the bottom right corner of the grid, travelling through all of the cells in either a horizontal, vertical or diagonal direction.

Every cell must be entered once only and your path should take you through the numbers in the sequence 1-2-3-4-1-2-3-4, etc.

Can you find the way?

1	2	1	2	1	2	1	4
3	4	3	3	4	3	3	2
2	4	3	4	1	2	1	3
1	2	2	4	4	3	4	2
1	4	1	3	2	1	3	1
2	3	4	1	3	2	4	2
1	2	4	4	1	1	3	3
4	3	1	3	2	2	4	4

Can you place the vessels into the diagram? Some parts of vessels or sea squares have already been filled in. A number to the right or below a row or column refers to the number of occupied squares in that row or column.

Any vessel may be positioned horizontally or vertically, but no part of a vessel touches part of any other vessel, either horizontally, vertically or diagonally.

Empty Area of Sea:

Aircraft Carrier:

Battleships:

Cruisers:

Submarines:

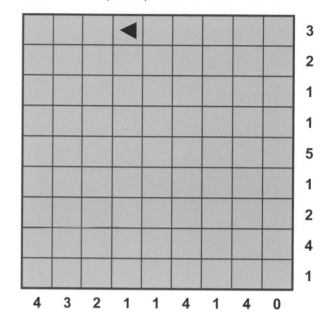

Can you fill each square in the bottom line with the correct digit?

Every square in the solution contains only one digit from each of the lines above, although two or more squares in the solution may contain the same digit.

At the end of every row is a score, which shows:

    a the number of digits placed in the correct finishing position on the bottom line, as indicated by a tick; and

    b the number of digits which appear on the bottom line, but in a different position, as indicated by a cross.

SCORE

8	1	1	5	✗
8	1	5	7	✓ ✗
3	7	5	5	✓
4	4	1	6	✗
2	4	7	2	✓
				✓ ✓ ✓ ✓

14

Draw a single continuous loop, by connecting the dots. No line may cross the path of another.

The figure inside each set of any four surrounding dots indicates the total number of surrounding lines.

```
2      1      1  1  2
 1        0  1  1  3     0
 1                 1     1
      1  2  1  2
    1     2  1  0     0
          1  3     1
 2        1  3           0
 1              0  3
 3     0           1        3
   1                 1     1
   2     0
   1  1     1     1     1  2
```

15

Each horizontal row and vertical column should contain different shapes and different numbers.

Every square will contain one number and one shape and no combination may be repeated anywhere else in the puzzle.

1   2   3   4   5

◇			②	
2		4		3
☆3		⬡	◇4	
4			1	
		☆1		

16

Given that the letters are valued 1-26 according to their places in the alphabet, can you crack the mystery code to reveal the missing letter?

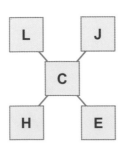

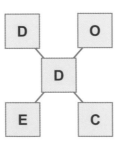

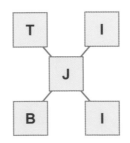

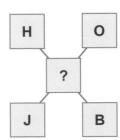

A set of dominoes is to be placed in four rows as shown below. The numbers indicate which values are shown on all the dominoes in each column and the relevant half of the domino in every row. Find out where each domino is placed by carefully comparing rows and columns to determine the possible positions of certain dominoes: for instance, if any column contains only one 6, then the domino 6/6 isn't in that column.

A set of dominoes consists of:

0/0, 0/1, 0/2, 0/3, 0/4, 0/5, 0/6, 1/1, 1/2, 1/3, 1/4, 1/5, 1/6, 2/2,

2/3, 2/4, 2/5, 2/6, 3/3, 3/4, 3/5, 3/6, 4/4, 4/5, 4/6, 5/5, 5/6, 6/6.

?	1, 3, 3, 4, 4, 6, 6, 6.	0, 1, 2, 3, 3, 4, 4, 4.	0, 2, 3, 3, 3, 4, 4, 5.	0, 0, 1, 1, 1, 6, 6, 6.	0, 1, 2, 5, 5, 5, 6, 6.	0, 1, 2, 2, 3, 4, 5, 5.	0, 0, 1, 2, 2, 2, 5, 5.
2, 2, 3, 4, 5, 6, 6.							
0, 0, 0, 0, 2, 4, 6.							
0, 1, 1, 2, 3, 4, 6.							
0, 1, 1, 1, 2, 5, 5.							
4, 4, 5, 5, 6, 6, 6.							
0, 3, 3, 4, 5, 5, 5.							
1, 1, 1, 2, 3, 3, 6.							
0, 2, 2, 3, 3, 4, 4.							

Place the eight tiles into the puzzle grid so that all adjacent numbers on each tile match up. Tiles may be rotated through 360 degrees, but none may be flipped over.

1	2
3	1

2	2
4	3

2	4
3	2

2	4
3	1

3	4
4	2

2	2
1	4

2	1
4	1

3	3
2	3

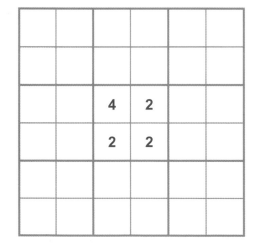

Place all twelve of the pieces into the grid. Any may be rotated or flipped over, but none may touch another, not even diagonally. The numbers outside the grid refer to the number of consecutive black squares; and each block is separated from the others by at least one white square. For instance, '3 2' could refer to a row with none, one or more white squares, then three black squares, then at least one white square, then two more black squares, followed by any number of white squares.

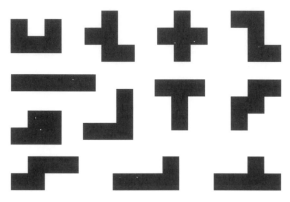

S
E
C
T
I
O
N

5

In the diagram below, which number should replace the question mark?

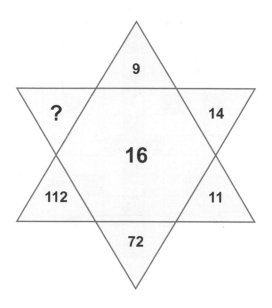

In the square below, change the positions of six numbers, one per horizontal row, vertical column and long diagonal line of six smaller squares, in such a way that the numbers in each row, column and long diagonal line total exactly 217. Any number may appear more than once in a row, column or line.

30	12	21	35	67	32
51	36	29	11	37	37
40	50	36	32	24	46
35	37	37	40	25	34
24	42	42	47	55	33
45	31	36	32	35	46

Every brick in this pyramid contains a number which is the sum of the two numbers below it, so that F=A+B, etc. Just work out the missing numbers!

O =

M =   N =

J = 231   K =   L =

F =   G =   H = 128   I = 233

A = 84   B =   C = 31   D =   E =

With the starter already given, can you fit all of the remaining listed numbers into this grid? Take care, this puzzle may not be as easy as it looks!

13	569	3684 ✓	31454	479359
39	599	4340	33565	500024
47	631	5763	34067	533621
56	773	6852	37440	537526
58	777	7494	67790	634273
67	926	7684	82844	712733
194	1657	8522	118636	745799
335	2238	8777	175213	757884
371	2359	9672	228729	811444
411	2565	9790	238867	862212
449	3575	21774	293724	891573
493	3599	23112	474239	943734

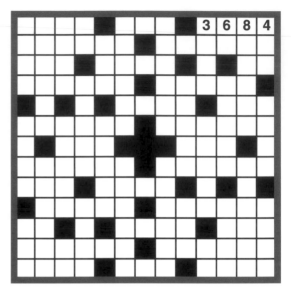

The chart gives directions to a hidden treasure behind the centre black square in the grid. Move the indicated number of spaces north, south, east and west (eg 4N means move four squares north) stopping at every square once only to arrive there. At which square should you start?

N

1E	3E	1E	4S	3S
2S	1S	3S	1W	4W
2S	2E	■	1N	1N
2E	2N	1N	2W	1W
4N	3E	4N	2W	2N

W ⇦   ⇨ E

⇩
S

Fill the grid so that every horizontal row and vertical column contains the numbers 1-5. The 'greater than' or 'less than' signs indicate where a number is larger or smaller than that in the neighbouring square.

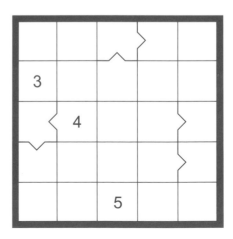

Each of the eight segments of the spider's web should be filled with a different number from 1 to 8, in such a way that every ring also contains a different number from 1 to 8.

The segments run from the outside of the spider's web to the centre, and the rings run all the way around.

Some numbers are already in place. Can you fill in the rest?

Every oval shape in this diagram contains a different letter of the alphabet from A to K inclusive. Use the clues to determine their locations. Reference in the clues to 'due' means in any location along the same horizontal or vertical line.

1   The B is next to and east of the H, which is next to and south of the A.

2   The D is next to and east of the K, which is next to and north of the E.

3   The F is next to and east of the J, which is further south than the D.

4   The I is further north than the C, but further south than the G, which is further south than the A.

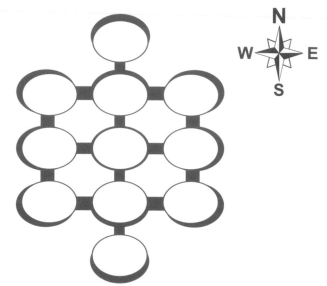

28

Fill the three empty circles with the symbols +, − and x in some order, to make a sum which totals the number in the centre. Each symbol must be used once and calculations are made in the direction of travel (clockwise).

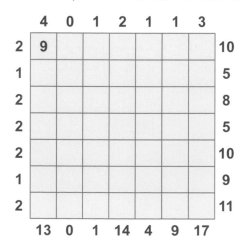

29

The numbers at the top and on the left side show the quantity of single-digit numbers (1-9) used in that row and column. The numbers at the bottom and on the right side show the sum of the digits. A number may appear more than once in a row or column, but no numbers are in squares that touch, even at a corner.

	4	0	1	2	1	1	3	
2	9							10
1								5
2								8
2								5
2								10
1								9
2								11
	13	0	1	14	4	9	17	

S E C T I O N

5

Using the numbers below, complete these six equations (three reading across and three reading downwards). Every number is used once.

1 2 3 4 5
6 7 8 9

	x		x		=	126
x		−		+		
	−		x		=	20
−		x		x		
	x		x		=	30
=		=		=		
71		20		36		

In the grid below, which number should replace the question mark?

3	10	17	24	31	38	45
164	171	178	185	192	199	52
157	276	283	290	297	206	59
150	269	332	?	304	213	66
143	262	325	318	311	220	73
136	255	248	241	234	227	80
129	122	115	108	101	94	87

When the box below is folded to form a cube, just one of the five options (A, B, C, D or E) can be produced. Which?

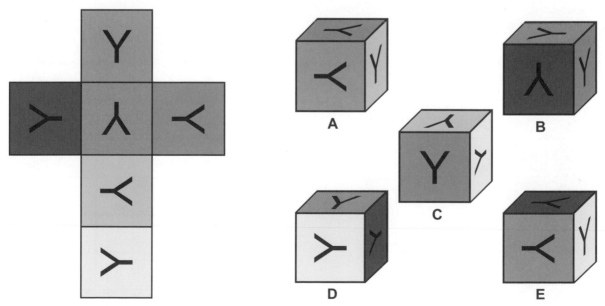

A

B

C

D

E

33

In this puzzle, an amateur coin collector has been out with his metal detector, searching for booty. He didn't have time to dig up all the coins he found, so has made a grid map, showing their locations, in the hope that if he loses the map, at least no-one else will understand it…

Those squares containing numbers are empty, but where a number appears in a square, it indicates how many coins are located in the squares (up to a maximum of eight) surrounding the numbered one, touching it at any corner or side. There is only one coin in any individual square.

Place a circle into every square containing a coin.

0				3					
		2			2	3	2		1
1					3		1		1
	1		1						
	2				5				
		1				2		5	
			0						
1		1		1	0		1		
		1		3				1	
	0						2		

34

Each symbol stands for a different number. In order to reach the correct total at the end of each row and column, what is the value of the circle, cross, pentagon, square and star?

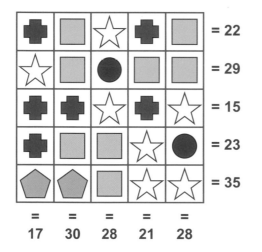

= 22
= 29
= 15
= 23
= 35

= 17
= 30
= 28
= 21
= 28

35

Every row and column of this grid should contain one each of the letters A, B, C, D, E and F. Each of the six shapes (marked by thicker lines) should also contain one each of the letters A, B, C, D, E and F. Can you complete the grid?

					A
					B
D					C
F		E			

36

A standard set of 28 dominoes has been laid out as shown. Can you draw in the edges of them all? The checkbox is provided as an aid and the domino already placed will help.

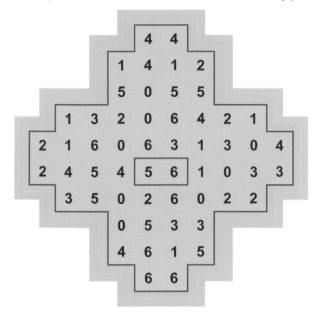

0-0	0-1	0-2	0-3	0-4	0-5	0-6

1-1	1-2	1-3	1-4	1-5	1-6	2-2

2-3	2-4	2-5	2-6	3-3	3-4	3-5

3-6	4-4	4-5	4-6	5-5	5-6	6-6
					✔	

37

Each of the small squares in the grid below contains either A, B or C. Each row, column, and diagonal line of six squares has exactly two of each letter. Can you tell the letter in each square?

Across

1. Each A is directly next to and right of a B
2. The Bs are next to each other
4. The Bs are further right than the As
5. The As are between the Cs

Down

1. The Cs are lower than the Bs
2. The Bs are lower than the Cs
3. The As are lower than the Cs
4. The As are lower than the Cs
6. The Cs are lower than the As

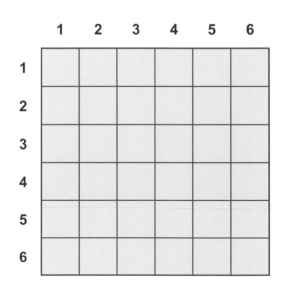

38

Every row and column in this grid originally contained one heart, one club, one diamond, one spade and two blank squares, although not necessarily in that order.

Every symbol with a black arrow refers to the first of the four symbols encountered when travelling in the direction of the arrow. Every symbol with a white arrow refers to the second of the four symbols encountered in the direction of the arrow.

Can you complete the original grid?

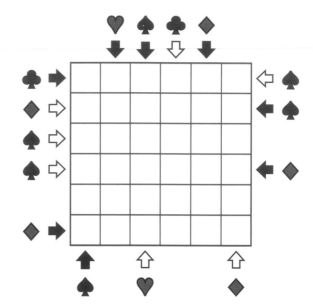

39

The blank squares below should be filled with whole numbers between 1 and 30 inclusive, any of which may occur more than once, or not at all.

The numbers in every horizontal row add up to the totals on the right, as do the two long diagonal lines; whilst those in every vertical column add up to the totals along the bottom.

							69
21	13		22	24	6		109
5		3	17	20		14	97
29	15	26	16		20	2	121
	24		1	3	27	7	93
7		21	18	15	6	19	92
	10	13		9		11	83
5	9	16			18		102

106	107	103	113	103	89	76	109

40

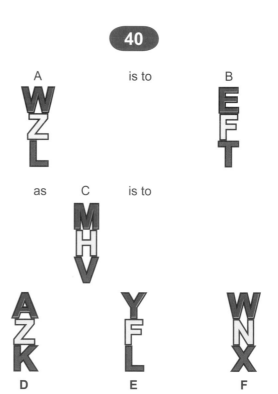

A   is to   B

as   C   is to

D   E   F

Can you place the hexagons into the grid, so that where any hexagon touches another along a straight line, the number in both triangles is the same? No rotation of any hexagon is allowed!

Twelve L-shapes like the ones here need to be inserted in the grid and each L has one hole in it.

There are three pieces of each of the four kinds shown here and any piece may be turned or flipped over before being put in the grid. No pieces of the same kind touch, even at a corner.

The pieces fit together so well that you cannot see any spaces between them; only the holes show.

Can you tell where the Ls are?

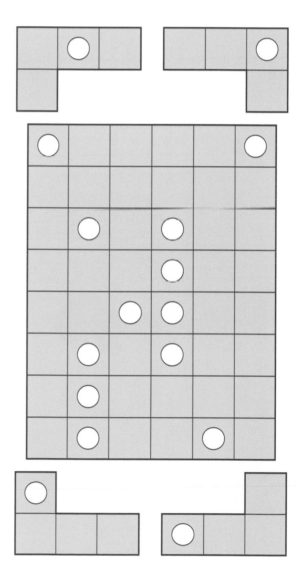

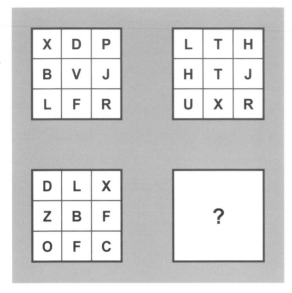

43

Which of the four lettered alternatives (A, B, C or D) fits most logically into the empty square?

X	D	P
B	V	J
L	F	R

L	T	H
H	T	J
U	X	R

D	L	X
Z	B	F
O	F	C

?

L	P	T
F	N	R
O	I	F

A

M	O	S
E	B	U
H	N	T

B

I	M	R
E	C	W
T	N	H

C

O	E	K
Q	G	E
D	B	Y

D

44

Which four pieces can be fitted together to form an exact copy of this shape?

A

B

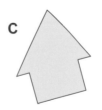

C

D

E

F

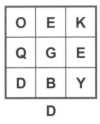

G

H

I

J

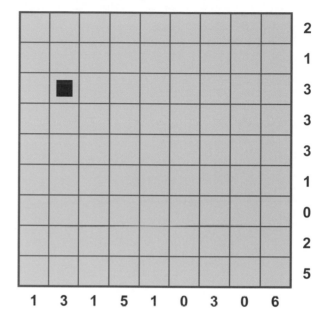

45

Can you place the vessels into the diagram? Some parts of vessels or sea squares have already been filled in. A number to the right or below a row or column refers to the number of occupied squares in that row or column.

Any vessel may be positioned horizontally or vertically, but no part of a vessel touches part of any other vessel, either horizontally, vertically or diagonally.

Empty Area of Sea: ≈

Aircraft Carrier: ◀■■▶

Battleships: ◀■▶ ◀■▶

Cruisers: ◀▶ ◀▶ ◀▶

Submarines: ● ● ● ●

Row numbers (top to bottom): 2, 1, 3, 3, 3, 1, 0, 2, 5

Column numbers (left to right): 1 3 1 5 1 0 3 0 6

46

Can you fill each square in the bottom line with the correct digit?

Every square in the solution contains only one digit from each of the lines above, although two or more squares in the solution may contain the same digit.

At the end of every row is a score, which shows:

a the number of digits placed in the correct finishing position on the bottom line, as indicated by a tick; and

b the number of digits which appear on the bottom line, but in a different position, as indicated by a cross.

SCORE

7	8	1	2	✓
5	4	4	7	✓ ✗ ✗
5	1	5	4	✓ ✗ ✗
3	4	7	4	✓ ✗
6	3	5	5	✓ ✓
				✓ ✓ ✓ ✓

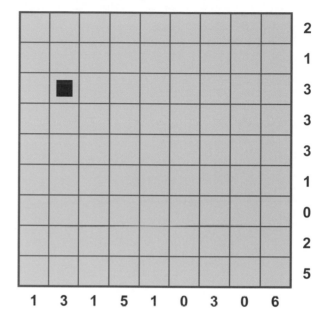

The grid should be filled with numbers from 1 to 6, so that each number appears just once in every row and column. The clues refer to the digit totals in the squares, eg A 1 2 3 = 6 means that the numbers in squares A1, A2 and A3 add up to 6.

1 E F 1 = 4

2 E 2 3 = 3

3 B C D 2 = 9

4 B 4 5 = 5

5 C 3 4 5 = 13

6 A B 3 = 5

7 D E 4 = 7

8 E F 6 = 10

9 D 5 6 = 4

10 F 2 3 = 9

	A	B	C	D	E	F
1						
2						
3						
4						
5						
6						

The object of this puzzle is to trace a single path from the top left corner to the bottom right corner of the grid, travelling through all of the cells in either a horizontal, vertical or diagonal direction.

Every cell must be entered once only and your path should take you through the numbers in the sequence 1-2-3-4-1-2-3-4, etc.

Can you find the way?

1	2	1	4	3	4	3	2
1	2	3	2	1	4	2	1
4	3	4	3	2	3	1	4
2	1	4	4	1	2	4	3
3	1	2	3	3	3	2	1
2	4	4	2	1	4	1	3
1	3	1	1	4	1	4	2
4	3	2	2	3	2	3	4

Draw a single continuous loop, by connecting the dots. No line may cross the path of another.

The figure inside each set of any four surrounding dots indicates the total number of surrounding lines.

```
  2      2      3          2
    0          2        2    1
    1  2  1    2              2
  3            1  1  1
      1              2    0
              0  3  1      1
  2  1  1              1    1
      2  2  2      2
  3      0  1            3      2
  1              1  1        3
      1      0  1  0
  2  2      2        1  2
```

Each horizontal row and vertical column should contain different shapes and different numbers.

Every square will contain one number and one shape and no combination may be repeated anywhere else in the puzzle.

	1	2	3	4	5

1	⬡	5	◯	
◯	□	◇		3
	5	□ 2		
			1	
3				5

Given that the letters are valued 1-26 according to their places in the alphabet, can you crack the mystery code to reveal the missing letter?

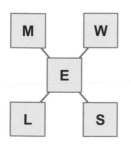

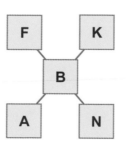

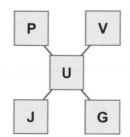

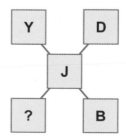

52

Which is the odd one out?

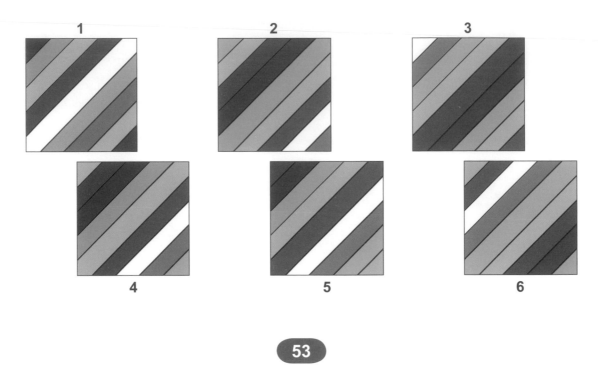

1   2   3

4   5   6

53

What number should replace the question mark?

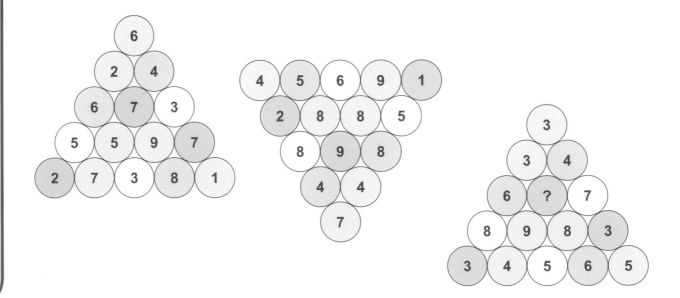

Place the eight tiles into the puzzle grid so that all adjacent numbers on each tile match up. Tiles may be rotated through 360 degrees, but none may be flipped over.

1	2
4	3

1	2
3	4

1	3
4	3

4	1
3	4

2	1
2	4

3	1
2	3

1	1
2	4

4	4
2	3

2	3				
4	3				

Place all twelve of the pieces into the grid. Any may be rotated or flipped over, but none may touch another, not even diagonally. The numbers outside the grid refer to the number of consecutive black squares; and each block is separated from the others by at least one white square. For instance, '3 2' could refer to a row with none, one or more white squares, then three black squares, then at least one white square, then two more black squares, followed by any number of white squares.

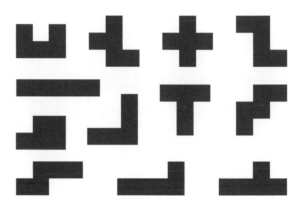

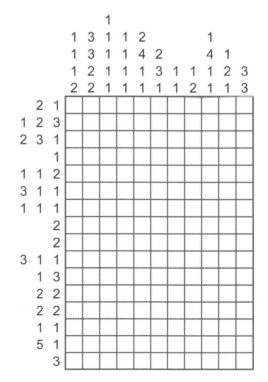

56

In the diagram below, what number should replace the question mark?

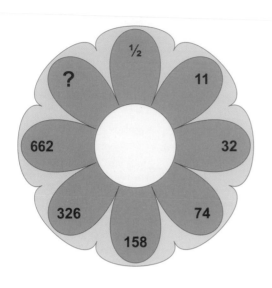

½ • ? • 11 • 662 • 32 • 326 • 74 • 158

57

In the square below, change the positions of six numbers, one per horizontal row, vertical column and long diagonal line of six smaller squares, in such a way that the numbers in each row, column and long diagonal line total exactly 166. Any number may appear more than once in a row, column or line.

42	15	18	27	24	28
33	27	35	16	31	19
19	14	27	35	17	22
36	38	31	46	11	31
22	27	36	41	23	33
20	13	35	28	48	28

58

Every brick in this pyramid contains a number which is the sum of the two numbers below it, so that F=A+B, etc. Just work out the missing numbers!

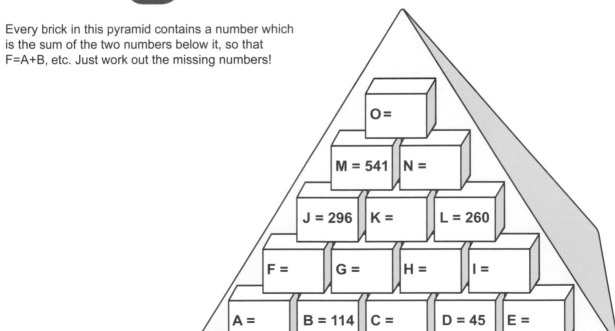

O =

M = 541   N =

J = 296   K =   L = 260

F =   G =   H =   I =

A =   B = 114   C =   D = 45   E =

With the starter already given, can you fit all of the remaining listed numbers into this grid? Take care, this puzzle may not be as easy as it looks!

30	129	6111	23142	202545
31	181	6123	26258	204876
39	185	7128	34863	351648
40	223	7390	36527	394000
42	291	8401 ✓	37220	640591
44	967	8498	43987	806742
55	3770	9112	46334	887639
58	3927	9729	46917	891838
63	4017	14733	52512	892180
72	4224	15126	68302	893601
88	5886	15931	104420	7318724
93	5961	22149	134438	7681918

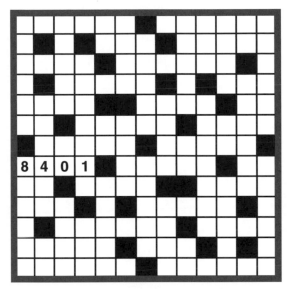

The chart gives directions to a hidden treasure behind the centre black square in the grid. Move the indicated number of spaces north, south, east and west (eg 4N means move four squares north) stopping at every square once only to arrive there. At which square should you start?

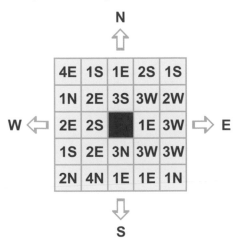

Fill the grid so that every horizontal row and vertical column contains the numbers 1-5. The 'greater than' or 'less than' signs indicate where a number is larger or smaller than that in the neighbouring square.

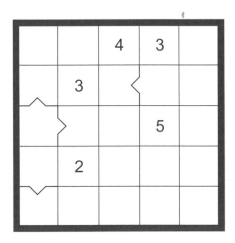

S
E
C
T
I
O
N

5

199

Each of the eight segments of the spider's web should be filled with a different number from 1 to 8, in such a way that every ring also contains a different number from 1 to 8.

The segments run from the outside of the spider's web to the centre, and the rings run all the way around.

Some numbers are already in place. Can you fill in the rest?

Every oval shape in this diagram contains a different letter of the alphabet from A to K inclusive. Use the clues to determine their locations. Reference in the clues to 'due' means in any location along the same horizontal or vertical line.

1 The B is next to and west of the C, which is due south of (but not next to) the G.

2 The E is further north than the A and further west than the G.

3 The F is due west of the K, which is due south of the I, which is further north than the H.

4 The J is next to and south of the K, which is further west than the D, which is due north of (but not next to) the A.

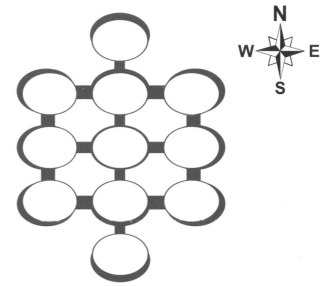

Fill the three empty circles with the symbols +, − and x in some order, to make a sum which totals the number in the centre. Each symbol must be used once and calculations are made in the direction of travel (clockwise).

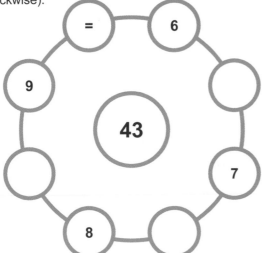

The numbers at the top and on the left side show the quantity of single-digit numbers (1-9) used in that row and column. The numbers at the bottom and on the right side show the sum of the digits. A number may appear more than once in a row or column, but no numbers are in squares that touch, even at a corner.

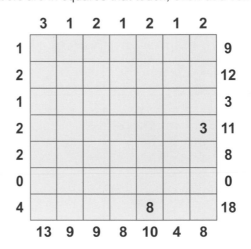

66

Using the numbers below, complete these six equations (three reading across and three reading downwards). Every number is used once.

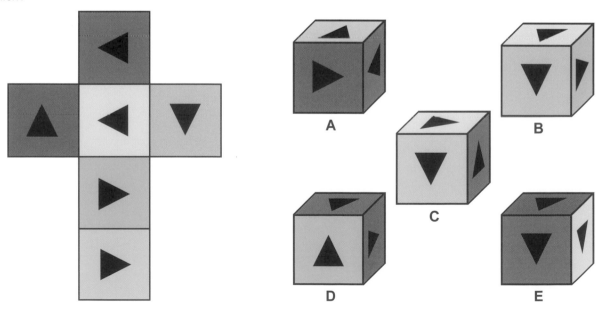

67

In the grid below, which number should replace the question mark?

15	45	41	82	79	158	156
8	24	20	40	37	74	72
13	39	35	70	67	134	132
5	15	?	22	19	38	36
16	48	44	88	85	170	168
10	30	26	52	49	98	96
18	54	50	100	97	194	192

68

When the box below is folded to form a cube, just one of the five options (A, B, C, D or E) can be produced. Which?

A

B

C

D

E

69

In this puzzle, an amateur coin collector has been out with his metal detector, searching for booty. He didn't have time to dig up all the coins he found, so has made a grid map, showing their locations, in the hope that if he loses the map, at least no-one else will understand it…

Those squares containing numbers are empty, but where a number appears in a square, it indicates how many coins are located in the squares (up to a maximum of eight) surrounding the numbered one, touching it at any corner or side. There is only one coin in any individual square.

Place a circle into every square containing a coin.

1		1				0			
				0					3
3			1				0		
		3					0		
	4		5		2	0			2
	3				1			3	
			4				2		
3		2	1						
	3		2		1		3		3
				0				2	

70

Every row and column of this grid should contain one each of the letters A, B, C, D, E and F. Each of the six shapes (marked by thicker lines) should also contain one each of the letters A, B, C, D, E and F. Can you complete the grid?

		B		A	
		D			C
	E				
F					

71

Each symbol stands for a different number. In order to reach the correct total at the end of each row and column, what is the value of the circle, cross, pentagon, square and star?

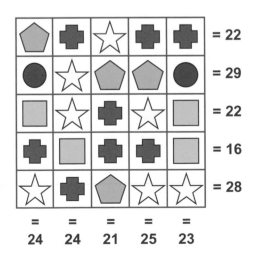

72

A standard set of 28 dominoes has been laid out as shown. Can you draw in the edges of them all? The check-box is provided as an aid and the domino already placed will help.

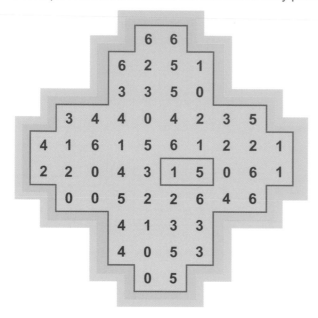

0-0	0-1	0-2	0-3	0-4	0-5	0-6

1-1	1-2	1-3	1-4	1-5	1-6	2-2
				✓		

2-3	2-4	2-5	2-6	3-3	3-4	3-5

3-6	4-4	4-5	4-6	5-5	5-6	6-6

73

Each of the small squares in the grid below contains either A, B or C. Each row, column, and diagonal line of six squares has exactly two of each letter. Can you tell the letter in each square?

Across

1 Each C is directly next to and right of a B

2 The Cs are between the Bs

4 The Bs are between the Cs

5 Each A is directly next to and right of a C

Down

1 The Cs are lower than the Bs

2 The Cs are between the Bs

4 The Cs are between the Bs

6 Each C is directly next to and below a B

204

	1	2	3	4	5	6
1						
2						
3						
4						
5						
6						

Every row and column in this grid originally contained one heart, one club, one diamond, one spade and two blank squares, although not necessarily in that order.

Every symbol with a black arrow refers to the first of the four symbols encountered when travelling in the direction of the arrow. Every symbol with a white arrow refers to the second of the four symbols encountered in the direction of the arrow.

Can you complete the original grid?

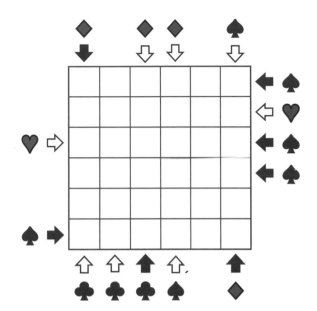

75

The blank squares below should be filled with whole numbers between 1 and 30 inclusive, any of which may occur more than once, or not at all.

The numbers in every horizontal row add up to the totals on the right, as do the two long diagonal lines; whilst those in every vertical column add up to the totals along the bottom.

							84
13		9	7	22	21		101
17	4		29		3	9	108
15		16	22	28		10	116
20	13	21			7	26	119
	11		25	16	23	5	94
27	6	19			10	30	115
	22	16	15	12	4		98
97	91	120	126	124	69	124	99

76

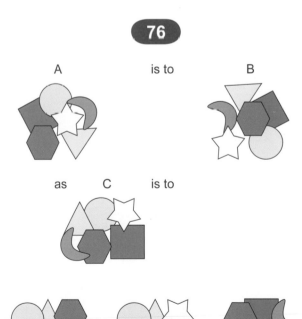

Can you place the hexagons into the grid, so that where any hexagon touches another along a straight line, the number in both triangles is the same? No rotation of any hexagon is allowed!

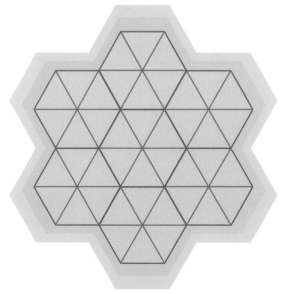

Twelve L-shapes like the ones here need to be inserted in the grid and each L has one hole in it.

There are three pieces of each of the four kinds shown here and any piece may be turned or flipped over before being put in the grid. No pieces of the same kind touch, even at a corner.

The pieces fit together so well that you cannot see any spaces between them; only the holes show.

Can you tell where the Ls are?

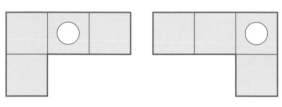

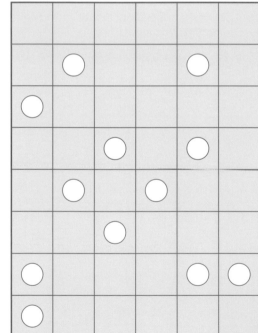

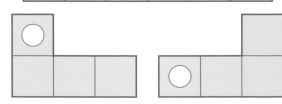

Draw walls to partition the grid into areas (some walls are already drawn in for you). Each area must contain two circles, area sizes must match those numbers shown next to the grid and each '+' must be linked to at least two walls.

2,   3,   6,   7,   7

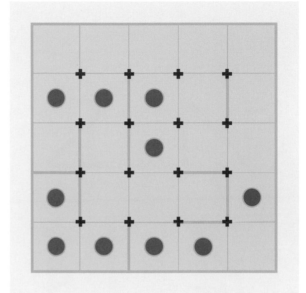

What number should replace the question mark?

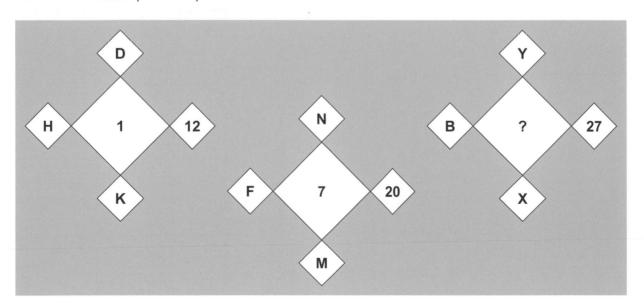

The object of this puzzle is to trace a single path from the top left corner to the bottom right corner of the grid, travelling through all of the cells in either a horizontal, vertical or diagonal direction.

Every cell must be entered once only and your path should take you through the numbers in the sequence 1-2-3-4-1-2-3-4, etc.

Can you find the way?

1	2	2	3	2	3	1	2
3	1	4	3	4	1	4	3
4	1	2	2	3	1	4	1
4	1	1	4	4	2	2	3
2	3	2	3	3	3	2	4
2	1	1	4	3	1	4	1
4	3	1	4	4	2	1	2
3	2	4	1	2	3	3	4

The grid should be filled with numbers from 1 to 6, so that each number appears just once in every row and column. The clues refer to the digit totals in the squares, eg A 1 2 3 = 6 means that the numbers in squares A1, A2 and A3 add up to 6.

1 C D E 3 = 9

2 C 4 5 = 11

3 D 4 5 6 = 13

4 A B 4 = 8

5 A B 5 = 6

6 A 1 2 = 7

7 B 1 2 = 8

8 F 4 5 = 5

9 A B 6 = 7

10 C D 1 = 6

11 E 5 6 = 6

12 C D 2 = 7

	A	B	C	D	E	F
1						
2						
3						
4						
5						
6						

83

Can you fill each square in the bottom line with the correct digit?

Every square in the solution contains only one digit from each of the lines above, although two or more squares in the solution may contain the same digit.

At the end of every row is a score, which shows:

a the number of digits placed in the correct finishing position on the bottom line, as indicated by a tick; and

b the number of digits which appear on the bottom line, but in a different position, as indicated by a cross.

SCORE

8	5	2	2	✓ ✗ ✗
5	6	6	7	✓
6	2	4	2	✗ ✗
4	4	1	7	✓
3	4	8	2	✗ ✗
				✓ ✓ ✓ ✓

84

Can you place the vessels into the diagram? Some parts of vessels or sea squares have already been filled in. A number to the right or below a row or column refers to the number of occupied squares in that row or column.

Any vessel may be positioned horizontally or vertically, but no part of a vessel touches part of any other vessel, either horizontally, vertically or diagonally.

Empty Area of Sea:

Aircraft Carrier:

Battleships:

Cruisers:

Submarines:

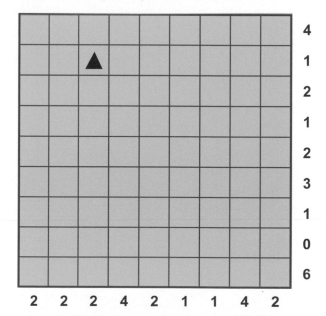

Column totals: 2 2 2 4 2 1 1 4 2

Row totals: 4 1 2 1 2 3 1 0 6

Draw a single continuous loop, by connecting the dots. No line may cross the path of another.

The figure inside each set of any four surrounding dots indicates the total number of surrounding lines.

```
  .   .   .   .   .   .   .   .   .   .
                1   1           3
  .   .   .   .   .   .   .   .   .   .
      3   2   0                 1   2
  .   .   .   .   .   .   .   .   .   .
    3                       1   2
  .   .   .   .   .   .   .   .   .   .
    2           0       1       2   0
  .   .   .   .   .   .   .   .   .   .
                1   3           1       1
  .   .   .   .   .   .   .   .   .   .
                3                       1
  .   .   .   .   .   .   .   .   .   .
    2       2       2       1   3
  .   .   .   .   .   .   .   .   .   .
    1                       1
  .   .   .   .   .   .   .   .   .   .
      3       0   0       1       1   2
  .   .   .   .   .   .   .   .   .   .
    2           1       3   2   2       3
  .   .   .   .   .   .   .   .   .   .
      1       0       1   1   1
  .   .   .   .   .   .   .   .   .   .
      1       1   2
  .   .   .   .   .   .   .   .   .   .
```

Each horizontal row and vertical column should contain different shapes and different numbers.

Every square will contain one number and one shape and no combination may be repeated anywhere else in the puzzle.

◇ = 1   ○ = 2   ☆ = 3   ⬡ = 4   ◻ = 5

		1		3
	☆		4	
		◇		
			5	
4	2		(1)	◇

Given that the letters are valued 1-26 according to their places in the alphabet, can you crack the mystery code to reveal the missing letter?

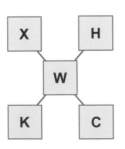

X   H
  W
K   C

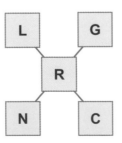

L   G
  R
N   C

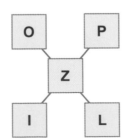

O   P
  Z
I   L

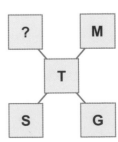

?   M
  T
S   G

A set of dominoes is to be placed in four rows as shown below. The numbers indicate which values are shown on all the dominoes in each column and the relevant half of the domino in every row. Find out where each domino is placed by carefully comparing rows and columns to determine the possible positions of certain dominoes: for instance, if any column contains only one 6, then the domino 6/6 isn't in that column.

A set of dominoes consists of:

0/0, 0/1, 0/2, 0/3, 0/4, 0/5, 0/6, 1/1, 1/2, 1/3, 1/4, 1/5, 1/6, 2/2,

2/3, 2/4, 2/5, 2/6, 3/3, 3/4, 3/5, 3/6, 4/4, 4/5, 4/6, 5/5, 5/6, 6/6.

	1, 1, 1, 1, 4, 4, 5, 6.	0, 0, 0, 2, 3, 4, 5, 6.	0, 0, 2, 2, 2, 3, 5, 6.	0, 0, 0, 1, 1, 4, 4, 4, 6.	0, 2, 2, 2, 3, 3, 6, 6.	3, 3, 3, 4, 4, 5, 5, 6.	1, 1, 2, 3, 5, 5, 5, 6.
2, 4, 4, 5, 5, 6, 6.							
1, 2, 3, 3, 6, 6, 6.							
0, 1, 3, 3, 4, 5, 6.							
1, 1, 1, 2, 3, 3, 4.							
1, 1, 2, 2, 4, 5, 5.							
0, 0, 1, 2, 2, 3, 6.							
0, 0, 0, 4, 5, 5, 6.							
0, 0, 2, 3, 4, 4, 5.							

Place the eight tiles into the puzzle grid so that all adjacent numbers on each tile match up. Tiles may be rotated through 360 degrees, but none may be flipped over.

Place all twelve of the pieces into the grid. Any may be rotated or flipped over, but none may touch another, not even diagonally. The numbers outside the grid refer to the number of consecutive black squares; and each block is separated from the others by at least one white square. For instance, '3 2' could refer to a row with none, one or more white squares, then three black squares, then at least one white square, then two more black squares, followed by any number of white squares.

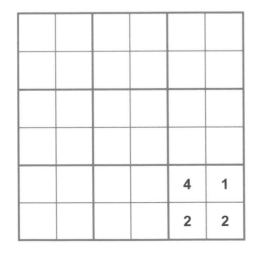

91

In the diagram below, which number should replace the question mark?

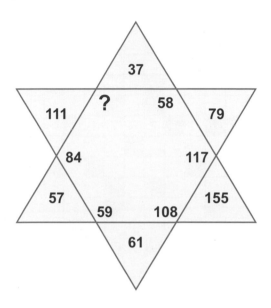

37

? 58

111

79

84

117

57

155

59 108

61

92

In the square below, change the positions of six numbers, one per horizontal row, vertical column and long diagonal line of six smaller squares, in such a way that the numbers in each row, column and long diagonal line total exactly 195. Any number may appear more than once in a row, column or line.

17	33	21	32	39	45
49	33	32	14	35	33
45	48	32	18	19	16
18	42	31	46	22	32
35	12	46	39	49	33
50	28	29	38	40	19

93

Every brick in this pyramid contains a number which is the sum of the two numbers below it, so that F=A+B, etc. Just work out the missing numbers!

O =

M =   N = 288

J = 269   K =   L =

F =   G =   H =   I = 88

A = 120   B = 63   C =   D =   E =

With the starter already given, can you fit all of the remaining listed numbers into this grid? Take care, this puzzle may not be as easy as it looks!

19	300	2434	7820	97403
28	333	2671 ✓	9876	98589
37	465	2677	19314	106527
40	483	2998	22234	280905
41	506	3386	34478	322990
62	513	3472	40837	431050
102	616	4196	50432	694555
163	631	4643	61046	730312
176	712	4667	69021	800566
201	720	5114	71352	900505
239	1192	5470	81738	5148944
295	1623	6047	90136	9061510

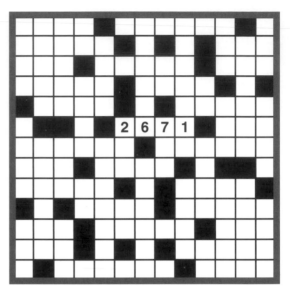

95

The chart gives directions to a hidden treasure behind the centre black square in the grid. Move the indicated number of spaces north, south, east and west (eg 4N means move four squares north) stopping at every square once only to arrive there. At which square should you start?

96

Fill the grid so that every horizontal row and vertical column contains the numbers 1-5. The 'greater than' or 'less than' signs indicate where a number is larger or smaller than that in the neighbouring square.

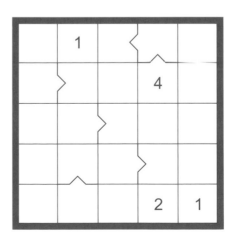

Each of the eight segments of the spider's web should be filled with a different number from 1 to 8, in such a way that every ring also contains a different number from 1 to 8.

The segments run from the outside of the spider's web to the centre, and the rings run all the way around.

Some numbers are already in place. Can you fill in the rest?

1

A standard set of 28 dominoes has been laid out as shown. Can you draw in the edges of them all? The check-box is provided as an aid and the domino already placed will help.

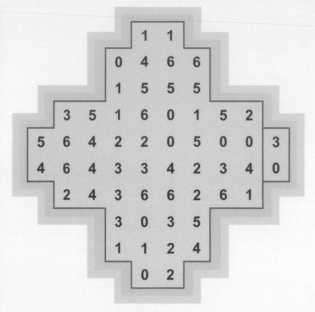

0-0	0-1	0-2	0-3	0-4	0-5	0-6
			✔			

1-1	1-2	1-3	1-4	1-5	1-6	2-2

2-3	2-4	2-5	2-6	3-3	3-4	3-5

3-6	4-4	4-5	4-6	5-5	5-6	6-6

2

Draw walls to partition the grid into areas (some walls are already drawn in for you). Each area must contain two circles, area sizes must match those numbers shown next to the grid and each '+' must be linked to at least two walls.

2,   3,   6,   7,   7

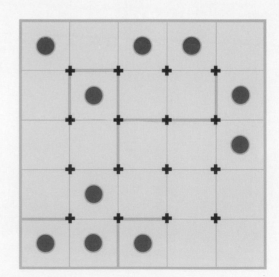

Every row and column in this grid originally contained one heart, one club, one diamond, one spade and two blank squares, although not necessarily in that order.

Every symbol with a black arrow refers to the first of the four symbols encountered when travelling in the direction of the arrow. Every symbol with a white arrow refers to the second of the four symbols encountered in the direction of the arrow.

Can you complete the original grid?

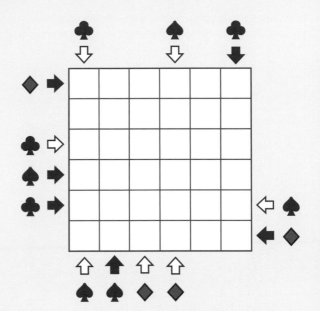

The blank squares below should be filled with whole numbers between 1 and 30 inclusive, any of which may occur more than once, or not at all.

The numbers in every horizontal row add up to the totals on the right, as do the two long diagonal lines; whilst those in every vertical column add up to the totals along the bottom.

								106
14	2	3			15	5	70	
10	22		15	12		7	95	
11	20		4		6	3	89	
11		18		17	5	16	113	
		28	8	4	6		102	
3	15	9	4	22			111	
		17		2	9	29	110	
68	105	123	112	84	78	120	155	

Draw in the missing hands on the final clock.

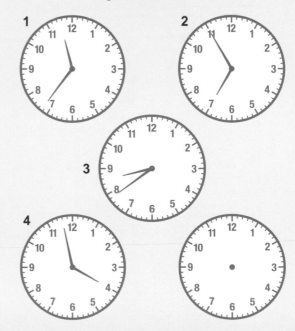

Can you place the hexagons into the grid, so that where any hexagon touches another along a straight line, the number in both triangles is the same? No rotation of any hexagon is allowed!

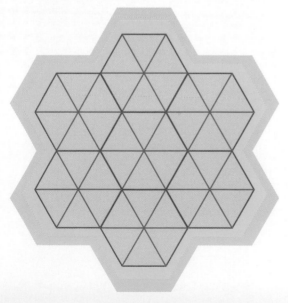

Twelve L-shapes like the ones here need to be inserted in the grid and each L has one hole in it.

There are three pieces of each of the four kinds shown here and any piece may be turned or flipped over before being put in the grid. No pieces of the same kind touch, even at a corner.

The pieces fit together so well that you cannot see any spaces between them; only the holes show.

Can you tell where the Ls are?

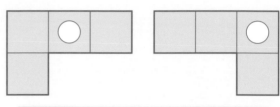

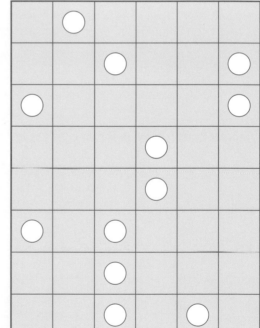

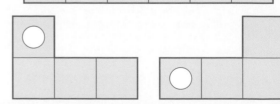

In this puzzle, an amateur coin collector has been out with his metal detector, searching for booty. He didn't have time to dig up all the coins he found, so has made a grid map, showing their locations, in the hope that if he loses the map, at least no-one else will understand it…

Those squares containing numbers are empty, but where a number appears in a square, it indicates how many coins are located in the squares (up to a maximum of eight) surrounding the numbered one, touching it at any corner or side. There is only one coin in any individual square.

Place a circle into every square containing a coin.

9

The grid should be filled with numbers from 1 to 6, so that each number appears just once in every row and column. The clues refer to the digit totals in the squares, eg A 1 2 3 = 6 means that the numbers in squares A1, A2 and A3 add up to 6.

1 D E 3 = 4

2 D 4 5 = 9

3 A B 4 = 9

4 E 1 2 = 8

5 B 1 2 3 = 8

6 C D 1 = 10

7 C D 2 = 3

8 F 2 3 = 10

9 A B 6 = 8

10 C 3 4 5 = 11

Each of the small squares in the grid below contains either A, B or C. Each row, column, and diagonal line of six squares has exactly two of each letter. Can you tell the letter in each square?

Across

1 Each C is directly next to and right of an A
2 The Bs are next to each other
3 The Bs are further right than the As
4 The Bs are further right than the As
6 The Bs are between the Cs

Down

1 No two letters the same are directly next to each other
4 No two letters the same are directly next to each other
5 No two letters the same are directly next to each other
6 Each A is directly next to and above a C

	1	2	3	4	5	6
1						
2						
3						
4						
5						
6						

11

The object of this puzzle is to trace a single path from the top left corner to the bottom right corner of the grid, travelling through all of the cells in either a horizontal, vertical or diagonal direction.

Every cell must be entered once only and your path should take you through the numbers in the sequence 1-2-3-4-1-2-3-4, etc.

Can you find the way?

1	3	2	1	4	3	2	1
3	2	4	1	1	2	4	3
2	4	1	4	2	4	3	2
1	3	3	2	3	4	1	4
4	4	2	1	1	2	1	3
3	3	1	4	2	3	1	2
2	4	2	2	3	4	4	3
1	3	4	1	3	1	2	4

Can you place the vessels into the diagram? Some parts of vessels or sea squares have already been filled in. A number to the right or below a row or column refers to the number of occupied squares in that row or column.

Any vessel may be positioned horizontally or vertically, but no part of a vessel touches part of any other vessel, either horizontally, vertically or diagonally.

Empty Area of Sea: ≈

Aircraft Carrier: ◀■■▶

Battleships: ◀■▶ ◀■▶

Cruisers: ◀▶ ◀▶ ◀▶

Submarines: ● ● ● ●

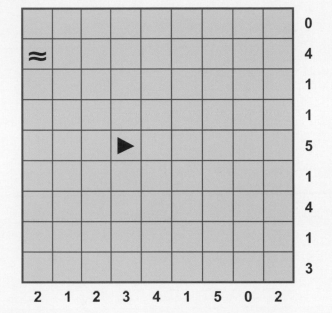

Can you fill each square in the bottom line with the correct digit?

Every square in the solution contains only one digit from each of the lines above, although two or more squares in the solution may contain the same digit.

At the end of every row is a score, which shows:

a the number of digits placed in the correct finishing position on the bottom line, as indicated by a tick; and

b the number of digits which appear on the bottom line, but in a different position, as indicated by a cross.

				SCORE
9	7	4	5	✗ ✗
3	5	9	5	✓ ✗ ✗
3	2	9	4	✗
1	9	7	9	✓
1	9	6	3	✗
				✓ ✓ ✓ ✓

S
E
C
T
I
O
N

6

221

14

Draw a single continuous loop, by connecting the dots. No line may cross the path of another.

The figure inside each set of any four surrounding dots indicates the total number of surrounding lines.

```
      1  2      3  2  2
 2       0  0                    2
 1       2              2     3
         1       0        2  2
      1  1       1           2  2
   3             2     3
         0       2     3  2  2
 2                  2
   2  1  3  2  1  1           2
                        1     1
   2     1     2     2     2
 2          2  1
```

15

Each horizontal row and vertical column should contain different shapes and different numbers.

Every square will contain one number and one shape and no combination may be repeated anywhere else in the puzzle.

1   2   3   4   5

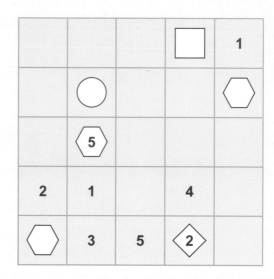

16

Given that the letters are valued 1-26 according to their places in the alphabet, can you crack the mystery code to reveal the missing letter?

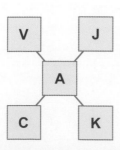

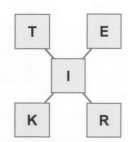

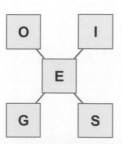

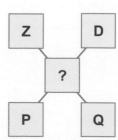

A set of dominoes is to be placed in four rows as shown below. The numbers indicate which values are shown on all the dominoes in each column and the relevant half of the domino in every row. Find out where each domino is placed by carefully comparing rows and columns to determine the possible positions of certain dominoes: for instance, if any column contains only one 6, then the domino 6/6 isn't in that column.

A set of dominoes consists of:

0/0, 0/1, 0/2, 0/3, 0/4, 0/5, 0/6, 1/1, 1/2, 1/3, 1/4, 1/5, 1/6, 2/2,

2/3, 2/4, 2/5, 2/6, 3/3, 3/4, 3/5, 3/6, 4/4, 4/5, 4/6, 5/5, 5/6, 6/6.

	0, 1, 1, 3, 3, 5, 5, 5.	0, 2, 2, 3, 3, 4, 4, 5.	0, 1, 1, 1, 4, 5, 6, 6.	0, 2, 2, 2, 3, 4, 5, 5.	0, 1, 2, 3, 3, 6, 6, 6.	0, 1, 1, 2, 2, 4, 6, 6.	0, 0, 3, 4, 4, 4, 5, 6.
1, 2, 2, 2, 3, 3, 4.							
0, 4, 5, 5, 5, 6, 6.							
0, 0, 0, 2, 2, 5, 6.							
0, 0, 1, 1, 2, 5, 6.							
1, 1, 3, 3, 3, 4, 5.							
0, 0, 1, 2, 2, 3, 4.							
1, 3, 3, 5, 5, 6, 6.							
1, 4, 4, 4, 4, 6, 6.							

Place the eight tiles into the puzzle grid so that all adjacent numbers on each tile match up. Tiles may be rotated through 360 degrees, but none may be flipped over.

Place all twelve of the pieces into the grid. Any may be rotated or flipped over, but none may touch another, not even diagonally. The numbers outside the grid refer to the number of consecutive black squares; and each block is separated from the others by at least one white square. For instance, '3 2' could refer to a row with none, one or more white squares, then three black squares, then at least one white square, then two more black squares, followed by any number of white squares.

Tiles for puzzle 18:

1	4
3	3

1	4
4	3

1	2
2	4

1	1
1	4

3	3
3	4

2	1
2	3

4	1
2	3

3	4
4	2

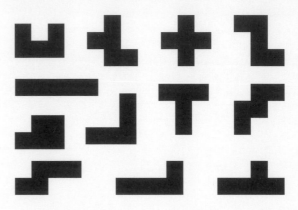

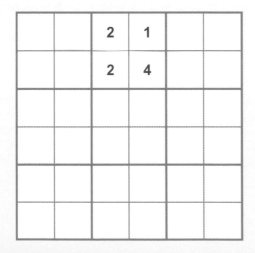

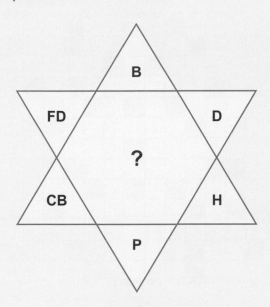

20

In the diagram below, which letters should replace the question mark?

B

FD

D

?

CB

H

P

21

In the square below, change the positions of six numbers, one per horizontal row, vertical column and long diagonal line of six smaller squares, in such a way that the numbers in each row, column and long diagonal line total exactly 211. Any number may appear more than once in a row, column or line.

23	23	26	35	22	57
27	35	23	20	36	34
43	46	35	37	28	39
42	48	36	63	19	33
22	47	52	46	42	22
18	32	33	40	39	43

22

Every brick in this pyramid contains a number which is the sum of the two numbers below it, so that F=A+B, etc. Just work out the missing numbers!

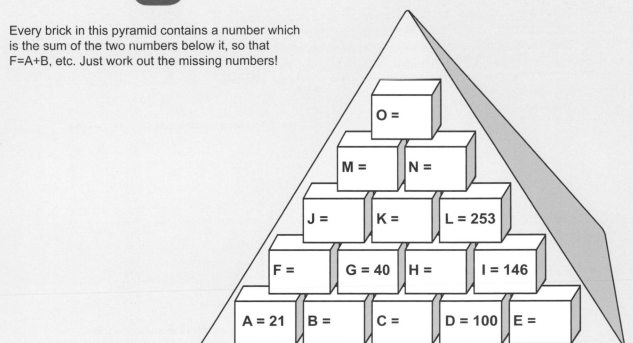

O =

M =   N =

J =   K =   L = 253

F =   G = 40   H =   I = 146

A = 21   B =   C =   D = 100   E =

With the starter already given, can you fit all of the remaining listed numbers into this grid? Take care, this puzzle may not be as easy as it looks!

14	434	824	5369	157952
19	472	910	5697	266131
28	482	934	7899	305782
38	526	943	9016 ✓	533099
56	562	1854	16736	559945
68	599	3009	23913	802936
140	659	3999	24310	2955503
160	677	4364	26080	3789277
184	743	4672	42726	3892870
200	776	4678	49724	4259147
205	777	5089	58844	6171179
383	804	5327	79883	6240305

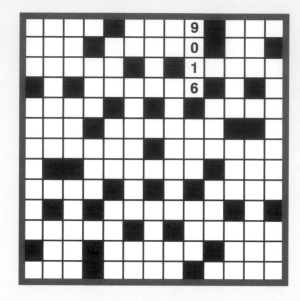

24

The chart gives directions to a hidden treasure behind the centre black square in the grid. Move the indicated number of spaces north, south, east and west (eg 4N means move four squares north) stopping at every square once only to arrive there. At which square should you start?

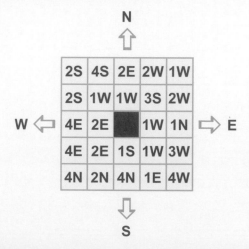

25

Fill the grid so that every horizontal row and vertical column contains the numbers 1-5. The 'greater than' or 'less than' signs indicate where a number is larger or smaller than that in the neighbouring square.

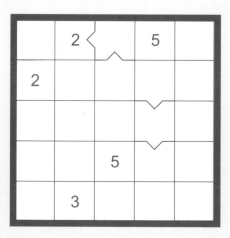

S E C T I O N

6

Each of the eight segments of the spider's web should be filled with a different number from 1 to 8, in such a way that every ring also contains a different number from 1 to 8.

The segments run from the outside of the spider's web to the centre, and the rings run all the way around.

Some numbers are already in place. Can you fill in the rest?

Every oval shape in this diagram contains a different letter of the alphabet from A to K inclusive. Use the clues to determine their locations. Reference in the clues to 'due' means in any location along the same horizontal or vertical line.

1 The A is next to and north of the C, which is next to and east of the D.

2 The B is next to and west of the J, which is next to and north of the I.

3 The E is next to and south of the K, which is next to and west of the B.

4 The I is next to and east of the F, which is next to and north of the H.

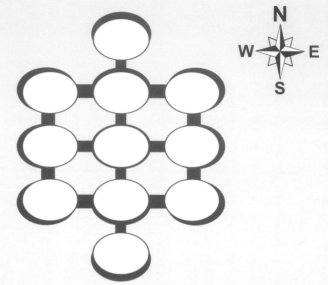

28

Fill the three empty circles with the symbols +, – and x in some order, to make a sum which totals the number in the centre. Each symbol must be used once and calculations are made in the direction of travel (clockwise).

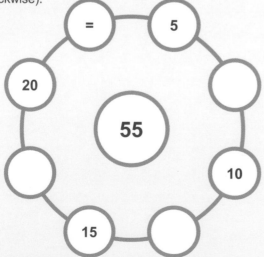

29

The numbers at the top and on the left side show the quantity of single-digit numbers (1-9) used in that row and column. The numbers at the bottom and on the right side show the sum of the digits. A number may appear more than once in a row or column, but no numbers are in squares that touch, even at a corner.

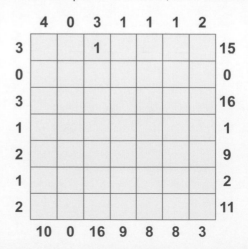

	4	0	3	1	1	1	2	
3			1					15
0								0
3								16
1								1
2								9
1								2
2								11
	10	0	16	9	8	8	3	

6

S E C T I O N

30

Using the numbers below, complete these six equations (three reading across and three reading downwards). Every number is used once.

1   2   3   4   5
  6   7   8   9

	+		−		=	5
×	■	−	■	×		
	+		+		=	16
×	■	×	■	−		
	×		−		=	27
=		=		=		
135		21		4		

31

In the grid below, which number should replace the question mark?

26	15	22	34	19	28	11
30	21	26	40	23	34	15
24	17	20	36	17	30	9
28	23	24	42	21	36	13
22	19	18	38	15	32	7
26	25	22	44	19	38	11
20	21	16	40	13	34	?

32

When the box below is folded to form a cube, just one of the five options (A, B, C, D or E) can be produced. Which?

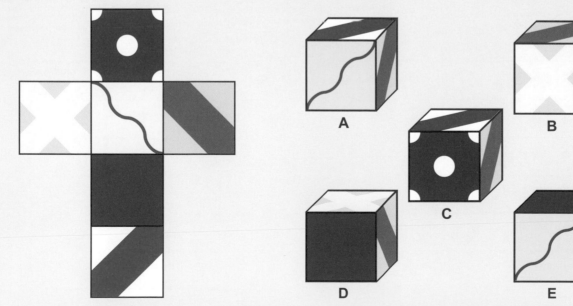

33

In this puzzle, an amateur coin collector has been out with his metal detector, searching for booty. He didn't have time to dig up all the coins he found, so has made a grid map, showing their locations, in the hope that if he loses the map, at least no-one else will understand it…

Those squares containing numbers are empty, but where a number appears in a square, it indicates how many coins are located in the squares (up to a maximum of eight) surrounding the numbered one, touching it at any corner or side. There is only one coin in any individual square.

Place a circle into every square containing a coin.

2					1		1		2
		2		1					
		3			1			3	
	4	5				1	2		1
				1			2		
3			1				3		2
	3	3		2					
			2		2			2	2
3									1
		2	1			1		2	

34

Each symbol stands for a different number. In order to reach the correct total at the end of each row and column, what is the value of the circle, cross, pentagon, square and star?

pentagon	cross	square	circle	pentagon	= 19
square	circle	cross	pentagon	square	= 14
pentagon	pentagon	cross	star	cross	= 28
pentagon	star	star	pentagon	star	= 36
circle	square	star	circle	square	= 14
=21	=21	=25	=24	=20	

35

Every row and column of this grid should contain one each of the letters A, B, C, D, E and F. Each of the six shapes (marked by thicker lines) should also contain one each of the letters A, B, C, D, E and F. Can you complete the grid?

			B		A
				C	
			D		
		F	E		

A standard set of 28 dominoes has been laid out as shown. Can you draw in the edges of them all? The check-box is provided as an aid and the domino already placed will help.

0-0	0-1	0-2	0-3	0-4	0-5	0-6

1-1	1-2	1-3	1-4	1-5	1-6	2-2
						✓

2-3	2-4	2-5	2-6	3-3	3-4	3-5

3-6	4-4	4-5	4-6	5-5	5-6	6-6

Each of the small squares in the grid below contains either A, B or C. Each row, column, and diagonal line of six squares has exactly two of each letter. Can you tell the letter in each square?

Across
  2 The As are next to each other
  4 The As are further right than the Cs
  5 The Cs are between the Bs

Down
  3 The As are between the Cs
  4 The As are next to each other
  5 The Bs are lower than the As
  6 The As are next to each other

	1	2	3	4	5	6
1						
2						
3						
4						
5						
6						

Every row and column in this grid originally contained one heart, one club, one diamond, one spade and two blank squares, although not necessarily in that order.

Every symbol with a black arrow refers to the first of the four symbols encountered when travelling in the direction of the arrow. Every symbol with a white arrow refers to the second of the four symbols encountered in the direction of the arrow.

Can you complete the original grid?

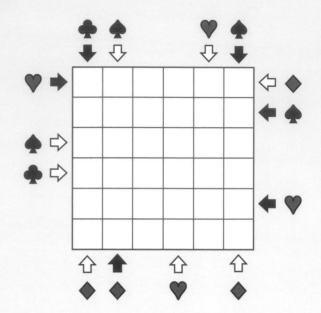

The blank squares below should be filled with whole numbers between 1 and 30 inclusive, any of which may occur more than once, or not at all.

The numbers in every horizontal row add up to the totals on the right, as do the two long diagonal lines; whilst those in every vertical column add up to the totals along the bottom.

							116
13		21		18	7	26	119
11	17	4			5	10	86
9	6	27	29			19	113
7	3	29	12				99
	13		16	22	4	7	88
		18	14	10	20	21	118
28	12	19	6		25		118
99	76	143	107	127	71	118	124

A   is to   B

as   C   is to

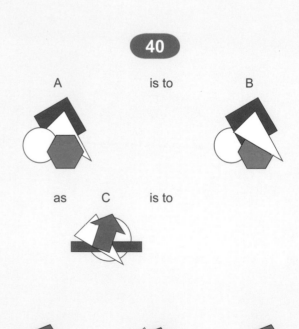

D   E   F

Can you place the hexagons into the grid, so that where any hexagon touches another along a straight line, the number in both triangles is the same? No rotation of any hexagon is allowed!

Twelve L-shapes like the ones here need to be inserted in the grid and each L has one hole in it.

There are three pieces of each of the four kinds shown here and any piece may be turned or flipped over before being put in the grid. No pieces of the same kind touch, even at a corner.

The pieces fit together so well that you cannot see any spaces between them; only the holes show.

Can you tell where the Ls are?

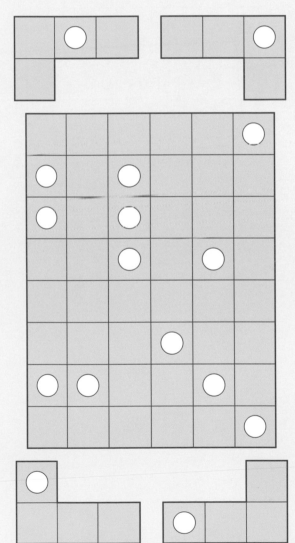

Which of the four lettered alternatives (A, B, C or D) fits most logically into the empty square?

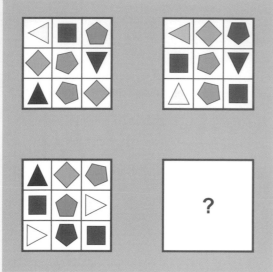

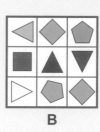

A

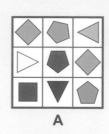

B

?

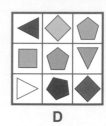

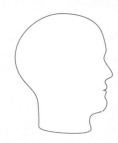

C

D

Which four pieces can be fitted together to form an exact copy of this shape?

A

B

C

D

E

F

G

H

I

J

45

Can you place the vessels into the diagram? Some parts of vessels or sea squares have already been filled in. A number to the right or below a row or column refers to the number of occupied squares in that row or column.

Any vessel may be positioned horizontally or vertically, but no part of a vessel touches part of any other vessel, either horizontally, vertically or diagonally.

Empty Area of Sea: ≈

Aircraft Carrier:

Battleships:

Cruisers:

Submarines:

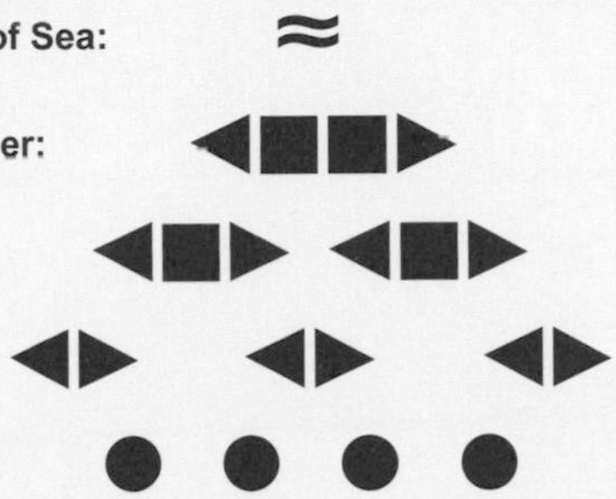

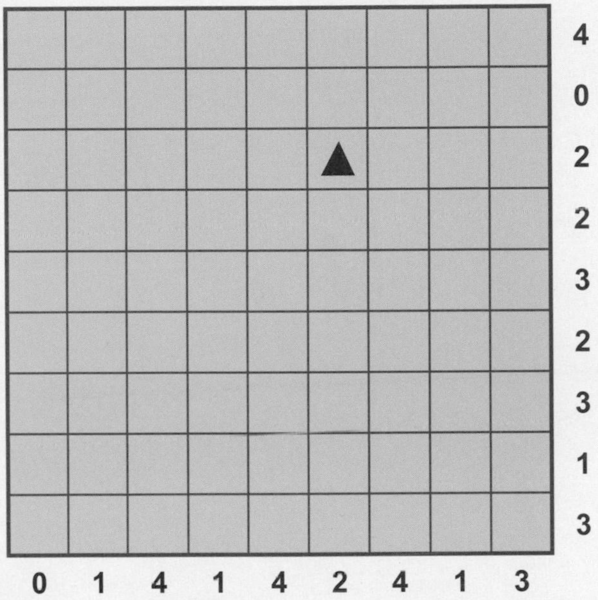

46

Can you fill each square in the bottom line with the correct digit?

Every square in the solution contains only one digit from each of the lines above, although two or more squares in the solution may contain the same digit.

At the end of every row is a score, which shows:

a the number of digits placed in the correct finishing position on the bottom line, as indicated by a tick; and

b the number of digits which appear on the bottom line, but in a different position, as indicated by a cross.

				SCORE
2	6	8	7	✓ ✗ ✗
4	6	2	2	✓ ✗ ✗
4	1	2	4	✗
3	7	7	2	✓
5	1	6	3	✓
				✓ ✓ ✓ ✓

The grid should be filled with numbers from 1 to 6, so that each number appears just once in every row and column. The clues refer to the digit totals in the squares, eg A 1 2 3 = 6 means that the numbers in squares A1, A2 and A3 add up to 6.

1 D 4 5 = 10

2 A B 4 = 8

3 B C 5 = 9

4 B 1 2 3 = 8

5 A 2 3 = 9

6 C 3 4 = 6

7 D E F 3 = 11

8 A B 6 = 3

9 F 1 2 = 10

10 C D 1 = 8

11 C D 2 = 3

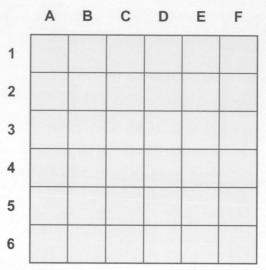

	A	B	C	D	E	F
1						
2						
3						
4						
5						
6						

The object of this puzzle is to trace a single path from the top left corner to the bottom right corner of the grid, travelling through all of the cells in either a horizontal, vertical or diagonal direction.

Every cell must be entered once only and your path should take you through the numbers in the sequence 1-2-3-4-1-2-3-4, etc.

Can you find the way?

1	1	4	3	1	2	3	2
2	3	2	4	2	4	1	3
2	4	1	3	1	4	3	4
1	3	2	4	1	2	2	1
4	4	1	3	4	1	3	2
3	2	1	2	3	3	4	3
1	3	2	4	1	2	4	3
4	2	3	4	1	1	2	4

49

Draw a single continuous loop, by connecting the dots. No line may cross the path of another.

The figure inside each set of any four surrounding dots indicates the total number of surrounding lines.

```
2      3  3  3      3  1
2         1  1            3
    1           0            2
3  0              1     1     2
      2                 2
         2  1  1     1        1
2  2  2  1                 1
            0           1     3
   2  1     1  3  2     3
1  2  1     0              1
                          3
         2  1     1  1
```

50

Each horizontal row and vertical column should contain different shapes and different numbers.

Every square will contain one number and one shape and no combination may be repeated anywhere else in the puzzle.

1   2   3   4   5

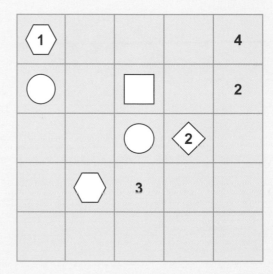

51

Given that the letters are valued 1-26 according to their places in the alphabet, can you crack the mystery code to reveal the missing letter?

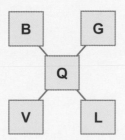

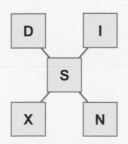

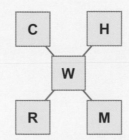

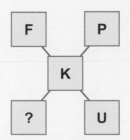

52

Which is the odd one out?

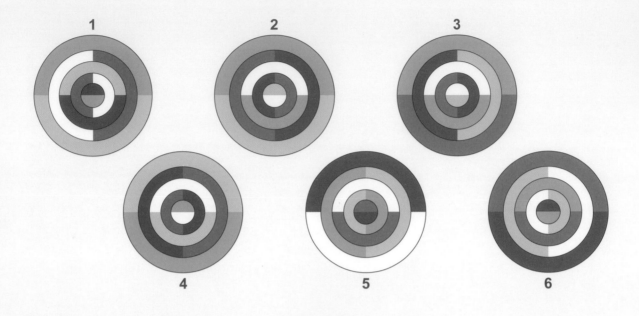

1   2   3

4   5   6

53

Which of the alternatives (1, 2, 3 or 4) should replace the question mark?

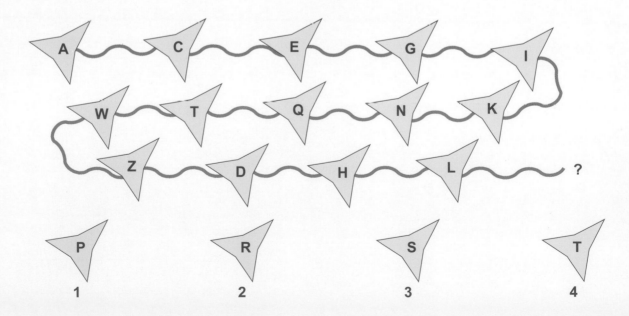

Place the eight tiles into the puzzle grid so that all adjacent numbers on each tile match up. Tiles may be rotated through 360 degrees, but none may be flipped over.

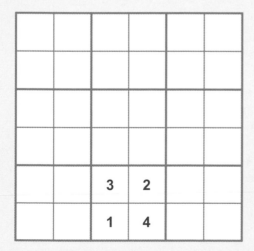

Place all twelve of the pieces into the grid. Any may be rotated or flipped over, but none may touch another, not even diagonally. The numbers outside the grid refer to the number of consecutive black squares; and each block is separated from the others by at least one white square. For instance, '3 2' could refer to a row with none, one or more white squares, then three black squares, then at least one white square, then two more black squares, followed by any number of white squares.

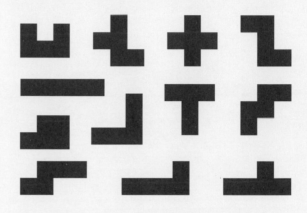

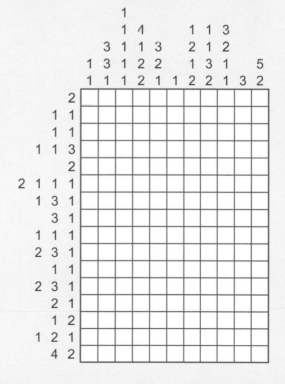

56

In the diagram below, what three-digit number should replace the question mark?

57

In the square below, change the positions of six numbers, one per horizontal row, vertical column and long diagonal line of six smaller squares, in such a way that the numbers in each row, column and long diagonal line total exactly 264. Any number may appear more than once in a row, column or line.

37	86	32	48	51	37
63	84	47	37	24	14
57	23	32	88	41	47
45	31	68	26	59	43
25	10	15	56	72	8
51	57	94	14	25	37

58

Every brick in this pyramid contains a number which is the sum of the two numbers below it, so that F=A+B, etc. Just work out the missing numbers!

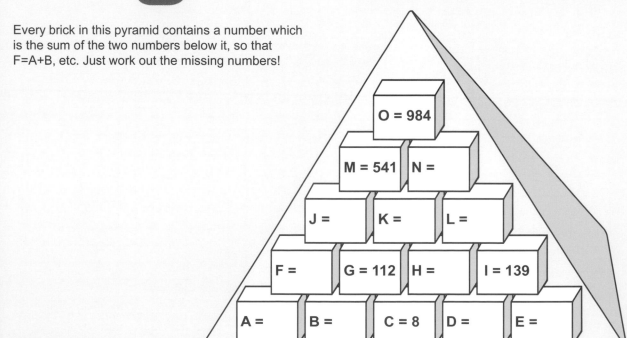

With the starter already given, can you fit all of the remaining listed numbers into this grid? Take care, this puzzle may not be as easy as it looks!

19	349	5694	46595	93171
20	552	6046	47588	98109
27	604	6271	51740	145693
34	736	6360	53376	290978
35	742	6651	58970	318935
42	939	9920	69436	354967
78	1148	14460	70050	387763
86	1570	20121	72198	390757
87	1617	24157	82494	2268327
93	2275	26429	89022	4149991
151	3354	30080	92293 ✓	8002355
239	4790	39480	93106	9330234

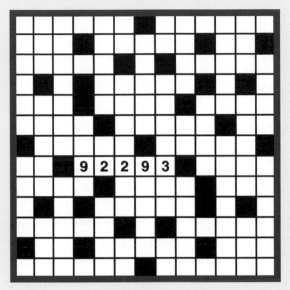

The chart gives directions to a hidden treasure behind the centre black square in the grid. Move the indicated number of spaces north, south, east and west (eg 4N means move four squares north) stopping at every square once only to arrive there. At which square should you start?

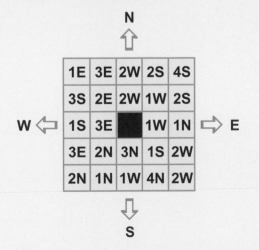

Fill the grid so that every horizontal row and vertical column contains the numbers 1-5. The 'greater than' or 'less than' signs indicate where a number is larger or smaller than that in the neighbouring square.

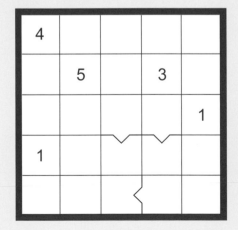

Each of the eight segments of the spider's web should be filled with a different number from 1 to 8, in such a way that every ring also contains a different number from 1 to 8.

The segments run from the outside of the spider's web to the centre, and the rings run all the way around.

Some numbers are already in place. Can you fill in the rest?

Every oval shape in this diagram contains a different letter of the alphabet from A to K inclusive. Use the clues to determine their locations. Reference in the clues to 'due' means in any location along the same horizontal or vertical line.

1 The A is further south than the G, which is further south than the I.

2 The D is further north than the J and further west than the H.

3 The F is next to and east of the A, which is due north of the E.

4 The I is next to and west of the C, which is due north of the B.

5 The K is next to and north of the D.

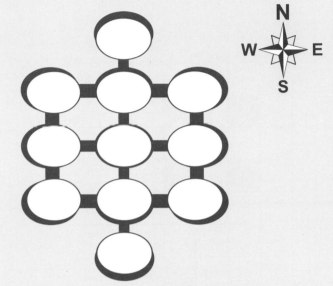

64

Fill the three empty circles with the symbols +, − and x in some order, to make a sum which totals the number in the centre. Each symbol must be used once and calculations are made in the direction of travel (clockwise).

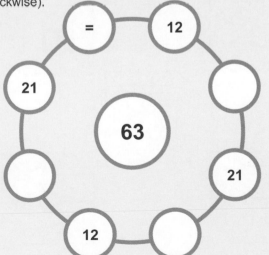

65

The numbers at the top and on the left side show the quantity of single-digit numbers (1-9) used in that row and column. The numbers at the bottom and on the right side show the sum of the digits. A number may appear more than once in a row or column, but no numbers are in squares that touch, even at a corner.

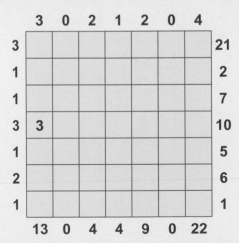

66

Using the numbers below, complete these six equations (three reading across and three reading downwards). Every number is used once.

1		2		3		4		5

| 6 | | 7 | | 8 | | 9 | | |

	−		×		=	27
−		+		−		
	×		−		=	21
+		+		×		
	×		+		=	15
=		=		=		
2		16		42		

67

In the grid below, which number should replace the question mark?

93	81	68	56	43	31	18
98	87	75	64	52	41	29
77	67	56	46	35	25	14
68	59	49	40	30	21	11
72	64	55	47	38	30	21
71	?	58	51	45	38	32
40	34	29	23	18	12	7

68

When the box below is folded to form a cube, just one of the five options (A, B, C, D or E) can be produced. Which?

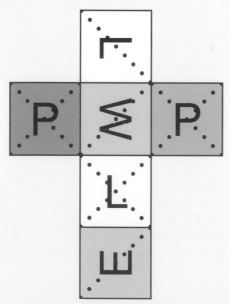

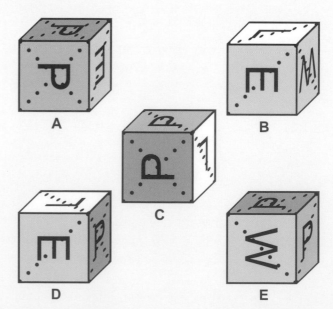

69

In this puzzle, an amateur coin collector has been out with his metal detector, searching for booty. He didn't have time to dig up all the coins he found, so has made a grid map, showing their locations, in the hope that if he loses the map, at least no-one else will understand it…

Those squares containing numbers are empty, but where a number appears in a square, it indicates how many coins are located in the squares (up to a maximum of eight) surrounding the numbered one, touching it at any corner or side. There is only one coin in any individual square.

Place a circle into every square containing a coin.

		0				0			1
	0		2			2			
					1				0
2				2	1			2	
	3						2		
			2				1		
4		4			0				3
			3	1			2		
			3		2			2	2
3		3					2		

70

Every row and column of this grid should contain one each of the letters A, B, C, D, E and F. Each of the six shapes (marked by thicker lines) should also contain one each of the letters A, B, C, D, E and F. Can you complete the grid?

C			B		A
D					
		E			
					F

71

Each symbol stands for a different number. In order to reach the correct total at the end of each row and column, what is the value of the circle, cross, pentagon, square and star?

●	☆	●	✚	●	= 39
☆	■	✚	✚	☆	= 28
✚	●	■	■	■	= 28
●	☆	●	☆	●	= 37
✚	●	⬠	⬠	■	= 36
= 37	= 32	= 37	= 31	= 31	

A standard set of 28 dominoes has been laid out as shown. Can you draw in the edges of them all? The check-box is provided as an aid and the domino already placed will help.

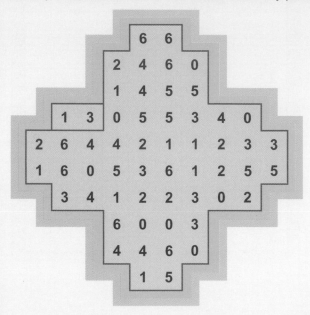

0-0	0-1	0-2	0-3	0-4	0-5	0-6

1-1	1-2	1-3	1-4	1-5	1-6	2-2
		✔				

2-3	2-4	2-5	2-6	3-3	3-4	3-5

3-6	4-4	4-5	4-6	5-5	5-6	6-6

73

Each of the small squares in the grid below contains either A, B or C. Each row, column, and diagonal line of six squares has exactly two of each letter. Can you tell the letter in each square?

Across

1 No two letters the same are directly next to each other
2 The Cs are between the Bs
3 No two letters the same are directly next to each other
4 Each B is directly next to and right of a C
5 The Bs are further right than the Cs

Down

1 The Cs are next to each other
2 No two letters the same are directly next to each other
3 No two letters the same are directly next to each other
6 The Bs are next to each other

	1	2	3	4	5	6
1						
2						
3						
4						
5						
6						

Every row and column in this grid originally contained one heart, one club, one diamond, one spade and two blank squares, although not necessarily in that order.

Every symbol with a black arrow refers to the first of the four symbols encountered when travelling in the direction of the arrow. Every symbol with a white arrow refers to the second of the four symbols encountered in the direction of the arrow.

Can you complete the original grid?

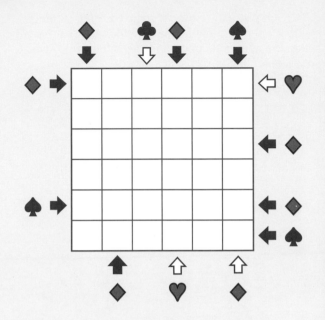

75

The blank squares below should be filled with whole numbers between 1 and 30 inclusive, any of which may occur more than once, or not at all.

The numbers in every horizontal row add up to the totals on the right, as do the two long diagonal lines; whilst those in every vertical column add up to the totals along the bottom.

76

							110
15	12	23	18		16		115
		9	14	24	2		98
2	17		25	22		13	97
		26	8	7	12	11	102
21		16	4		29	14	132
3	15			22	28	1	109
	12	7		30	17	10	101

95	120	117	90	127	110	95	101

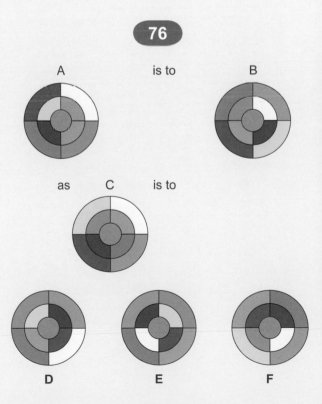

Can you place the hexagons into the grid, so that where any hexagon touches another along a straight line, the number in both triangles is the same? No rotation of any hexagon is allowed!

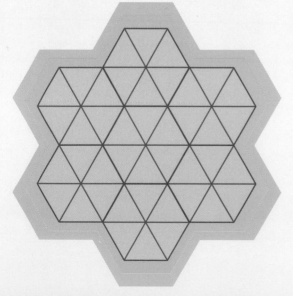

Twelve L-shapes like the ones here need to be inserted in the grid and each L has one hole in it.

There are three pieces of each of the four kinds shown here and any piece may be turned or flipped over before being put in the grid. No pieces of the same kind touch, even at a corner.

The pieces fit together so well that you cannot see any spaces between them; only the holes show.

Can you tell where the Ls are?

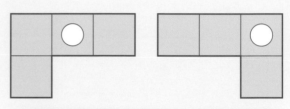

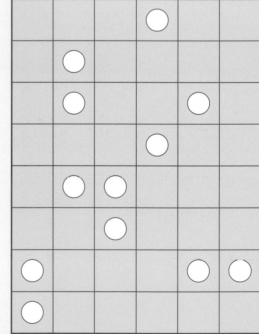

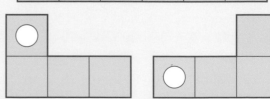

Draw walls to partition the grid into areas (some walls are already drawn in for you). Each area must contain two circles, area sizes must match those numbers shown next to the grid and each '+' must be linked to at least two walls.

2, 3, 4, 5, 5, 6

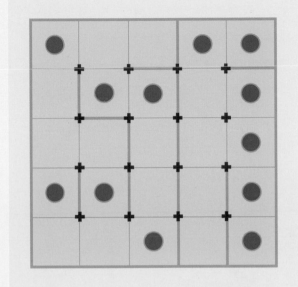

What number should replace the question mark?

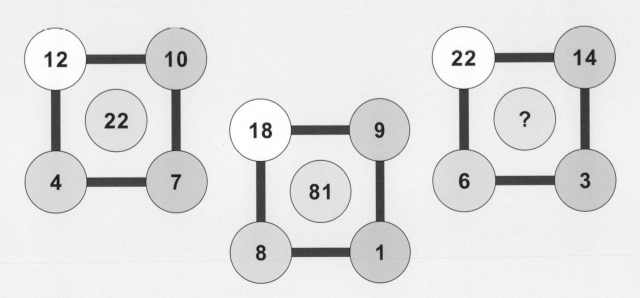

The object of this puzzle is to trace a single path from the top left corner to the bottom right corner of the grid, travelling through all of the cells in either a horizontal, vertical or diagonal direction.

Every cell must be entered once only and your path should take you through the numbers in the sequence 1-2-3-4-1-2-3-4, etc.

Can you find the way?

1	1	4	3	4	3	4	2
2	3	2	3	2	1	1	3
2	1	4	2	1	4	2	4
1	3	3	1	3	2	1	3
4	2	4	3	1	2	1	4
3	1	4	2	4	3	3	4
2	4	1	4	3	2	1	2
1	2	3	2	1	4	3	4

The grid should be filled with numbers from 1 to 6, so that each number appears just once in every row and column. The clues refer to the digit totals in the squares, eg A 1 2 3 = 6 means that the numbers in squares A1, A2 and A3 add up to 6.

1 D 4 5 = 5

2 A B 4 = 7

3 E F 5 = 7

4 A 1 2 = 11

5 B 5 6 = 11

6 E 1 2 3 = 13

7 B C D 1 = 9

8 C 3 4 = 3

9 B C 2 = 6

10 F 1 2 = 3

11 A B 3 = 6

	A	B	C	D	E	F
1						
2						
3						
4						
5						
6						

Can you fill each square in the bottom line with the correct digit?

Every square in the solution contains only one digit from each of the lines above, although two or more squares in the solution may contain the same digit.

At the end of every row is a score, which shows:

  a the number of digits placed in the correct finishing position on the bottom line, as indicated by a tick; and

  b the number of digits which appear on the bottom line, but in a different position, as indicated by a cross.

				SCORE
2	7	1	7	✓✓
8	2	5	7	✓✗
8	4	5	6	✗
7	3	8	7	✗
6	8	5	7	✗
				✓✓✓✓

84

Can you place the vessels into the diagram? Some parts of vessels or sea squares have already been filled in. A number to the right or below a row or column refers to the number of occupied squares in that row or column.

Any vessel may be positioned horizontally or vertically, but no part of a vessel touches part of any other vessel, either horizontally, vertically or diagonally.

Empty Area of Sea: ≈

Aircraft Carrier: ◀■■▶

Battleships: ◀■▶ ◀■▶

Cruisers: ◀▶ ◀▶ ◀▶

Submarines: ● ● ● ●

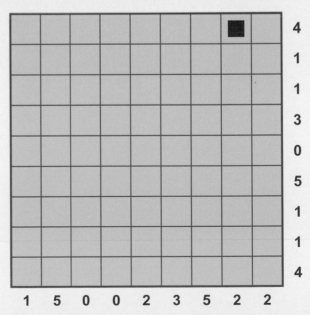

Draw a single continuous loop, by connecting the dots. No line may cross the path of another.

The figure inside each set of any four surrounding dots indicates the total number of surrounding lines.

```
  2     3     2  1     3
   0     1           3     1
    2  2        0
 3     2           2  1  1
    1              2
 2                 0        1
 2     2  0              1  3

 1  2           0  1  1  3
    2  1  0
    1                 0     3
 3  2  2     2  3  3        3
```

Each horizontal row and vertical column should contain different shapes and different numbers.

Every square will contain one number and one shape and no combination may be repeated anywhere else in the puzzle.

| 1 | 2 | 3 | 4 | 5 |

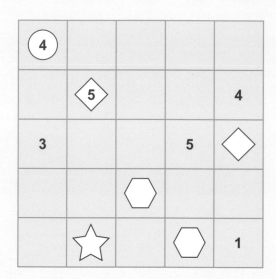

Given that the letters are valued 1-26 according to their places in the alphabet, can you crack the mystery code to reveal the missing letter?

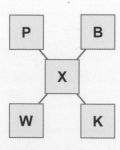
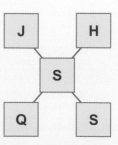
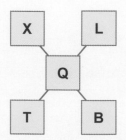
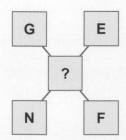

Place the eight tiles into the puzzle grid so that all adjacent numbers on each tile match up. Tiles may be rotated through 360 degrees, but none may be flipped over.

2	3
4	1

4	1
1	1

1	3
1	2

1	1
4	3

1	4
4	3

4	2
4	2

3	1
2	3

2	4
1	3

		4	3		
		4	1		

Place all twelve of the pieces into the grid. Any may be rotated or flipped over, but none may touch another, not even diagonally. The numbers outside the grid refer to the number of consecutive black squares; and each block is separated from the others by at least one white square. For instance, '3 2' could refer to a row with none, one or more white squares, then three black squares, then at least one white square, then two more black squares, followed by any number of white squares.

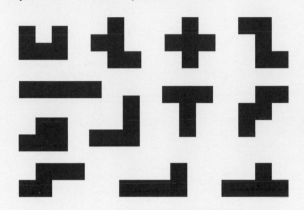

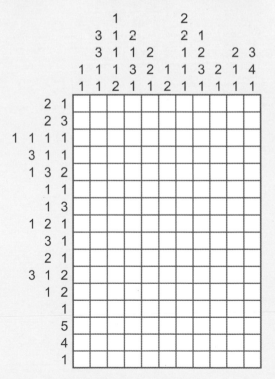

90

In the diagram below, which number should replace the question mark?

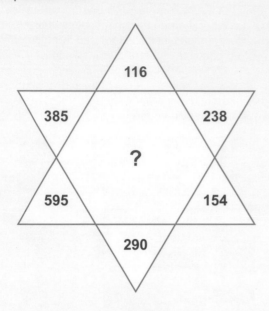

116

385   238

?

595   154

290

91

In the square below, change the positions of six numbers, one per horizontal row, vertical column and long diagonal line of six smaller squares, in such a way that the numbers in each row, column and long diagonal line total exactly 240. Any number may appear more than once in a row, column or line.

38	38	47	37	32	38
54	47	55	36	4	27
35	26	12	70	77	64
49	12	72	10	18	60
26	18	38	43	78	57
20	82	36	34	12	38

92

Every brick in this pyramid contains a number which is the sum of the two numbers below it, so that F=A+B, etc. Just work out the missing numbers!

O=

M = 558   N =

J =   K =   L =

F =   G = 134   H =   I = 154

A = 29   B = 52   C =   D =   E =

With the starter already given, can you fit all of the remaining listed numbers into this grid? Take care, this puzzle may not be as easy as it looks!

14	447	983	8373	50179
39	502	992	8741	57010
42	595	1109	9144	57703
51	642	1401 ✓	9917	98061
63	659	2193	14845	177633
86	695	2573	19420	263713
184	697	2793	25794	272648
186	740	2978	26288	326802
288	765	4891	29161	345531
297	782	5577	34965	551328
343	852	6056	42941	713409
391	924	7689	48650	765243

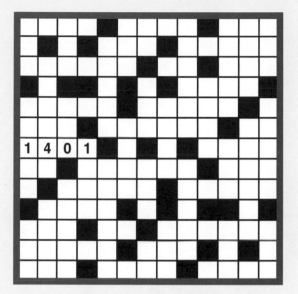

The chart gives directions to a hidden treasure behind the centre black square in the grid. Move the indicated number of spaces north, south, east and west (eg 4N means move four squares north) stopping at every square once only to arrive there. At which square should you start?

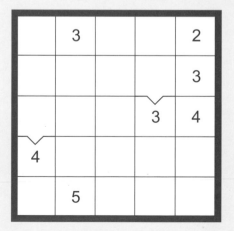

Fill the grid so that every horizontal row and vertical column contains the numbers 1-5. The 'greater than' or 'less than' signs indicate where a number is larger or smaller than that in the neighbouring square.

Each of the eight segments of the spider's web should be filled with a different number from 1 to 8, in such a way that every ring also contains a different number from 1 to 8.

The segments run from the outside of the spider's web to the centre, and the rings run all the way around.

Some numbers are already in place. Can you fill in the rest?

No 1

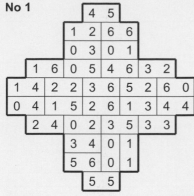

```
        4 5
      1 2 6 6
      0 3 0 1
  1 6 0 5 4 6 3 2
1 4 2 2 3 6 5 2 6 0
0 4 1 5 2 6 1 3 4 4
  2 4 0 2 3 5 3 3
      3 4 0 1
      5 6 0 1
        5 5
```

No 2

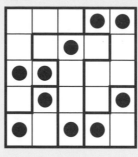

No 3

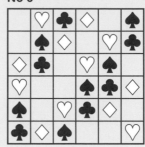

No 4

							115
3	29	6	30	4	17	10	99
18	21	19	9	29	14	15	125
28	27	4	8	9	18	7	101
25	20	16	9	22	10	15	117
1	17	28	14	2	3	22	87
4	21	18	30	13	7	17	110
24	8	30	10	16	11	2	101
103	143	121	110	95	80	88	48

No 5

The minute hand moves forward by 11 minutes and the hour hand moves back by 3 hours each time.

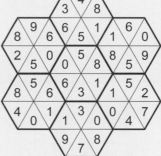

No 6

No 7

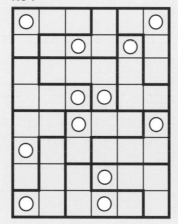

No 8

No 9

4	3	2	5	6	1
6	2	1	4	5	3
2	5	3	6	1	4
3	1	5	2	4	6
5	4	6	1	3	2
1	6	4	3	2	5

No 10

A	C	C	A	B	B
B	A	B	C	C	A
A	B	C	B	C	A
B	C	A	B	A	C
C	A	A	C	B	B
C	B	B	A	A	C

No 11

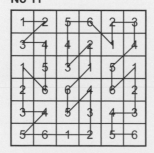

```
1 2 5 6 2 3
3 4 4 2 1 4
1 5 3 1 5 1
2 6 6 4 6 2
3 4 5 3 4 3
5 6 1 2 5 6
```

No 12

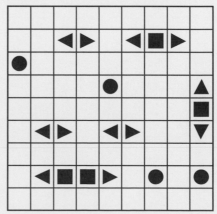

257

No 13

2888

No 14

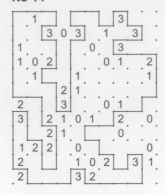

No 15

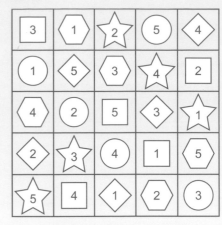

No 16

The sum total of the values of the letter in the top right and central squares is equal to the sum total of the values of the letters in the other squares. Thus the missing value is 1, so the missing letter is A.

No 17

4	5	1	3	6	1	1
6	4	2	3	6	4	3

0	2	0	4	3	6	3
1	5	0	4	5	1	0

5	5	1	0	0	5	6
5	0	1	2	6	6	3

2	4	4	2	3	3	1
6	0	2	2	2	4	5

No 18

2	4	4	4	4	2
3	1	1	3	3	3
3	1	1	3	3	3
2	2	2	1	1	1
2	2	2	1	1	1
2	4	4	4	4	3

No 19

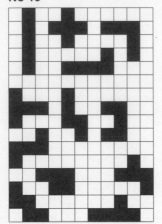

No 20

A – Assign a number to each letter according to its place in the alphabet, so E=5, F=6, M=13, W=23 and C=3, making a total of 50. The total in the centre is 51, so the missing letter is A (=1).

No 21

14	**21**	10	23	14	14
25	26	18	21	**2**	4
22	9	**6**	28	21	10
12	9	30	4	17	24
9	8	6	11	32	**30**
14	23	26	**9**	10	14

No 22

A=143, B=54, C=63, D=73, E=106, F=197, G=117, H=136, I=179, J=314, K=253, L=315, M=567, N=568, O=1135.

No 23

2	7	5	6		2	4	6		7	6	8	8
4		1	8		7		1	0	7	9		8
8	9	7		4	8	9	4		8	6	3	5
	5	4	6	6	7		7	5	3	3	4	0
9	2		4		1	4	9	6			5	
4	3	3	7	9	0		3	7	6	3	6	1
9		2	2	6				9	1	9		8
1	1	5	2	3	5		2	6	7	8	4	3
	0			6	5	0	5		0		9	0
2	0	4	8	9	1		2	6	4	3	8	
8	3	6	7		1	1	3	0		7	8	5
3		3	3	4	6		0		2	3		8
7	7	6	5		8	3	7		5	7	4	3

No 24

1S	1E	2W	2W	1W
1E	1E	1E	1S	**1N**
2E	1S	■	1E	1S
1S	2E	2W	1W	1S
2N	2N	1E	2W	2W

No 25

4	1	3	2	5
1	3	5	4	2
3	2	4	5	1
5	4	2	1	3
2	5	1	3	4

No 26

No 27

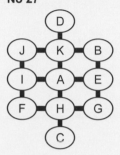

No 28

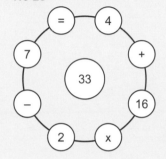

No 30

8	+	5	x	9	=	117
−	■	−	■	x		
1	x	2	+	3	=	5
+	■	x	■	+		
6	+	4	−	7	=	3
=		=		=		
13		12		34		

No 31

17 – The numbers in each vertical column total 98.

No 32

E

No 29

6						6
			7			
	5				1	
7			7		4	
6		9		5		1

No 34

Circle = 2, cross = 9, pentagon = 1, square = 5, star = 6.

No 33

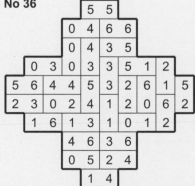

No 35

D	B	F	C	A	E
C	E	B	A	D	F
F	D	C	B	E	A
E	A	D	F	B	C
A	C	E	D	F	B
B	F	A	E	C	D

No 36

			5	5				
		0	4	6	6			
		0	4	3	5			
0	3	0	3	3	5	1	2	
5	6	4	4	5	3	2	6	1	5
2	3	0	2	4	1	2	0	6	2
	1	6	1	3	1	0	1	2	
		4	6	3	6			
		0	5	2	4			
			1	4				

259

No 37

A	B	B	C	C	A
C	B	A	C	B	A
C	A	B	A	B	C
B	C	C	A	A	B
A	C	A	B	C	B
B	A	C	B	A	C

No 40
E (378 x 2 = 756)

No 42

No 38

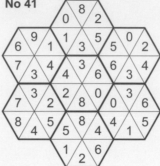

No 41

No 45

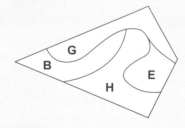

No 39

							101
21	25	7	17	20	16	13	119
30	22	28	15	24	1	8	128
4	12	18	11	25	13	9	92
21	7	15	2	16	27	20	108
12	19	25	3	29	14	26	128
2	18	10	22	9	1	24	86
17	13	19	14	26	23	12	124
107	116	122	84	149	95	112	105

No 43
C – They are all reflections (horizontal or vertical) of one another.

No 44

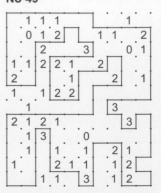

No 46
9591

No 47

2	6	1	5	4	3
3	4	2	6	1	5
4	1	5	2	3	6
6	3	4	1	5	2
5	2	3	4	6	1
1	5	6	3	2	4

No 48

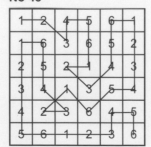

No 49

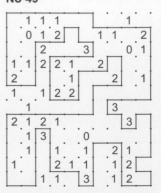

No 50

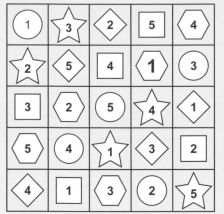

No 51

The sum total of the values of the letters in the top right, central and bottom left squares equals that of the sum total of the value of the letters in the top left and bottom right squares. Thus the missing value is 19, so the missing letter is S.

No 52

F – It has an even number of yellow squares.

No 53

D – The man's eyes look towards his hat if blue, and away from his hat if red.

No 54

4	1	1	1	1	3
2	4	4	4	4	4
2	4	4	4	4	4
2	1	1	4	4	3
2	1	1	4	4	3
3	2	2	3	3	2

No 56

36 – The number in the lowest left box is the cube and the number in the lowest right box is the square of the number in the top box.

No 55

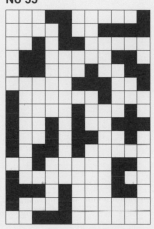

No 57

25	**3**	10	28	43	21
30	21	25	**8**	25	21
27	32	**21**	17	10	23
18	34	25	25	**12**	16
15	27	23	32	11	**22**
15	13	26	20	29	27

No 58

A=50, B=60, C=32, D=94, E=66, F=110, G=92, H=126, I=160, J=202, K=218, L=286, M=420, N=504, O=924.

No 59

6	0	3		3	4	1	7	2		9	6	9
1		5	3	3	2	1		7	3	9	2	
1	3	5		8	8	7		4	0	5	5	7
0		4	4	8		7	6	1	2	9		1
6	7	5	9		5	5	5	0		9	4	5
	0		4	2	9		6	6	6	4	4	4
1	0	8	2		9	4	1		6	9	3	9
9	3	3	3	1	0		5	0	0		7	
9	6	6		9	9	7	2		2	3	3	7
6		2	5	4	8	6		2	5	1		3
4	6	2	2	2		5	8	0		2	6	9
	7	4	0	1		9	3	4	1	3		7
7	8	6		5	7	1	6	4		1	6	3

No 60

2E	2E	1W	1E	2S
1N	1S	1W	1W	1W
1S	2E		2S	1S
1E	2E	1N	1W	2N
2N	1W	1W	1E	2W

No 61

4	1	3	2	5
3	4	2	5	1
2	3	5	**1**	4
1	**5**	4	3	2
5	**2**	1	4	3

No 62

No 63

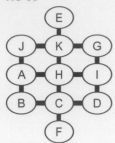

```
        E
   J    K    G
   A    H    I
   B    C    D
        F
```

No 64

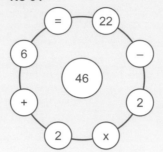

(ring: =, 22, –, 2, x, 2, +, 6; centre: 46)

No 65

1					
		1		8	
2					
			3		4
7		1			
			7		
7		9			9

No 66

7	x	4	–	5	=	23
+	■	+	■	+		
9	–	6	x	2	=	6
–	■	x	■	x		
8	x	3	x	1	=	24
=		=		=		
8		30		7		

No 67

18 – The totals of the numbers in the horizontal rows increases by 10.

No 68

B

No 69

			1	3	●	●	2	1	
1	●	1		●	●	●			●
1			2	1		●	3		●
	1	●	1		2	●	4	4	●
0						●	●		
		●	●		0				1
	●	6	●				0	1	
2	●			●	3		1	2	●
1		4	●		2	●		●	2
	0	2	●	2		●	3		

No 70

D	E	F	C	B	A
B	D	A	F	E	C
A	F	B	D	C	E
C	A	E	B	D	F
F	B	C	E	A	D
E	C	D	A	F	B

No 71

Circle = 7, cross = 3, pentagon = 6,
square = 2, star = 1.

No 72

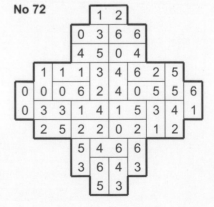

No 73

A	B	B	C	C	A
A	C	A	B	B	C
C	A	B	C	A	B
C	B	A	B	C	A
B	C	C	A	A	B
B	A	C	A	B	C

No 74

No 75

								125
29	14	3	13	7	12	25	103
20	28	2	16	21	15	17	119
4	20	6	11	21	10	26	98
6	17	28	22	14	13	27	127
30	29	4	9	5	15	23	115
19	17	16	24	12	13	20	121
21	13	14	30	25	11	22	136

| 129 | 138 | 73 | 125 | 105 | 89 | 160 | 12 |

No 76

E – It is the total number of degrees of the internal angles.

No 77

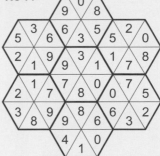

No 78

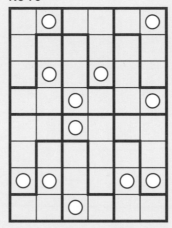

No 79

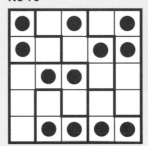

No 80

A – Starting top left, all odd numbers increase by 14 and even numbers by 12 from set to set.

No 81

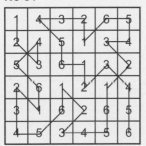

No 82

5	3	2	6	1	4
4	5	1	2	3	6
6	4	5	1	2	3
2	1	6	3	4	5
3	2	4	5	6	1
1	6	3	4	5	2

No 83

7757

No 84

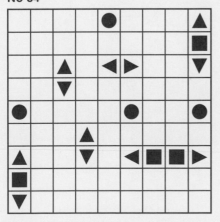

No 85

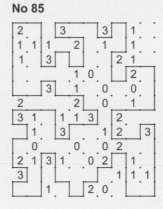

No 86

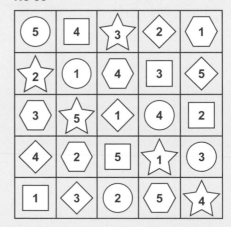

No 87

The sum total of the values of the letters in the outer squares minus the value of the letter in the central square is 50. Thus the missing value is 3, so the missing letter is C.

No 90

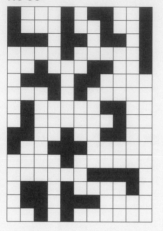

No 88

2	6	5	6	3	0	4
4	3	6	6	3	0	1

1	1	5	1	3	0	5
2	3	1	0	0	2	2

3	4	4	2	2	2	5
4	4	6	2	6	3	5

0	5	5	6	5	1	6
4	0	4	0	3	1	1

No 89

2	3	3	4	4	3
3	1	1	3	3	2
3	1	1	3	3	2
2	1	1	3	3	1
2	1	1	3	3	1
1	4	4	2	2	4

No 91

29 – The numbers in opposite points of the star total the number in the centre.

No 93

A=118, B=73, C=27, D=102, E=91, F=191, G=100, H=129, I=193, J=291, K=229, L=322, M=520, N=551, O=1071.

No 92

25	31	**17**	35	11	25
12	**42**	36	15	34	5
31	20	14	**32**	36	11
12	15	22	26	31	38
39	6	21	26	12	**40**
25	30	34	10	**20**	25

No 94

1	4	7		2	8	8		1	6	1		3
6	0	6		3	5	9	6	6		7	8	9
9	5	8	7	0		7		9	9	6	5	0
3		6		1	0	7	3	1		6	0	
3	3	4	3	0		4	0		8	9	9	2
	8		0		8	9	5	9	0			0
2	8	5	6	1	1		1	6	0	7	4	6
0			8	5	4	1	7		0		7	
2	8	2	0		5	5		9	4	9	0	9
	9	0		9	6	4	0	4		7		8
2	8	8	5	0		8		2	9	0	3	8
5	8	5		2	8	8	3	9		7	8	7
2		1	0	8		5	7	0		6	9	4

No 95

1S	**1W**	1E	1S	2S
2S	1S	1N	2W	1N
2E	1W		2S	1W
1E	1S	2N	1W	2N
2E	1W	2E	1N	1N

No 96

3	5	2	4	1
2	3	1	5	4
5	**4**	3	1	2
1	2	4	3	**5**
4	1	5	2	3

No 97

264

No 1

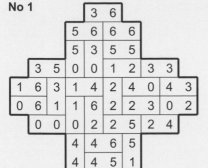

		3	6						
	5	6	6	6					
	5	3	5	5					
3	5	0	0	1	2	3	3		
1	6	3	1	4	2	4	0	4	3
0	6	1	1	6	2	2	3	0	2
	0	0	0	2	2	5	2	4	
		4	4	6	5				
		4	4	5	1				
		1	1						

No 2

No 3

No 4

8	13	17	2	30	28	7	**105**
21	24	18	10	4	9	3	89
17	22	15	27	16	18	13	128
12	23	2	24	19	9	17	106
5	14	25	15	29	30	21	139
16	19	28	2	11	6	15	97
1	12	20	8	16	10	25	92
80	127	125	88	125	110	101	131

Top-right corner value: **101**

No 5

The hour hand alternately gains 3 and 7 hours and the minute hand alternately loses 7 and 3 minutes each time.

No 6

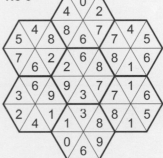

No 7

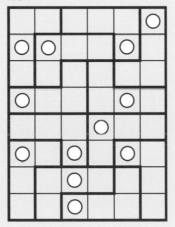

No 8

No 9

6	5	4	2	3	1
5	4	1	3	6	2
2	3	6	1	4	5
1	6	3	5	2	4
4	2	5	6	1	3
3	1	2	4	5	6

No 10

B	C	C	B	A	A
A	A	B	C	B	C
B	C	A	A	C	B
C	A	C	B	A	B
A	B	B	C	C	A
C	B	A	A	B	C

No 11

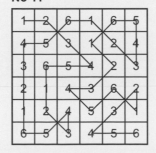

No 12

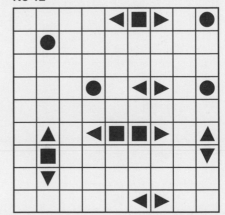

265

No 13
2218

No 16
The sum total of the values of the letters in the outer squares divided by ten equals the value of the letter in the central square. Thus the missing value is 19, so the missing letter is S.

No 19

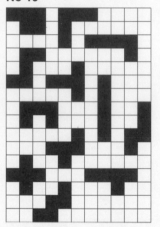

No 14

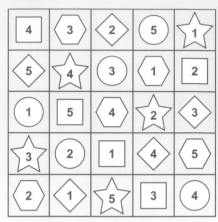

No 15

No 17

4	6	3	1	6	4	6
2	1	3	3	0	1	5

6	3	3	4	5	0	2
6	2	0	0	5	1	2

2	1	3	4	5	4	2
5	5	6	6	0	4	0

1	1	3	3	4	6	0
2	1	4	5	5	2	0

No 18

1	2	2	4	4	3
3	2	2	3	3	3
3	2	2	3	3	3
3	4	4	2	2	1
3	4	4	2	2	1
1	1	1	3	3	4

No 20
C – Each letter in opposite points of the star is opposite in position in the alphabet, so R is 9th from the end and I is 9th from the beginning, T is 7th from the end and G is 7th from the beginning, and X is 3rd from the end and C is 3rd from the beginning.

No 21

53	**11**	14	36	42	21
14	31	34	50	**32**	16
34	36	**29**	29	27	22
33	47	58	3	9	27
33	27	2	33	26	**56**
10	25	40	**26**	41	35

No 22
A=86, B=67, C=75, D=121, E=68, F=153, G=142, H=196, I=189, J=295, K=338, L=385, M=633, N=723, O=1356.

No 23

1	8	9	1	■	2	4	8	5	■	8	9	6
4	■	8	■	6	3	5	■	6	■	3	2	■
9	4	1	5	4	■	6	■	6	2	0	6	6
4	0	■	7	9	3	4	2	1	■	7	3	2
6	3	2	5	■	7	■	4	■	8	9	1	3
■	5	■	1	9	5	0	9	2	■	■	■	7
6	5	6	1	2	■	■	2	9	6	3	0	■
6	■	7	7	1	9	2	6	■	8	■	■	■
2	3	3	7	■	8	■	1	■	3	3	2	7
3	0	8	■	5	9	2	7	4	7	■	6	2
5	0	4	9	1	■	0	■	9	6	5	0	7
■	7	7	■	4	■	7	5	3	■	8	■	5
4	3	2	■	7	7	3	1	■	6	2	3	8

No 24

1E	2S	2W	1W	1W
1S	1E	1W	1W	1S
1S	1E	■	1S	2N
2E	**1S**	2E	2N	2N
2E	1W	2E	2N	1W

No 25

5	4	1	2	3
1	**3**	2	5	4
4	2	5	3	1
3	5	4	1	2
2	1	3	4	5

No 26

No 27

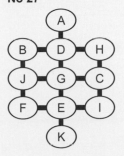

No 28

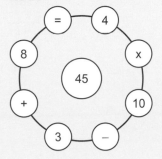

No 30

5	+	7	−	8	=	4
−	■	+	■	+		
1	x	9	+	2	=	11
x	■	−	■	−		
4	x	6	−	3	=	21
=		=		=		
16		10		7		

No 31

46 – The numbers in the vertical
columns decrease by 12, 11, 10, 9, 8,
7 and 6.

No 32

D

No 29

			8		2		
	3						
				9		6	
9		2					
				5		1	
2		8			5		

No 34

Circle = 7, cross = 2, pentagon = 1,
square = 9, star = 4.

No 35

C	E	D	B	F	A
D	A	B	E	C	F
E	B	F	A	D	C
B	C	A	F	E	D
F	D	E	C	A	B
A	F	C	D	B	E

No 33

No 36

No 37

A	A	B	C	B	C
A	B	C	C	A	B
C	C	A	B	B	A
C	A	A	B	C	B
B	C	B	A	C	A
B	B	C	A	A	C

No 38

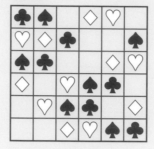

No 39

							117

19	8	10	14	6	20	24	101
25	30	2	26	9	17	7	116
27	3	25	2	12	16	5	90
17	15	27	18	8	7	20	112
13	16	23	1	6	14	28	101
21	19	20	24	5	30	14	133
4	8	22	13	24	9	19	99

126	99	129	98	70	113	117	147

No 40

F – The outer and inner shapes are reversed and the triangle makes a 90 degree turn.

No 41

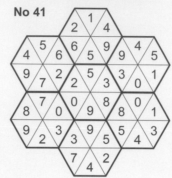

No 42

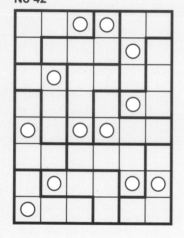

No 43

B – The whole set of nine squares makes a quarter turn clockwise every time.

No 44

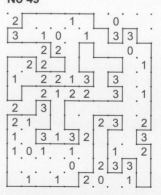

No 45

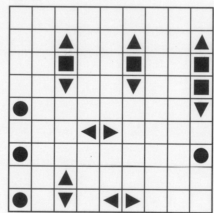

No 46

2229

No 47

6	2	4	3	5	1
4	6	1	2	3	5
5	1	2	6	4	3
3	4	5	1	6	2
1	3	6	5	2	4
2	5	3	4	1	6

No 48

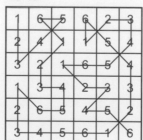

No 49

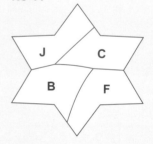

No 50

(5×5 grid of numbered shapes)

4	5	2	1	3
2	1	5	3	4
3	2	4	5	1
1	4	3	2	5
5	3	1	4	2

No 51

Starting clockwise from the top left square, the value of the second letter is added to the first, the third is subtracted and the fourth added, to give the value of the central square. Thus the missing value is 17, so the missing letter is Q.

No 52

2 – 4 is a mirror image of 3 and 5 is a mirror image of 1.

No 53

C – Starting top centre and moving anticlockwise, the colours are those of the rainbow, in order, with the next colour becoming the first in the next shape.

No 54

4	4	4	1	1	2
4	4	4	1	1	3
4	4	4	1	1	3
3	2	2	2	2	4
3	2	2	2	2	4
2	1	1	3	3	3

No 56

24 – Add the number to the left to the number at the top and subtract the number to the right to get the number inside the triangle.

No 58

A=136, B=9, C=7, D=10, E=125, F=145, G=16, H=17, I=135, J=161, K=33, L=152, M=194, N=185, O=379.

No 55

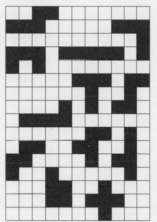

No 57

32	16	**20**	25	38	32
34	**27**	29	15	28	30
40	32	27	**21**	12	31
9	48	28	33	17	28
15	21	32	33	32	**30**
33	19	27	36	**36**	12

No 59

9	4	8	8	1	9	■	5	1	0	2	6	2
■	7	1	■	7	2	4	0	0	■	2	5	■
6	0	3	9	5	■	0	■	1	0	0	6	2
0	■	1	■	5	9	6	8	8	■	9	■	5
3	2	7	■	7	0	0	0	■	1	0	3	1
5	0	3	4	■	1	3	4	3	2	■	4	4
■	3	5	7	8	0	■	6	2	5	7	5	■
2	1	■	7	5	0	4	6	■	9	9	5	3
8	6	5	6	■	2	8	3	3	■	5	9	4
0	■	0	■	3	8	9	5	4	■	0	■	4
4	1	0	6	7	■	1	■	2	4	4	1	7
■	7	3	■	5	7	6	8	7	■	6	4	■
9	6	8	0	9	6	■	3	6	0	0	3	7

No 62

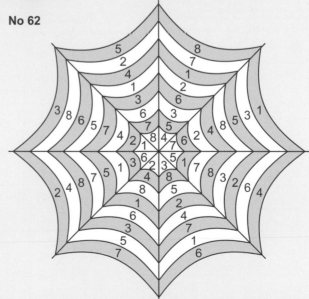

No 60

1S	1S	1W	3W	**1W**
3S	1S	1N	1S	1W
2E	3E	■	3W	1S
1E	1E	1S	3W	2N
1E	3E	3N	1N	1W

No 61

3	**2**	4	1 < 5	
1	4	2	5	3
4	1	5 > 3	2	
2	**5**	3 < 4	1	
5	3	1	**2**	4

No 63

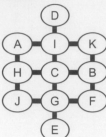

No 64

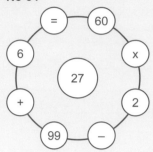

No 65

2			4			
					4	
	9		2			
9		3				9
				8		
8		9				8

No 66

4	x	1	x	3	=	12
x		+		−		
7	−	6	x	2	=	2
+		+		+		
9	−	5	x	8	=	32
=		=		=		
37		12		9		

No 67

66 – The numbers in each horizontal row decrease by 7, 5, 3, 8, 6, 4 and 2.

No 68

C

No 69

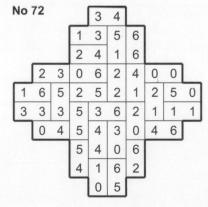

No 70

E	C	D	B	F	A
A	E	F	C	B	D
F	A	E	D	C	B
C	B	A	E	D	F
D	F	B	A	E	C
B	D	C	F	A	E

No 71

Circle = 4, cross = 9, pentagon = 2, square = 7, star = 80.

No 72

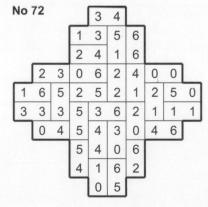

No 73

B	C	C	A	B	A
A	A	B	C	C	B
B	A	C	B	A	C
A	C	A	B	C	B
C	B	B	C	A	A
C	B	A	A	B	C

No 74

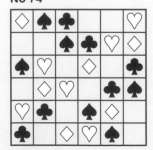

No 75

14	18	23	3	21	2	17	98
5	9	22	11	15	12	28	102
20	7	29	12	18	30	24	140
13	14	16	5	4	21	19	92
7	15	25	6	16	11	25	105
18	17	23	26	20	12	5	121
1	30	6	14	21	28	3	103

95

78	110	144	77	115	116	121	88

No 76

D – In A and B, the sequence of the number of sides is 8-6-4/6-5-4 and in C and D the sequence is 4-5-6/4-6-8.

No 77

No 78

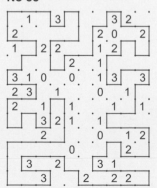

No 79

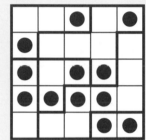

No 80

D – The outer letters swap with their horizontal, vertical and diagonal opposites, then move clockwise one place around the central Y.

No 81

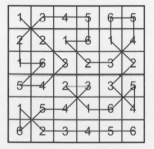

No 82

1	3	2	6	5	4
4	6	5	3	1	2
3	1	4	2	6	5
5	2	3	1	4	6
2	4	6	5	3	1
6	5	1	4	2	3

No 83

6881

No 84

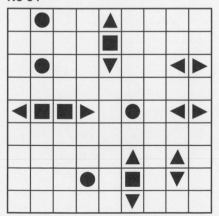

No 85

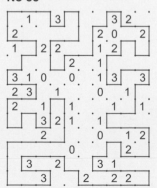

No 86

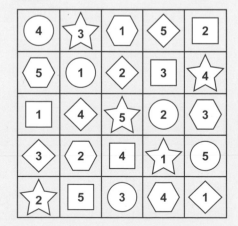

No 87

The sum total of the values of the letters in the top left and central squares is the value in the bottom right square. The value in the top right minus that in the middle square is the value in the bottom left square. Thus the missing value is 8, so the missing letter is H.

No 90

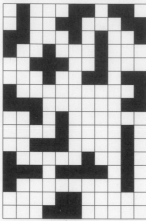

No 88

5	1	3	6	4	6	4
4	1	0	5	4	3	1

1	5	1	0	6	1	2
6	3	5	0	2	2	2

1	5	0	6	6	6	2
3	5	5	0	4	6	4

0	0	0	3	2	2	3
4	2	1	3	3	5	4

No 93

A=39, B=9, C=12, D=60, E=35, F=48, G=21, H=72, I=95, J=69, K=93, L=167, M=162, N=260, O=422.

No 89

2	3	3	1	1	4
2	2	2	1	1	4
2	2	2	1	1	4
3	1	1	2	2	3
3	1	1	2	2	3
2	3	3	4	4	2

No 91

9 – Each single digit number divides nine times into the number in the opposite point of the star.

No 92

44	18	30	26	52	**44**
60	35	18	25	39	37
21	**59**	35	51	25	23
57	43	39	**19**	17	39
18	27	**50**	51	39	29
14	32	42	42	**42**	42

No 94

4	8	2	1		6	4	8	7		3	2	8
9		5	8	3	9	1		7	1	4	1	4
7	4	4	8	0	3		4	9	1	9	4	9
	1	0		9		1		5	9	0	2	3
2	9	3	8	1		2	6	9	7	5		9
6	7		3	8	5	8	9	2		4		
7	8	9	5		9	4	2		3	0	1	2
	8		3	0	9	7	4	4		7	3	
5		1	4	0	6	0		6	9	9	7	2
7	2	9	8	2		9		1		2	2	
1	0	1	9	0	4		3	9	5	8	3	5
6	8	0	6	1		3	8	7	0	5		3
6	6	9		6	9	3	0		1	9	9	9

No 95

2E	1S	1W	2S	1W
3E	3E	3S	1W	3S
2N	1S		2S	2N
2N	1E	2E	3W	1W
2N	2N	2N	2W	2N

No 96

4	**2**	3	**5**	1
3	4	2	1	5
2	1	5	4	3
5	3	1	**2**	4
1	5	**4**	3	**2**

No 97

No 1

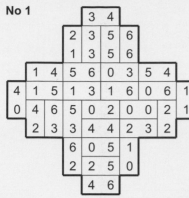

No 2

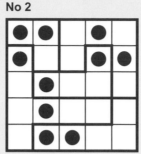

No 3

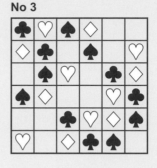

No 4

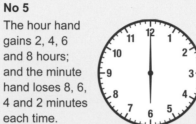

16	17	23	4	9	11	20	100
10	14	15	7	16	24	13	99
18	5	28	30	1	19	26	127
6	12	14	22	20	13	21	108
2	15	27	17	8	18	28	115
25	16	12	20	24	5	4	106
10	14	26	4	18	19	13	104

87	93	145	104	96	109	125	106

120

No 5

The hour hand gains 2, 4, 6 and 8 hours; and the minute hand loses 8, 6, 4 and 2 minutes each time.

No 6

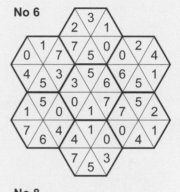

No 7

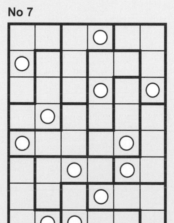

No 8

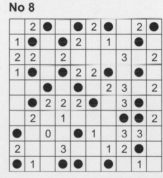

No 9

1	6	2	5	3	4
2	3	5	6	4	1
6	4	1	3	5	2
4	2	3	1	6	5
3	5	4	2	1	6
5	1	6	4	2	3

No 10

B	A	C	A	B	C
A	C	B	C	A	B
A	C	B	C	A	B
C	B	A	A	B	C
C	B	A	B	C	A
B	A	C	B	C	A

No 11

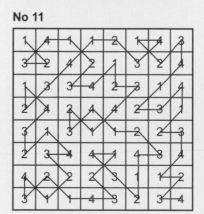

No 12

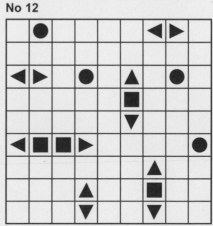

273

No 13

7771

No 16

The value of the letter in the central square is the difference between the sum total of the values of the letters in the top left and bottom right squares and the sum total of the values of the letters in the top right and bottom left squares. Thus the missing value is 16, so the missing letter is P.

No 14

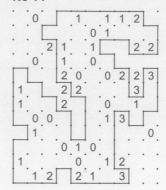

No 15

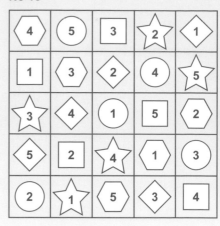

No 17

2	3	5	0	4	2	3
6	5	5	6	4	0	6

3	2	4	6	5	1	4
3	2	0	1	4	4	2

2	4	0	6	3	3	6
5	6	0	5	0	4	6

2	1	1	2	5	1	5
1	0	3	3	1	1	0

No 18

1	3	3	2	2	1
4	1	1	3	3	3
4	1	1	3	3	3
2	2	2	4	4	4
2	2	2	4	4	4
4	3	3	1	1	1

No 19

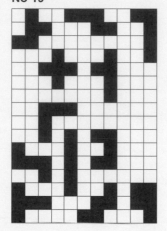

No 20

39 – Working clockwise from the top, the figures represent the running total of numbers in preceding two points of the star, ending with the number in the centre.

No 21

37	52	**10**	77	51	37
69	66	39	28	20	42
54	20	38	**56**	61	35
35	19	84	12	46	**68**
32	30	57	26	**74**	45
37	**77**	36	65	12	37

No 22

A=138, B=90, C=86, D=84, E=8, F=228, G=176, H=170, I=92, J=404, K=346, L=262, M=750, N=608, O=1358.

No 23

7	9	1		4	4	9	6		1	0	7	6
0		6	7	6	6		5	1	4		3	0
5	2	6	0		0		1		6	2	3	8
1	5		5	7	8	3	2	9	6		4	
	4	4	3	4	8		8	5	5	6	0	2
9	4	6	0		8	7	6	5		2	8	0
7		4	8	4			5	4	2		6
4	3	3		3	8	4	1		5	3	1	6
2	9	7	9	0	5		5	8	1	4	8
	0		9	9	3	2	1	0	9		2	4
3	9	4	9		1		0		1	8	7	9
6	2		9	2	5		8	5	5	7		4
7	0	0	7		7	0	9	0		9	8	4

No 24

2E	2S	2E	3S	1W
1N	1E	2E	2W	3S
3E	3E	■	1N	2W
1N	3N	1W	1E	2W
3N	2E	1W	3W	2W

No 25

2	3	**1**	4	**5**
4	2	5	**3**	1
3	**1**	**4**	5	2
5	4	>2	1	3
1	**5**	3	2	4

No 26

No 27

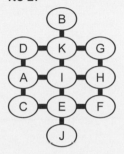

No 28

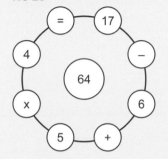

No 29

9				9	
		4			1
6				6	
		4			6
			7		
	2				7
			8		

No 30

4	x	7	–	9	=	19
–	■	x	■	+		
1	x	6	x	3	=	18
x	■	+	■	–		
5	+	8	x	2	=	26
=		=		=		
15		50		10		

No 31

4 – The numbers in each horizontal row total 42, 44, 46, 48, 50, 52 and 54.

No 32

E

No 33

1	2	●	2	2	●	●	2	1	1
●	2		●		4	●		3	●
	1		3	●				●	●
			●						2
●	3	●			1		●	2	
	●	2		0		●	3	●	
2		1				3			●
●		1			●	●	1	2	2
2	●			1				2	●
	1				●	2	●		

No 34

Circle = 6, cross = 9, pentagon = 4, square = 7, star = 5.

No 35

C	E	D	F	B	A
E	B	A	D	F	C
D	A	F	B	C	E
A	F	B	C	E	D
B	D	C	E	A	F
F	C	E	A	D	B

No 36

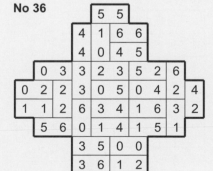

SOLUTIONS

No 37

C	A	A	B	C	B
B	A	C	C	B	A
C	B	B	A	A	C
B	C	C	A	A	B
A	C	B	C	B	A
A	B	A	B	C	C

No 38

No 39

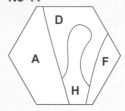

118

19	28	5	2	15	18	20	107
6	29	1	27	24	11	19	117
16	21	23	3	1	30	12	106
25	30	6	15	4	14	23	117
27	2	22	26	8	19	3	107
9	28	7	5	12	27	13	101
21	6	14	25	17	23	10	116

123	144	78	103	81	142	100	131

No 40

F – The pattern is reflected and turned 90 degrees.

No 41

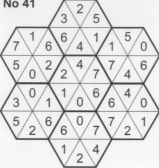

No 42

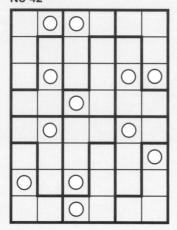

No 43

C – The centre number indicates the position of the letter to the left from the start of the alphabet and the letter to the right from the end of the alphabet.

No 44

D A F H (in hexagon)

No 45

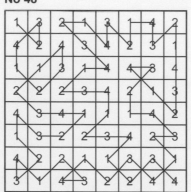

No 46

4818

No 47

4	3	2	6	1	5
2	4	6	5	3	1
5	6	3	1	2	4
3	5	1	2	4	6
1	2	5	4	6	3
6	1	4	3	5	2

No 48

No 49

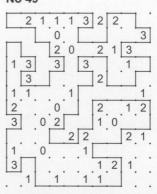

276

No 50

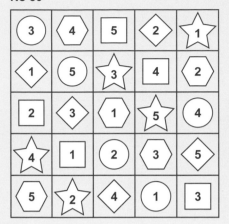

No 51

The value of the letter in the bottom right square is the sum total of the values in the top squares minus that of the values in the bottom left and centre. Thus the missing value is 5, so the missing letter is E.

No 52

4 – The others contains shapes with differing numbers of sides.

No 53

B – In each new set of four, the number of points increases by one and the shapes with the same depth of inset move one place clockwise.

No 54

4	4	4	3	3	2
1	1	1	3	3	4
1	1	1	3	3	4
3	2	2	2	2	1
3	2	2	2	2	1
3	1	1	4	4	1

No 56

19 – The top right number, minus its diagonal opposite gives the same total as the top left figure minus its diagonal opposite.

No 55

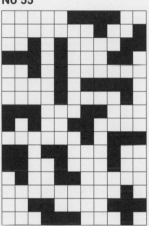

No 57

38	5	33	31	68	48
47	37	29	30	38	42
43	56	37	33	27	27
37	58	38	41	8	41
35	43	53	37	30	25
23	24	33	51	52	40

No 58

A=47, B=18, C=12, D=139, E=73, F=65, G=30, H=151, I=212, J=95, K=181, L=363, M=276, N=544, O=820.

No 59

1		9	3	6		3	8	9	5	9	4	9
5	2	3	7	0	5	5		1	2	6	8	0
5	1	4	3	2		7	1	5	0	8	5	0
0		9		2	7	6		6	0			6
6	6	9	9		3		8	8		7	3	9
	0		5	7	9	3		5	1	2	0	3
7	6	3	7	5	8		2	5	2	0	6	0
2	2	4	0	9		1	0	5	0		3	
2	8	6		3	8		0		3	3	7	4
7		7	8		4	9	0	4		4		7
1	8	4	6	6	2	2		2	5	8	8	3
6	6	0	4	7		8	8	0	2	4	2	3
7	5	9	4	4	9	9		4	0	8		2

No 62

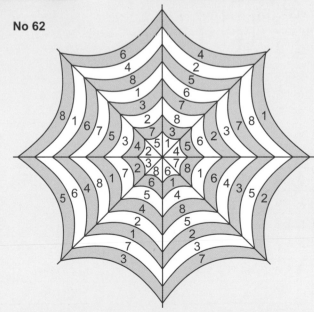

No 60

2E	1W	2E	3S	1S
3S	1W	2S	1N	1W
1E	2E		1W	2S
1E	3N	2W	1S	1N
2N	3N	3N	2W	2W

No 61

1	4	3	2	5
5	2	1	3	4
3	5	4	1	2
2	1	5	4	3
4	3	2	5	1

No 63

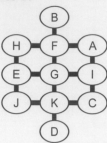

No 64

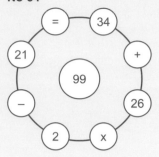

No 65

3		9		1			
							9
			7				
	1						2
					9		
5							9
		2		6			

No 66

5	+	3	+	1	=	9
+	■	–		+		
4	+	2	x	7	=	42
x	■	x	■	+		
8	x	6	+	9	=	57
=		=		=		
72		6		17		

No 67

22 – Reading down each column, the sequence of numbers is the first number minus 1 equals the second number plus 2 equals the third number minus 3 equals the fourth number plus 4 equals the fifth number minus 5 equals the sixth number plus 6 equals the seventh number.

No 68

B

No 69

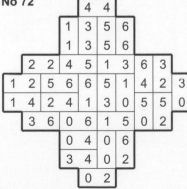

No 70

F	D	C	E	B	A
A	C	E	F	D	B
E	A	B	D	C	F
B	E	A	C	F	D
D	B	F	A	E	C
C	F	D	B	A	E

No 71

Circle = 6, cross = 2, pentagon = 9, square = 7, star = 4.

No 72

			4	4				
	1	3	5	6				
	1	3	5	6				
2	2	4	5	1	3	6	3	
1	2	5	6	6	5	1	4	2	3
1	4	2	4	1	3	0	5	5	0
3	6	0	6	1	5	0	2	
		0	4	0	6			
		3	4	0	2			
			0	2				

No 73

B	A	C	A	B	C
A	C	A	C	B	B
B	B	A	A	C	C
C	C	B	B	A	A
A	A	C	B	C	B
C	B	B	C	A	A

No 74

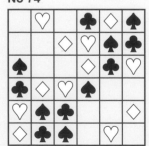

No 75

21	17	1	18	25	5	8	**95**
6	15	19	24	20	12	7	**103**
25	10	30	19	2	24	9	**119**
2	23	12	16	7	16	27	**103**
30	15	19	28	25	1	4	**122**
17	13	6	24	14	8	12	**94**
3	27	11	2	13	26	5	**87**

104	**120**	**98**	**131**	**106**	**92**	**72**	**120**

No 76

D – The shape is repeated, then both are turned and combined into one shape.

No 78

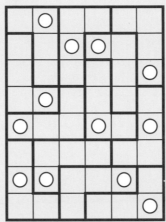

No 77

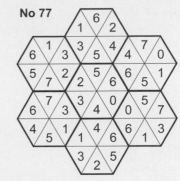

No 79

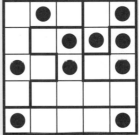

No 80

A – From left to right, the sum of the numbers in the vertical columns is 30, 31 and 32.

No 81

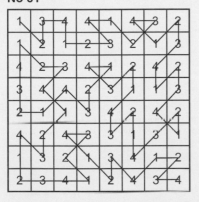

No 82

4	5	1	6	2	3
1	2	3	5	6	4
2	6	5	3	4	1
3	1	4	2	5	6
6	3	2	4	1	5
5	4	6	1	3	2

No 83

3211

No 84

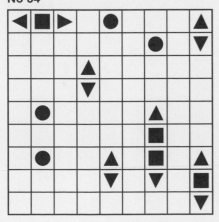

No 85

(grid puzzle solution)

No 86

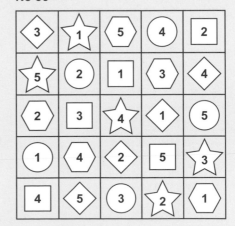

No 87

The value of the letter in the central square is the value of the letter in each top square minus the value of the letter in the bottom square diagonal opposite. Thus the missing value is 14, so the missing letter is N.

No 90

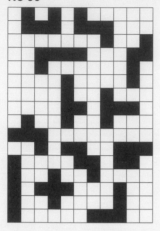

No 88

6	5	0	3	5	4	5
6	4	0	3	3	3	1

0	4	3	0	2	5	5
6	4	2	1	6	6	0

0	2	2	1	1	1	4
3	0	1	6	1	4	6

6	2	2	1	5	4	4
3	5	2	3	5	2	0

No 93

A=78, B=85, C=145, D=144, E=138, F=163, G=230, H=289, I=282, J=393, K=519, L=571, M=912, N=1090, O=2002.

No 89

2	4	4	1	1	1
1	3	3	3	3	1
1	3	3	3	3	1
4	1	1	3	3	2
4	1	1	3	3	2
4	3	3	2	2	1

No 91

91 – Working clockwise from the top, 127–49=78+23=101–10=91.

No 92

37	13	22	44	84	**39**
46	39	42	**24**	44	44
52	77	39	7	18	46
18	**50**	44	71	16	40
22	41	47	48	**32**	49
64	19	**45**	45	45	21

No 94

4	9	6	3	8	■	5	0	1	■	4	7	7
■	4	3	■	8	1	3	■	6	5	1	0	1
8	9	6	3	0	■	3	■	6	1	6	3	2
■	7	■	6	1	2	3	0	■	7	■	8	
2	6	9	7	3	■	2	8	■	4	6	5	8
2	■	6	7	■	5	2	1	9	9	■	3	
1	4	3	0	9	8	■	2	0	0	9	4	4
■	5	■	5	2	8	9	4	■	5	4	■	9
7	6	5	2	■	3	8	■	7	7	1	4	7
9	■	6	■	5	4	1	0	8	■	1		
3	3	5	6	2	■	4	■	9	7	5	0	5
8	6	0	6	6	■	1	9	2	■	1	7	
9	7	7	■	8	3	9	■	8	7	6	3	9

No 95

3S	2E	3S	3W	2W
1S	1S	1W	3W	2W
3E	2N	■	1E	2N
1S	2E	1N	1S	2N
1E	1N	**2E**	3N	1N

No 96

4	5	1	3	**2**
2<	3	**5**	4	1
5	**2**	4	1<	3
3	1	**2**	5	**4**
1<	**4**	3	2	5

No 97

No 1

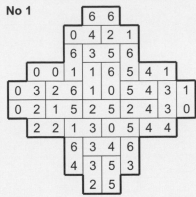

```
        6 6
      0 4 2 1
      6 3 5 6
  0 0 1 1 6 5 4 1
0 3 2 6 1 0 5 4 3 1 0
0 2 1 5 2 5 2 4 3 0
  2 2 1 3 0 5 4 4
      6 3 4 6
      4 3 5 3
        2 5
```

No 2

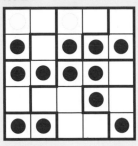

No 3

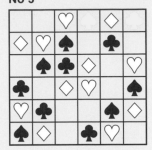

No 4

70							

28	16	2	18	21	24	5	**114**
6	14	17	20	9	1	19	**86**
23	12	2	11	13	15	30	**106**
22	8	27	18	17	12	8	**112**
2	4	7	29	21	25	18	**106**
5	10	26	3	12	14	28	**98**
16	22	21	1	17	18	9	**104**
102	**86**	**102**	**100**	**110**	**109**	**117**	**106**

No 5

Clocks gain 3 hours 33 minutes, 2 hours 33 minutes, 1 hour 33 minutes and finally 33 minutes each time.

No 6

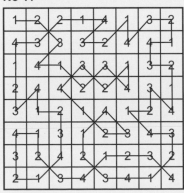

No 7

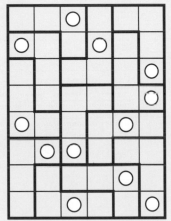

No 8

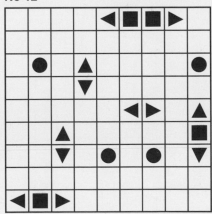

No 9

1	2	4	3	6	5
6	3	5	2	1	4
5	1	3	4	2	6
2	4	6	1	5	3
3	6	1	5	4	2
4	5	2	6	3	1

No 10

B	B	A	C	C	A
B	C	B	A	C	A
C	A	A	B	B	C
C	A	C	B	A	B
A	B	C	C	A	B
A	C	B	A	B	C

No 11

No 12

No 13

8766

No 16

The value of the letter in the central square is the square root of the sum total of the values of the letters in the outer squares. Thus the missing value is 6, so the missing letter is F.

No 19

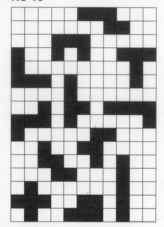

No 14

```
    1   2 2           1
  3 2     2         1
    1 3 2 2 3       3
  1 0     1     1
    1 3 2 1       2
    0 2       2 2     3   2
  1             1   2 1   3
                  0
  2 2 1     3       1 2
        0         1
  3 1           0       2
    1 1 1 1 2 2     3
```

No 15

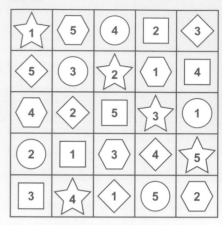

No 17

3	1	5	4	5	5	1
2	1	4	6	2	5	2

3	4	0	6	0	2	3
3	4	1	6	6	0	6

6	6	5	2	0	0	2
1	2	6	4	0	5	2

4	0	5	1	5	4	1
3	3	3	4	1	0	3

No 18

1	1	1	2	2	1
4	3	3	4	4	2
4	3	3	4	4	2
1	1	1	4	4	3
1	1	1	4	4	3
1	2	2	3	3	2

No 20

J – Assign a number to each letter according to its place in the alphabet, so W=23, M=13, L=12, B=2, Q=17 and G=7. Subtract each of the lower value from that in the opposite point of the star, thus 10 each time: J=10.

No 21

56	8	**18**	72	84	24
61	43	36	**25**	47	50
64	55	43	21	27	52
12	67	47	65	**27**	44
17	**71**	54	61	11	48
52	18	64	18	66	**44**

No 22

A=29, B=72, C=69, D=138, E=110, F=101, G=141, H=207, I=248, J=242, K=348, L=455, M=590, N=803, O=1393.

No 23

4	4	3	4	6	■	2	7	4	2	8	■	7
8	■	7	9	3	■	8	■	7	5	4	1	8
8	2	2	■	3	5	6	1	1	■	3	3	3
5	■	1	6	8	7	5	■	5	1	2	2	■
■	8	3	6	■	9	3	6	■	9	3	5	3
9	9	■	1	2	2	■	9	4	2	2	■	2
4	3	3	4	■	4	■	2	■	7	3	8	3
4	■	2	6	4	4	■	2	6	3	■	7	3
8	7	2	1	■	1	6	0	■	2	6	0	■
■	6	4	0	8	■	9	0	1	2	0	■	7
9	7	2	■	8	3	4	3	3	■	6	5	1
1	6	0	4	6	■	5	■	7	3	2	■	1
0	■	9	7	9	5	6	■	7	3	3	6	9

No 24

3S	3E	1E	3W	1S
3S	1W	1N	2S	1W
2E	1N	■	3W	3W
1E	3N	2E	1W	1S
2E	2E	3N	2N	3W

No 25

2	3	1	5	4
5	1	4	3	2
1	2	3	4	5
3	4	5	2	1
4	5	2	1	3

No 26

No 27

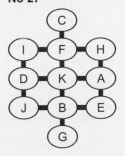

No 28

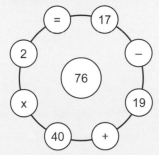

No 29

1		9			
				4	
	6		4		
8		8		1	
1		9		3		5

No 30

9	+	4	+	8	=	21
+		−		x		
3	+	1	x	5	=	20
x		x		−		
6	+	2	+	7	=	15
=		=		=		
72		6		33		

No 31

24 – Reading down each column, take
6 from each preceding number until the
central number, after which add 7 to
each preceding number.

No 32

B

No 33

(grid puzzle)

No 34

Circle = 3, cross = 7, pentagon = 9,
square = 2, star = 4.

No 35

E	D	F	C	B	A
A	C	B	F	E	D
B	F	A	E	D	C
C	B	E	D	A	F
D	A	C	B	F	E
F	E	D	A	C	B

No 36

(crossword-style number grid)

No 37

A	C	B	A	B	C
C	C	B	A	A	B
B	A	C	C	B	A
C	B	A	B	C	A
A	B	C	B	A	C
B	A	A	C	C	B

No 40

D – The letters occupy the same position counting back through the alphabet.

No 42

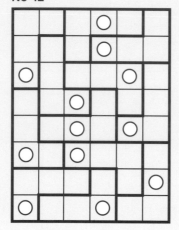

No 38

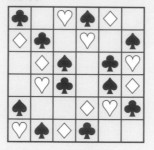

No 41

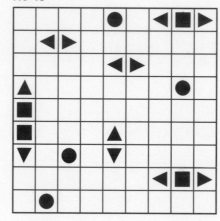

No 45

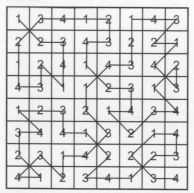

No 39

							135
12	25	5	14	28	4	11	99
13	16	1	10	17	20	27	104
21	7	22	15	30	18	29	142
8	9	6	23	16	28	16	106
17	22	12	14	5	22	13	105
20	15	2	30	4	11	10	92
24	3	8	14	21	17	6	93

115	97	56	120	121	120	112	95

No 43

D – The shapes remain the same throughout, but the colours move three places anticlockwise, except for the central colour, which remains red.

No 44

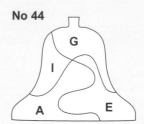

No 46

6861

No 47

1	5	4	6	3	2
2	3	1	5	4	6
5	4	6	2	1	3
4	2	3	1	6	5
6	1	5	3	2	4
3	6	2	4	5	1

No 48

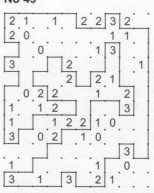

No 49

No 50

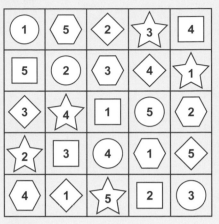

No 51

The value of the central letter is the sum total of the letters in the left squares minus the sum total of the letters in the right squares. Thus the missing value is 18, so the missing letter is R.

No 52

E – In the blue squares, the odd numbers are in red/even numbers in blue; in the pink squares, the odd numbers are in blue/even numbers in red.

No 53

B – Deduct from each digit in turn, every time allocating the total to a letter of the alphabet where A=1, B=2, etc. Thus 15–14=1 and 1=A, 21–14=7 and 7=G, 19–14=5 and 6=E. So 30–14=16 and 16=P.

No 54

2	4	4	2	2	3
2	3	3	4	4	3
2	3	3	4	4	3
3	2	2	1	1	3
3	2	2	1	1	3
1	4	4	2	2	3

No 56

7 – On diametrically opposite petals, the higher number is the square of the lower number.

No 58

A=99, B=30, C=102, D=128, E=25, F=129, G=132, H=230, I=153, J=261, K=362, L=383, M=623, N=745, O=1368.

No 55

No 57

63	2	30	37	**99**	29
75	43	35	18	45	**44**
42	**53**	43	55	24	43
43	72	45	**31**	25	44
20	69	**54**	67	15	35
17	21	53	52	52	65

No 59

1		4	1	5		3	7	3	9		2
6	8	0		6	1	5	6	9		4	5	0
4	8	4	6	8	0		7	9	3	0	3
0		0		2	3	5	7		5		2
6	7	9	4	8		7	9		1	5	9	5
4	2			7	5	3	2	6	1		8	1
	7	4	9	2	9		2	3	2	1	5
2	4		1	1	4	5	6	6		1	3
9	3	3	0		8	9		6	1	2	5	0
7		7		1	3	4	8		4		2
9	6	2	1	6		8	2	1	2	4	4
4	8	0		3	1	4	8	6		3	7	0
0		5	6	8	1		5	2	4		4

No 62

No 60

3S	**1E**	1S	3W	1S
1S	2E	3S	1N	3W
2E	2E		1E	2N
3E	1N	1W	1S	2W
3N	1W	2E	2W	1N

No 61

3	2	1	4	**5**
1	4	5	**3**	2
4	3	2	5	1
2	5	3	1	4
5	1	**4**	2	**3**

No 63

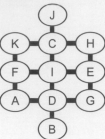

No 64

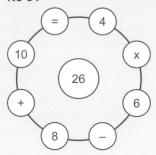

No 65

		4		4		9
5						
		7			1	
9						
			6		1	
	7					
				1		7

No 66

3	x	9	+	2	=	29
x		+		x		
5	x	4	–	1	=	19
+		–		x		
6	x	8	+	7	=	55
=		=		=		
21		5		14		

No 67

6 – Reading along each row, deduct each number from the preceding number.

No 68

A

No 69

1		0	2	●		●	●	●	1
●					●	3		3	3
			2	●				1	●	●
0			2	●	3				
		1			●			0	
			●	3	2		0		
	●		3	2	●			●	2
2	●					●	3	●	5	●
		●				2	●	4	●	●
●	3	●	2					●	3

No 70

E	C	D	B	F	A
C	A	F	D	B	E
B	D	E	F	A	C
F	E	B	A	C	D
D	B	A	C	E	F
A	F	C	E	D	B

No 71

Circle = 2, cross = 3, pentagon = 9, square = 4, star = 5.

No 72

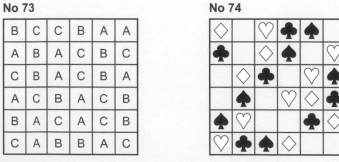

No 73

B	C	C	B	A	A
A	B	A	C	B	C
C	B	A	C	B	A
A	C	B	A	C	B
B	A	C	A	C	B
C	A	B	B	A	C

No 74

♢		♡	♣	♠	
♣		♢	♠		♡
	♢	♣		♡	♠
	♠		♡	♢	♣
♠	♡		♣		♢
♡	♣	♠	♢		

No 75

							103
8	22	27	19	4	5	10	95
11	17	12	26	30	21	1	118
29	15	13	14	16	28	4	119
18	23	16	13	12	24	8	114
25	2	27	21	3	19	20	117
30	14	7	24	10	6	25	116
2	9	13	20	26	1	17	88
123	102	115	137	101	104	85	77

No 76

E – The largest shape doubles in quantity and becomes the inside shape, one of the outer shapes becomes the largest shape, and the inside shape moves outside and doubles in quantity.

No 77

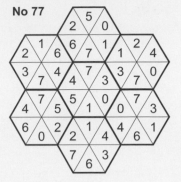

No 78

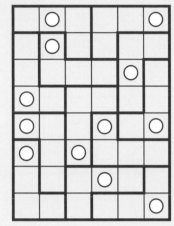

No 79

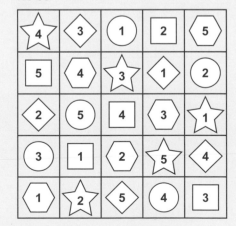

No 80

C – Starting at the top left and working clockwise to the centre, alternately add 15 and subtract nine each time.

No 81

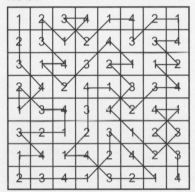

No 82

2	6	1	3	4	5
5	1	4	2	6	3
6	3	2	5	1	4
4	5	3	1	2	6
1	4	5	6	3	2
3	2	6	4	5	1

No 83

5774

No 84

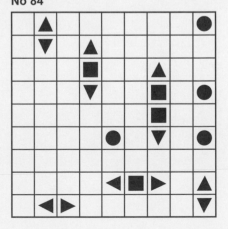

No 85

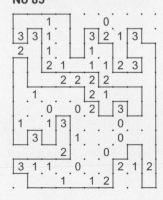

No 86

4	3	1	2	5
5	4	3	1	2
2	5	4	3	1
3	1	2	5	4
1	2	5	4	3

No 87

The value of the letter in the bottom left square is equal to that in the top left multiplied by that in the central square. The value in the bottom right is equal to that in the top right multiplied by that in the central square. Thus the missing value is 18, so the missing letter is R.

No 90

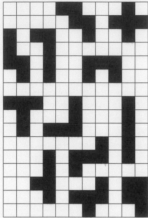

No 88

6	0	1	2	5	2	0
5	2	3	2	3	5	5

2	0	4	2	4	6	6
6	4	1	4	3	0	1

6	0	1	1	4	1	1
6	0	0	1	6	2	5

6	5	3	4	4	2	3
3	5	0	4	5	3	3

No 93

A=90, B=38, C=03, D=41, E=118, F=128, G=41, H=44, I=159, J=169, K=85, L=203, M=254, N=288, O=542.

No 89

2	4	4	4	4	1
4	2	2	3	3	4
4	2	2	3	3	4
3	1	1	2	2	1
3	1	1	2	2	1
2	4	4	2	2	1

No 91

96 – Assign a number to each letter according to its place in the alphabet. Each letter multiplied by that in the opposite point of the star equals 96.

No 92

35	15	26	**52**	58	79
72	44	51	31	**45**	22
79	48	**44**	8	34	52
25	56	45	80	39	20
30	64	46	49	23	**53**
24	**38**	53	45	66	39

No 94

8	3	3	■	4	5	7	3	7	■	5	4	2
5	■	7	6	4	■	2	5	4	5	6	2	1
6	0	7	6	6	■	3	■	6	7	3	2	4
2	■	8	5	9	7	6	5	■	4	6	■	1
8	3	3	0	■	0	■	8	7	2	4	4	1
1	4	2	■	1	7	0	8	9	■	1	6	■
■	6	6	2	7	3	■	5	5	2	2	6	■
3	9	■	2	2	4	7	6	■	3	0	2	■
4	6	3	8	9	6	■	3	■	1	3	6	2
1	■	6	2	■	1	7	3	3	5	3	■	5
8	6	1	0	5	■	5	■	3	0	4	5	5
1	2	2	9	3	4	9	■	1	6	9	■	5
2	1	6	■	6	4	7	2	0	■	8	6	9

No 95

3S	3E	1W	2S	1S
3S	**2E**	1N	3W	2S
2N	1E	■	1E	3W
2E	2E	1S	3N	1S
2N	1N	3N	2W	1W

No 96

1	2	3	4	5
2	**3**	5	1	4
4	**1**	2	5	**3**
5	4	1	3	2
3	5	4	2	1

No 97

No 1

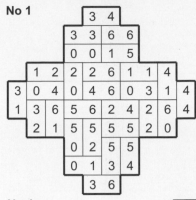

		3	4				
	3	3	6	6			
	0	0	1	5			
1	2	2	2	6	1	1	4
3	0	4	0	4	6	0	3	1	4
1	3	6	5	6	2	4	2	6	4
	2	1	5	5	5	5	2	0
		0	2	5	5			
		0	1	3	4			
		3	6				

No 2

No 3

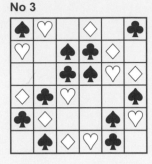

No 4

							128
25	14	4	20	12	19	7	101
15	10	16	23	21	8	9	102
22	13	26	1	17	2	30	111
20	5	14	25	18	6	12	100
21	13	12	22	24	8	19	119
11	29	27	6	7	19	23	122
30	1	28	10	15	17	9	110
144	85	127	107	114	79	109	138

No 5

Clocks gain 2 hours 19 minutes, 2 hours 29 minutes, 2 hours 39 minutes and 2 hours 49 minutes.

No 6

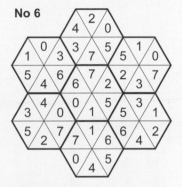

No 7

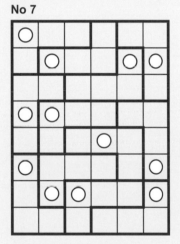

No 8

No 9

1	3	4	2	6	5
5	1	2	3	4	6
2	6	5	1	3	4
6	5	3	4	2	1
3	4	6	5	1	2
4	2	1	6	5	3

No 10

A	B	A	C	C	B
C	B	B	A	C	A
B	A	C	C	A	B
B	C	B	A	A	C
C	A	C	B	B	A
A	C	A	B	B	C

No 11

No 12

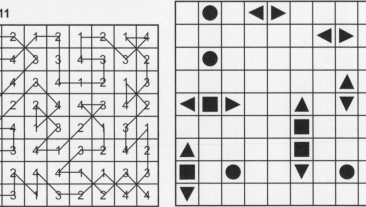

S
O
L
U
T
I
O
N
S

No 13
1777

No 16
The values of the letters in the top squares are multiplied together, as are those in the bottom squares. The value of the letter in the central square is the number of times the product of the lower squares divides into that of the upper squares. Thus the missing value is 6, so the missing letter is F.

No 19

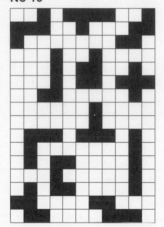

No 14

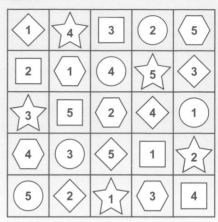

No 15

◇1	☆4	□3	○2	⬡5
□2	⬡1	○4	☆5	◇3
☆3	□5	⬡2	◇4	○1
⬡4	○3	◇5	□1	☆2
○5	◇2	☆1	⬡3	□4

No 17

6	4	3	6	5	2	2
4	0	0	6	0	0	2

6	3	4	1	1	2	0
1	1	2	1	5	5	0

6	4	4	6	6	5	5
3	4	5	0	5	3	5

3	2	3	1	6	1	1
4	3	3	0	2	4	2

No 18

3	2	2	3	3	3
1	4	4	2	2	3
1	4	4	2	2	3
1	2	2	2	2	4
1	2	2	2	2	4
3	1	1	4	4	3

No 20
88 – In opposite points of the star, the lower number is multiplied by the central number and the result is divided by two to equal the higher number, so 11x16 divided by two = 88.

No 21

30	12	21	**55**	67	32
51	36	**45**	11	37	37
40	50	36	32	24	**35**
35	**46**	37	40	25	34
24	42	42	47	**29**	33
37	31	36	32	35	46

No 22
A=84, B=58, C=31, D=97, E=136, F=142, G=89, H=128, I=233, J=231, K=217, L=361, M=448, N=578, O=1026.

No 23

2	5	6	5	■	1	9	4	■	3	6	8	4
2	3	8	8	6	7	■	7	4	5	7	9	9
3	3	5	■	3	5	9	9	■	7	■	1	3
8	6	2	2	1	2	■	3	3	5	6	5	■
■	2	■	1	■	1	6	5	7	■	7	7	7
7	1	2	7	3	3	■	9	4	3	7	3	4
6	■	3	7	1	■	■	■	4	4	9	■	9
8	1	1	4	4	4	■	5	0	0	0	2	4
4	1	1	■	5	7	6	3	■	6	■	2	■
■	8	2	8	4	4	■	7	5	7	8	8	4
5	6	■	5	■	2	3	5	9	■	7	7	3
6	3	4	2	7	3	■	2	9	3	7	2	4
9	6	7	2	■	9	2	6	■	9	7	9	0

No 24

1E	3E	1E	4S	3S
2S	1S	3S	1W	4W
2S	2E	■	1N	1N
2E	2N	1N	2W	1W
4N	3E	4N	2W	2N

No 25

5	3	2 >	1	4
3	1	4	2	5
2 <	**4**	1	5 >	3
1	5	3	4 >	2
4	2	**5**	3	1

No 26

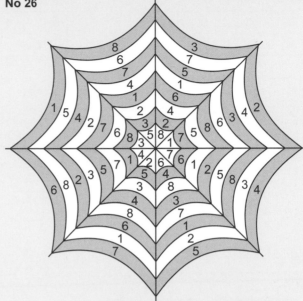

No 27

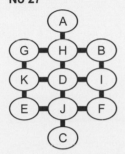

No 28

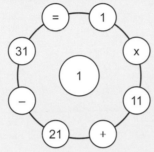

No 29

9								1
			5					
1							7	
		1		4				
1								9
			9					
2						9		

No 30

9	x	7	x	2	=	126
x	■	−	■	+		
8	−	3	x	4	=	20
−	■	x	■	x		
1	x	5	x	6	=	30
=		=		=		
71		20		36		

No 31

339 – From the top left corner, follow a clockwise path around and spiral towards the centre, adding 7 to each number every time.

No 32

E

No 33

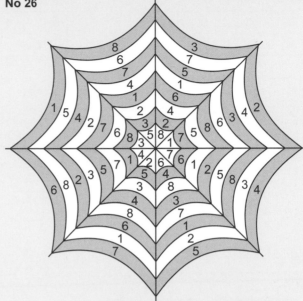

No 34

Circle = 2, cross = 1, pentagon = 8, square = 7, star = 6.

No 35

E	D	B	F	C	A
C	A	F	E	D	B
D	E	A	B	F	C
F	B	E	C	A	D
A	F	C	D	B	E
B	C	D	A	E	F

No 36

A number grid puzzle solution.

No 37

B	A	C	C	B	A
A	C	C	B	B	A
B	A	A	C	C	B
A	C	A	B	C	B
C	B	B	A	A	C
C	B	B	A	A	C

No 38

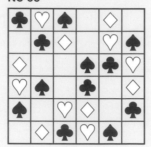

No 39

							69

21	13	12	22	24	6	11	109
5	30	3	17	20	8	14	97
29	15	26	16	13	20	2	121
19	24	12	1	3	27	7	93
7	6	21	18	15	6	19	92
20	10	13	16	9	4	11	83
5	9	16	23	19	18	12	102

106	107	103	113	103	89	76	109

No 40

F – Each letter requires one fewer stroke of the pen than the one above it, ie 4, 3 and 2.

No 41

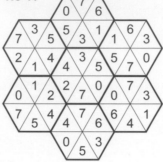

No 42

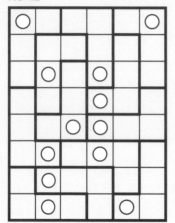

No 43

A – Assign a number to each letter according to its position in the alphabet. These values are divisible by four in the top row, two in the middle row and three in the bottom row.

No 44

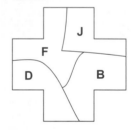

No 45

(grid with symbols)

No 46

7455

No 47

2	6	5	4	3	1
6	3	1	5	2	4
3	2	4	6	1	5
4	1	6	2	5	3
5	4	3	1	6	2
1	5	2	3	4	6

No 48

(grid puzzle solution)

No 49

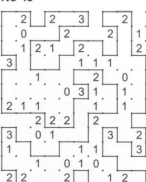

No 50

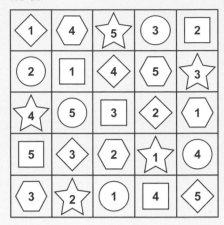

No 51

The value of the letter in the central square is equal to the difference between the sum total of the values in the top squares and the sum total of the values in the bottom squares. Thus the missing value is 17, so the missing letter is Q.

No 52

1 – The brown and pink bands have reversed places in the sequence of colours.

No 53

6 – The sum of the five balls in each side of the triangle is the same as the sum of the three central balls.

No 54

2	3	3	4	4	2
4	3	3	1	1	2
4	3	3	1	1	2
4	2	2	3	3	4
4	2	2	3	3	4
1	1	1	4	4	1

No 56

1334 – Working clockwise from the top, double each number, then add 10.

No 58

A=25, B=114, C=43, D=45, E=127, F=139, G=157, H=88, I=172, J=296, K=245, L=260, M=541, N=505, O=1046.

No 55

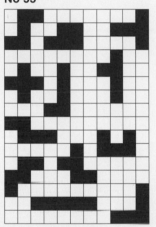

No 57

42	15	18	27	**36**	28
33	27	35	16	31	**24**
19	**46**	27	35	17	22
36	38	31	**19**	11	31
22	27	**20**	41	23	33
14	13	35	28	48	28

No 59

2	0	2	5	4	5		3	5	1	6	4	8
0		3		2	9	1		2	2	1	4	9
4	0	1	7		6	4	0	5	9	1		2
8		4	6	9	1	7		1		1	8	1
7	1	2	8			3	9	2	7		8	8
6	3		1	5	9	3	1		3	7	7	0
	4	3	9	8	7		1	5	1	2	6	
8	4	0	1		2	6	2	5	8		3	1
9	3		8	4	9	8			7	3	9	0
1	8	5		6		3	6	5	2	7		4
8		8	9	3	6	0	1		4	2	2	4
3	4	8	6	3		2	2	3		2		2
8	0	6	7	4	2		3	9	4	0	0	0

No 62

No 60

4E	1S	1E	2S	1S
1N	2E	3S	3W	2W
2E	2S		1E	3W
1S	2E	**3N**	3W	3W
2N	4N	1E	1E	1N

No 61

1	5	**4**	3	2
2	**3**	1	4	5
4	1	2	**5**	3
5	**2**	3	1	4
3	4	5	2	1

No 63

No 64

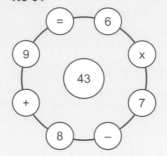

No 65

	9					
			8		4	
3						
		8				3
6				2		
4		1		8		5

No 66

8	x	6	x	1	=	48
x	■	–	■	+		
5	–	4	+	7	=	8
x	■	x	■	x		
9	–	3	–	2	=	4
=		=		=		
360		6		16		

No 67

11 – Reading across each row, multiply the first number by 3, then deduct 4, then multiply by 2, then deduct 3, then multiply by 2, then deduct 2.

No 68

A

No 69

1	●	1				0		●	●
				0					3
3	●		1			0		●	
●	●	3		●			0		●
	4	●	5		2	0			2
3	●	●	●		1			3	●
	●		4				2	●	●
3	●	2	1	●				●	●
●	3		2			1		3	●
		●		0			●	2	

No 70

E	F	B	C	A	D
A	B	D	E	F	C
D	E	C	F	B	A
C	A	E	B	D	F
B	D	F	A	C	E
F	C	A	D	E	B

No 71

Circle = 8, cross = 4, pentagon = 3, square = 2, star = 7.

No 72

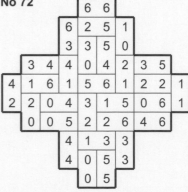

No 73

A	B	C	B	C	A
B	C	A	C	B	A
B	A	A	C	C	B
A	C	B	B	A	C
C	A	C	A	B	B
C	B	B	A	A	C

No 74

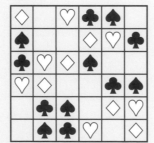

No 75

							84
13	11	9	7	22	21	18	101
17	4	27	29	19	3	9	108
15	24	16	22	28	1	10	116
20	13	21	14	18	7	26	119
2	11	12	25	16	23	5	94
27	6	19	14	9	10	30	115
3	22	16	15	12	4	26	98
97	91	120	126	124	69	124	99

No 76

D – The green and blue shapes change places, as do the mauve and yellow shapes, and the pink and orange shapes.

No 77

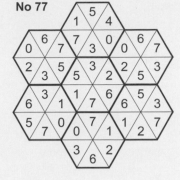

No 78

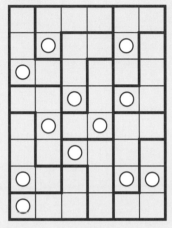

No 79

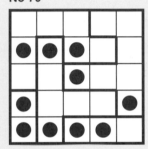

No 80

3 – Assign a number to each letter according to its position in the alphabet: B+Y(2+25)=27–X(24)=3.

No 81

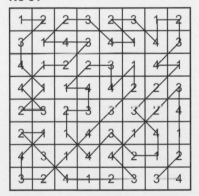

No 82

6	5	4	2	3	1
1	3	2	5	6	4
4	2	3	1	5	6
2	6	5	4	1	3
5	1	6	3	4	2
3	4	1	6	2	5

No 83

2827

No 84

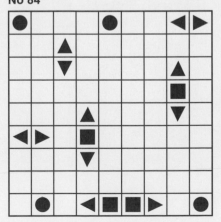

No 85

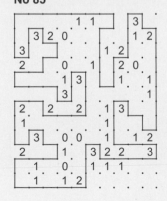

No 86

5	4	1	2	3
3	5	2	4	1
1	3	4	5	2
2	1	5	3	4
4	2	3	1	5

No 87

The value of the letter in the central square is half that of the sum total of the value of the letters in the other squares. Thus the missing value is 1, so the missing letters is A.

No 90

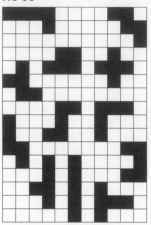

No 88

5	4	2	4	6	6	5
1	2	3	6	6	3	6

1	0	6	4	3	5	3
1	3	2	1	3	4	1

1	5	5	1	2	4	2
6	0	2	0	2	3	1

4	6	0	0	0	5	5
4	0	0	4	2	3	5

No 93

A=120, B=63, C=23, D=34, E=54, F=183, G=86, H=57, I=88, J=269, K=143, L=145, M=412, N=288, O=700.

No 89

1	2	2	3	3	2
4	1	1	1	1	4
4	1	1	1	1	4
3	3	3	4	4	1
3	3	3	4	4	1
4	4	4	2	2	2

No 91

74 – The number in the angles of the central hexagon is half of the total of the numbers in the adjacent points of the star, so 111+37=148 and half of 148 is 74.

No 92

17	33	21	**40**	39	45
49	**32**	32	14	35	33
45	48	32	18	19	**33**
18	42	**35**	46	22	32
16	12	46	39	49	33
50	28	29	38	**31**	19

No 94

4	1	9	6	■	2	8	0	9	0	5	■	1
6	9	0	2	1	■	0	■	0	■	1	7	6
6	3	1	■	6	1	0	4	6	■	3	3	3
7	1	3	5	2	■	5	1	1	4	■	0	■
■	4	6	4	3	■	6	■	5	0	4	3	2
3	■	7	■	2	6	7	1	■	6	1	6	
4	3	1	0	5	0	■	1	0	6	5	2	7
7	2	0	■	1	1	9	2	■	0	■	■	7
2	2	2	3	4	■	0	■	2	4	3	4	■
■	9	■	7	8	2	0	■	9	7	4	0	3
2	9	5	■	9	8	5	8	9	■	4	8	3
3	0	0	■	4	■	0	■	8	1	7	3	8
9	■	6	9	4	5	5	5	■	9	8	7	6

No 95

4S	**1W**	1S	4S	1W
3E	2S	1S	2S	1N
3E	2S	■	1E	3W
1N	3E	2W	1W	2N
3N	3N	4N	1E	2W

No 96

4	**1**	2	3	5
5	2	1	**4**	3
1	4	3	5	2
2	3	5	1	4
3	5	4	**2**	**1**

No 97

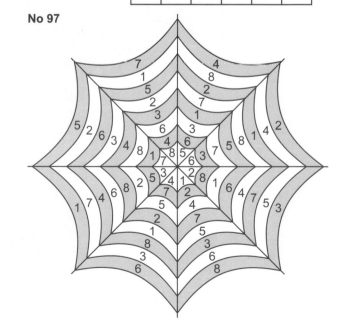

No 1

```
        1 1
      0 4 6 6
      1 5 5 5
  3 5 1 6 0 1 5 2
5 6 4 2 2 0 5 0 0 3 0
4 6 4 3 3 4 2 3 4 0
  2 4 3 6 6 2 6 1
      3 0 3 5
      1 1 2 4
        0 2
```

No 2

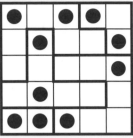

No 3

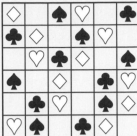

No 4

							106
14	2	3	21	10	15	5	70
10	22	20	15	12	9	7	95
11	20	28	4	17	6	3	89
11	16	18	30	17	5	16	113
17	9	28	8	4	6	30	102
3	15	9	4	22	28	30	111
2	21	17	30	2	9	29	110

68	105	123	112	84	78	120	155

No 5

The clock moves back 4 hours 41 minutes, forwards 1 hour 44 minutes, back 4 hours 41 minutes and forwards 1 hour 44 minutes.

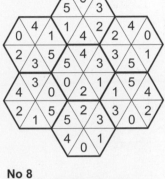

No 6

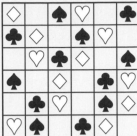

No 7

No 8

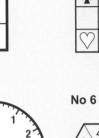

No 9

3	1	6	4	2	5
5	3	1	2	6	4
2	4	5	1	3	6
4	5	2	6	1	3
1	6	4	3	5	2
6	2	3	5	4	1

No 10

A	C	B	A	C	B
B	B	C	C	A	A
A	A	B	B	C	C
C	A	A	C	B	B
B	C	C	B	A	A
C	B	A	A	B	C

No 11

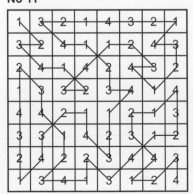

No 12

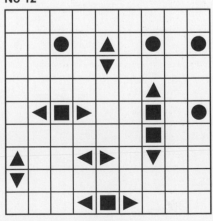

No 13

5559

No 16

The values of the letters in the outer squares are added together and the individual digits of the sum are added together until a single digit (1-9) is produced: this is the value of the letter in the central square. Thus the missing value is 63 and 6+3=9, so the missing letter is I.

No 14

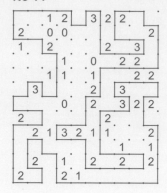

No 15

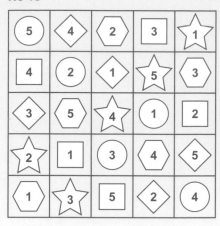

No 17

1	2	4	2	3	2	3
5	4	0	5	6	6	5

5	2	6	2	0	0	0
5	0	1	2	1	6	0

3	3	1	5	3	1	4
0	3	1	0	2	2	4

3	5	5	3	6	1	6
1	4	6	4	6	4	4

No 18

3	2	2	1	1	1
1	2	2	4	4	1
1	2	2	4	4	1
2	4	4	3	3	4
2	4	4	3	3	4
3	1	1	3	3	3

No 19

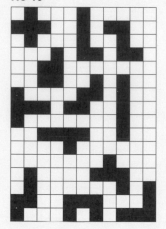

No 20

ABH – Assign a number to each letter according to its place in the alphabet, then start from the top and work clockwise, doubling the value each time, so B=2, D=4, H=8, P=16, CB=32, FD=64 and ABH=128.

No 21

23	23	26	35	**47**	57
63	35	23	20	36	34
43	46	35	37	28	**22**
42	48	36	**33**	19	33
22	**27**	52	46	42	22
18	32	**39**	40	39	43

No 22

A=21, B=33, C=07, D=100, E=46, F=54, G=40, H=107, I=146, J=94, K=147, L=253, M=241, N=400, O=641.

No 23

```
4 6 7 8 ■ 5 3 6 9 ■ 4 3 4
8 2 4 ■ 2 6 0 8 0 ■ 2 8 ■
2 4 3 1 0 ■ 0 ■ 1 6 7 3 6
■ 0 ■ 8 0 2 9 3 6 ■ 2 ■ 1
4 3 6 4 ■ 9 ■ 8 ■ 5 6 9 7
2 0 5 ■ 1 5 7 9 5 2 ■ ■ 1
5 5 9 9 4 5 ■ 2 6 6 1 3 1
9 . ■ 3 0 5 7 8 2 ■ 6 7 7
1 8 5 4 ■ 0 ■ 7 ■ 5 0 8 9
4 ■ 8 ■ 5 3 3 0 9 9 ■ 9 ■
7 9 8 8 3 ■ 9 ■ 4 9 7 2 4
■ 1 4 ■ 2 3 9 1 3 ■ 7 7 7
8 0 4 ■ 7 8 9 9 ■ 4 6 7 2
```

No 24

2S	4S	2E	2W	1W
2S	1W	1W	3S	2W
4E	2E	■	1W	1N
4E	2E	1S	1W	3W
4N	2N	4N	1E	4W

No 25

1	2	3	5	4
2	1	4	3	5
4	5	1	2	3
3	4	5	1	2
5	3	2	4	1

No 26

No 27

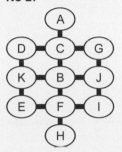

No 28

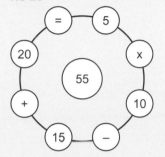

No 29

6		1			8
1		7		8	
					1
1		8			
					2
2			9		

No 30

3	+	4	−	2	=	5
x	■	−	■	x		
9	+	1	+	6	=	16
x	■	x	■	−		
5	x	7	−	8	=	27
=		=		=		
135		21		4		

No 31

5 – In the first column, add 4 to the first number, subtract 6 from the second, add 4 to the third, etc; in the second column, add 6 to the first number, subtract 4 from the second, etc; then repeat this process for the remaining columns, adding and subtracting 4 and/or 6 alternately.

No 32

C

No 33

(grid puzzle solution)

No 34

Circle = 2, cross = 4, pentagon = 6, square = 1, star = 8.

No 35

E	D	C	B	F	A
F	B	A	E	D	C
A	E	D	F	C	B
D	C	F	A	B	E
C	A	B	D	E	F
B	F	E	C	A	D

No 36

(diamond grid solution)

No 37

A	B	B	A	C	C
C	B	C	A	A	B
C	A	A	B	C	B
B	C	B	C	A	A
B	C	A	C	B	A
A	A	C	B	B	C

No 38

No 39

							116
13	20	21	14	18	7	26	119
11	17	4	16	23	5	10	86
9	6	27	29	15	8	19	113
7	3	29	12	24	2	22	99
1	13	25	16	22	4	7	88
30	5	18	14	10	20	21	118
28	12	19	6	15	25	13	118

99	76	143	107	127	71	118	124

No 40

E – Numbering the shapes 1, 2, 3, 4 from the top of the pile, the order changes to 3, 1, 4, 2.

No 41

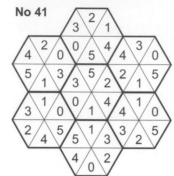

No 42

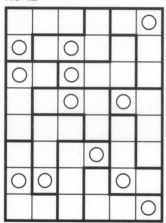

No 43

D – Reading each set clockwise from the top left to the centre, the shapes alternate between having 3, 4 and 5 sides.

No 44

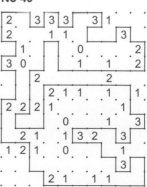

No 45

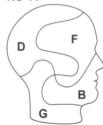

No 46

2862

No 47

6	1	3	5	2	4
4	3	2	1	5	6
5	4	1	2	6	3
2	6	5	4	3	1
3	5	4	6	1	2
1	2	6	3	4	5

No 48

No 49

No 50

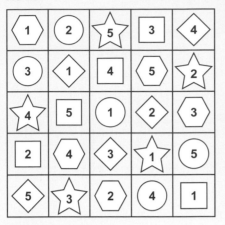

No 51

Working clockwise from the top left square, the value of the letter in each square increases by 5. The central square has a letter equal to the value missing from the sequence. Thus the missing value is 26, so the missing letter is Z.

No 52

3 – In the others, any two colours the same are reflected either horizontally or vertically; in 3, yellow, pink and blue do not follow this rule.

No 53

1 – Following the line around, the alphabetical order (from A to Z, then starting at A again) skips one between each letter in the top row, two in the middle row and three in the bottom row.

No 54

2	4	4	1	1	4
2	3	3	3	3	3
2	3	3	3	3	3
2	3	3	2	2	1
2	3	3	2	2	1
2	1	1	4	4	3

No 56

133 – Starting from the top and working clockwise, double each number then deduct 5 to get the next number.

No 58

A=117, B=104, C=08, D=88, E=51, F=221, G=112, H=96, I=139, J=333, K=208, L=235, M=541, N=443, O=984.

No 55

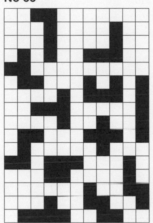

No 57

37	**59**	32	48	51	37
63	84	47	**32**	24	14
57	23	**8**	88	41	47
45	31	68	26	**51**	43
25	10	15	56	72	**86**
37	57	94	14	25	37

No 59

3	5	4	9	6	7		2	9	0	9	7	8
1	5	1		9	8	1	0	9		3	4	
8	2	4	9	4		4		2	0	1	2	1
9		9		3	9	4	8	0		0		6
3	4	9		6	3	6	0		6	6	5	1
5	6	9	4		3	0	0	8	0		8	7
	5	1	7	4	0		2	6	4	2	9	
1	9		9	2	2	9	3		6	2	7	1
1	5	7	0		3	3	5	4		6	0	4
4		0		2	4	1	5	7		8		5
8	9	0	2	2		7		5	3	3	7	6
	3	5		7	2	1	9	8		2	3	9
3	9	0	7	5	7		3	8	7	7	6	3

No 60

1E	3E	2W	2S	4S
3S	2E	2W	1W	2S
1S	**3E**		1W	1N
3E	2N	3N	1S	2W
2N	1N	1W	4N	2W

No 61

4	3	5	1	2
2	**5**	1	**3**	4
3	2	4	5	**1**
1	4	3	2	5
5	1	2	4	3

No 62

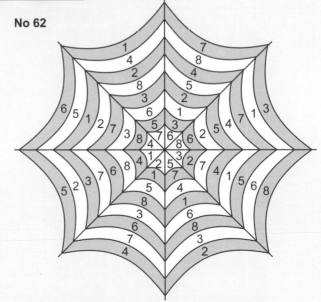

No 63

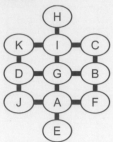

No 64

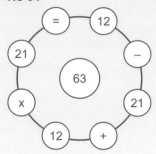

No 65

8			4		9
	2				
					7
3		2		5	
					5
2			4		
					1

No 66

5	–	2	x	9	=	27
–		+		–		
4	x	6	–	3	=	21
+		+		x		
1	x	8	+	7	=	15
=		=		=		
2		16		42		

No 67

64 – In the first row, deduct 12 then 13 from each successive number; in the second row, deduct 11 then 12; in the third, deduct 10 then 11; in the fourth, deduct 9 then 10; in the fifth, deduct 8 then 9; in the sixth, deduct 7 then 6; and in the seventh, deduct 6 then 5.

No 68

D

No 69

.	.	0	●	.	0	.	●	1
.	0	.	2	.	.	2	.	.
.	.	.	●	.	1	●	●	.	0
2	●	.	.	2	1	.	●	2
●	3	.	●	.	.	.	2	.
●	.	.	2	.	.	.	1	●	●
4	●	4	●	.	0	.	.	.	3
●	●	●	3	1	.	.	2	●
●	●	●	3	.	2	●	.	2	2
3	●	3	.	●	.	.	2	●

No 70

C	D	B	F	E	A
B	A	F	E	C	D
D	C	A	B	F	E
A	F	E	D	B	C
F	E	C	A	D	B
E	B	D	C	A	F

No 71

Circle = 9, cross = 7, pentagon = 8, square = 4, star = 5.

No 72

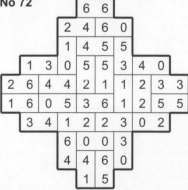

No 73

A	B	C	B	A	C
B	C	A	C	B	A
C	A	B	A	C	B
C	B	A	A	C	B
A	C	C	B	B	A
B	A	B	C	A	C

No 74

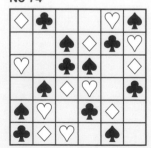

No 75

15	12	23	18	4	16	27	115
20	10	9	14	24	2	19	98
2	17	12	25	22	6	13	97
14	24	26	8	7	12	11	102
21	30	16	4	18	29	14	132
3	15	24	16	22	28	1	109
20	12	7	5	30	17	10	101

95	120	117	90	127	110	95	101

110

No 80

72 – Subtract the number at the top right from that at the top left, then multiply the result by the sum total of the numbers in the bottom two circles to get the central number.

No 81

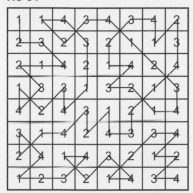

No 76

D – Red swaps places with dark blue, yellow with pink, light blue with orange, and purple with green.

No 78

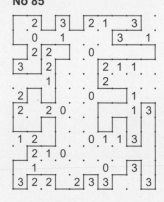

No 82

6	1	5	3	4	2
5	2	4	6	3	1
2	4	1	5	6	3
4	3	2	1	5	6
1	6	3	4	2	5
3	5	6	2	1	4

No 77

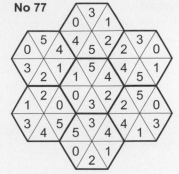

No 79

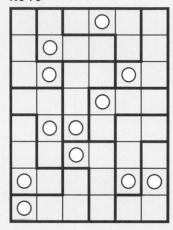

No 83

2218

No 84

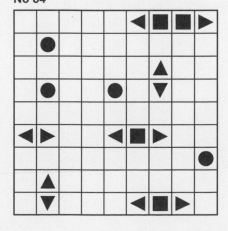

No 85

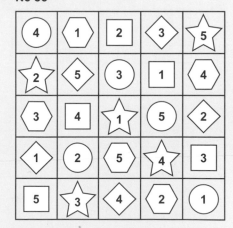

No 86

4	1	2	3	5
2	5	3	1	4
3	4	1	5	2
1	2	5	4	3
5	3	4	2	1

No 87

The value of the letter in the top left square is added to that in the bottom right. The value of the letter in the top right square is subtracted from that in the bottom left. The average of both products is the value of the letter in the central square. Thus the missing value is 11, so the missing letter is K.

No 88

2	4	4	3	3	2
2	4	4	1	1	1
2	4	4	1	1	1
1	3	3	1	1	4
1	3	3	1	1	4
3	2	2	4	4	3

No 89

No 90

2.5 – The lower number in each point of the star divides into its opposite higher number by 2.5.

No 91

38	38	47	**47**	32	38
54	**64**	55	36	4	27
35	26	12	70	77	**20**
49	12	72	10	**37**	60
26	18	**18**	43	78	57
38	82	36	34	12	38

No 92

A=29, B=52, C=82, D=127, E=27, F=81, G=134, H=209, I=154, J=215, K=343, L=363, M=558, N=706, O=1264.

No 93

6	0	5	6		2	1	9	3		4	4	7
4		0		1	8	4		2	6	2	8	8
2	7	2	6	4	8		8	6		9	9	2
	6		8		3		8	7	4	1		
2	5	7	9	4		9	8	0	6	1		1
9	2	4		5	5	1	3	2	8		3	9
1	4	0	1		5		5	7		9	1	4
6	3		1	7	7	6	3	3		8	5	2
1		5	0	1	7	9		4	8	6	5	0
	2	7	9	3		5		9			3	
6	9	7		4	2		2	6	3	7	1	3
5	7	0	1	0		5	9	5		6		4
9	8	3		9	9	1	7		2	5	7	3

No 94

3S	4S	1S	3S	2W
3S	3E	1E	3W	1S
1E	2N		3W	2W
2E	**3E**	1S	1N	1S
4N	3N	1E	4N	4N

No 95

1	**3**	5	4	**2**
2	4	1	5	**3**
5	1	2	**3**	**4**
4	2	3	1	5
3	**5**	4	2	1

No 96

6

304